A DECADE OF UPHEAVAL

PRINCETON STUDIES IN
CONTEMPORARY CHINA

Mary Gallagher and Yu Xie, Series Editors

A Decade of Upheaval: The Cultural Revolution in Rural China, Dong Guoqiang
and Andrew G. Walder

*Governing the Urban in China and India: Land Grabs, Slum Clearance, and the
War on Air Pollution,* Xuefei Ren

China's Urban Champions: The Politics of Spatial Development, Kyle A. Jaros

The Contentious Public Sphere: Law, Media, and Authoritarian Rule in China,
Ya-Wen Lei

A Decade of Upheaval

THE CULTURAL REVOLUTION
IN RURAL CHINA

DONG GUOQIANG

ANDREW G. WALDER

PRINCETON UNIVERSITY PRESS

PRINCETON & OXFORD

Copyright © 2021 by Princeton University Press

Princeton University Press is committed to the protection of copyright and the intellectual property our authors entrust to us. Copyright promotes the progress and integrity of knowledge. Thank you for supporting free speech and the global exchange of ideas by purchasing an authorized edition of this book. If you wish to reproduce or distribute any part of it in any form, please obtain permission.

Requests for permission to reproduce material from this work should be sent to permissions@press.princeton.edu

Published by Princeton University Press
41 William Street, Princeton, New Jersey 08540
6 Oxford Street, Woodstock, Oxfordshire OX20 1TR

press.princeton.edu

All Rights Reserved

ISBN 9780691213224
ISBN (pbk.) 9780691213217
ISBN (e-book) 9780691214979

British Library Cataloging-in-Publication Data is available

Editorial: Bridget Flannery-McCoy and Alena Chekanov
Production Editorial: Mark Bellis
Cover Design: Karl Spurzem
Production: Brigid Ackerman
Publicity: Kate Hensley and Kathryn Stevens
Copyeditor: Molan Goldstein

Cover Credit: image courtesy of author

This book has been composed in Arno

Printed on acid-free paper. ∞

Printed in the United States of America

10 9 8 7 6 5 4 3 2 1

CONTENTS

ILLUSTRATIONS

Figures

Maps

Photos

Tables

PREFACE

THIS BOOK, the first sustained analysis of political conflict during the Cultural Revolution in a rural Chinese county, yields a number of novel observations. First, despite its remote and marginal location on the border of several provinces, and despite being one of the poorest and least urbanized places in the country, Feng County suffered from deep and enduring factional divisions and violent civil strife. Second, these conflicts survived beyond the imposition of military control and suppression of rebel organizations, and factional animosities endured throughout the Cultural Revolution, to be extinguished only after the death of Mao. Third, military intervention, long understood to have reimposed order across China, instead was a catalyst for the formation of factional warfare and actually served to perpetuate it. Fourth, each twist and turn in national politics emanating from Beijing over the decade had a large impact on the balance of political forces in the county. Had we thought that these upheavals were largely concentrated in cities and nearby suburbs, and had we supposed that the upheavals were limited to the first few years of this decade, Feng County's history challenges what we thought we knew.

The decade-long political struggle that we portray in this book draws on an unusual level of evidentiary detail. Through contacts cultivated independently with networks of now-retired former activists, local officials, and soldiers, and local collectors of Cultural Revolution memorabilia, we have gained access to an unusually wide array of documentary sources, as well as interviews with key participants in the events of the period. The documentary sources include the flow of directives and notices from authorities in Beijing throughout the decade, along with similar directives from Jiangsu provincial authorities in Nanjing and the prefectural authorities in Xuzhou. In addition, we draw on an extensive collection of documents and directives from Feng County authorities, beginning with its party committee during the last months before its collapse, and the Feng County Revolutionary Committee after its establishment in 1969. We also draw on internal bulletins and documents issued by a range of interim authorities in the county during the long period that it remained under some form of military control—March 1967 to September 1969.

We supplement these streams of official documents with unofficial materials issued by each of the county's two political factions. These include handbills and wall posters, selected copies of periodicals, and chronologies of events. We also draw on a collection of confessions and self-criticisms written by individuals and by leaders of factions, and several unpublished memoirs and book drafts compiled by individuals who were involved in these events or who were tasked by the county's post-Mao government to compile a chronicle of the decade.

Also important are interviews with sixteen former activists and leaders of both factions, among them students, workers, and cadres. Even more essential than these oral testimonies, however, are the work notebooks and diaries kept by six individuals who were deeply involved in the events of the period. These detailed notes were kept at the time these events occurred. Especially valuable were notes taken during conferences, study classes, and other meetings. Unlike official documents and materials issued by factions, these notebooks and diaries take us inside some of the most important but otherwise inaccessible meetings of factions, government officials, and military units. They were kept by leaders of both civilian factions, by military officers assigned to the county, and by individuals who conducted investigations on behalf of the county's Revolutionary Committee after it was formed in 1969. Preserved over the years and shared with us, these written sources are even more valuable than oral reminiscences of the kind that can be elicited in interviews conducted decades after the fact. They give accurate chronologies of event sequences, and they present the words and sentiments of actors as they were originally recorded, not as they were recalled or reconstructed long afterward. These work notebooks and diaries are useful anchors for interviews with participants, and they provide interviewees with an opportunity to clarify gaps or ambiguities in the written record.

All of the sources that we cite in this account are recorded in the list of primary sources in the bibliography, following a standard alphabetized list of secondary sources. As a guide to readers in evaluating this documentation, we have arrayed in chronological order all of the primary materials that we cite in footnotes. The backgrounds of the individuals who sat for interviews, and those whose notebooks we draw upon, are listed separately, in alphabetical order. Interviewees who are listed by name consented to be identified in this publication; those who did not are listed by number. We also provide a glossary of names for several dozen people whose names appear more than once in this account, divided into separate lists of factional activists, civilian officials, and military officers. Additionally, we have included a concise chronology of the decade's events to help clarify the many twists and turns to this story.

Readers will become aware that our key informant is Zhang Liansheng, who was a high school senior in 1966. Zhang was one of the top students at Feng County Middle School, and he had every expectation that he would pass the national entrance exam in the spring of that year and attend university in the fall. Instead, the entrance examinations were canceled, and he was drawn into political activism in his school, eventually becoming a major rebel leader and a founder of one of the county's two factional alliances. He was intimately involved in all of the major political events in the county over the next decade, attending many of the key meetings of his faction's leadership and taking part in all of the negotiation sessions that military and civilian authorities organized in their fruitless efforts to reconcile the two warring factions. For a long period in the early 1970s, Zhang was isolated for highly coercive interrogations as an alleged counterrevolutionary, only to be released and vindicated as political tides shifted. In the mid-1970s, he was an activist in a region-wide protest movement by individuals who had suffered persecution in recent campaigns to consolidate political order. He has submitted to many hours of interviews, and the voluminous notebooks in which he recorded his experiences over these years are a major foundation for several of the chapters in this book.

Although we have also drawn on materials from the opposed faction, they are not as abundant as those provided by Zhang and his colleagues. We do draw on interviews with individuals from the other faction, but we did not have a key informant that provided us with the same level of access. We are conscious that the narrative that we have reconstructed in this book does not provide similar insight into the opposed faction's viewpoints. This is probably reflected in our account, which tends to portray Zhang's opponents as the aggressors. This may show Zhang's faction in an unfairly favorable light, but we are confident that the overall structure of the conflict and the key developments over the years are presented here in a way that is consistent with evidence provided by both sides and by military sources.

We are grateful to the many individuals who shared with us their reminiscences, notebooks, diaries, and the documents, handbills, and other materials in their possession. The identity of these individuals will in most cases remain anonymous. However, we would like to give special thanks to Ji Langyou, Sun

Tao, and Hui Mingsheng, residents of Feng County who were too young to have been involved in the events described in this book. Interested in this period of local history, these individuals assembled personal collections of documents and other materials. When they learned of our research project, they generously donated their collections to us, asking only to be acknowledged in our publications. These materials enriched our sources, especially regarding the faction opposed to Zhang Liansheng.

We would like to acknowledge research support provided to us by our current academic homes, Fudan University and Stanford University. Nanjing University, where Dong Guoqiang was a student and faculty member from 1981 until he moved to Fudan in 2015, generously sponsored our previous research on the history of Nanjing's Cultural Revolution. Our research on Feng County has drawn upon, and in fact was inspired by, our previous work on Jiangsu's provincial capital. We would also like to acknowledge Stanford's Humanities Center and Freeman-Spogli Institute for International Studies, which granted Dong a fellowship during the 2008–2009 academic year, providing us with the opportunity to begin our very rewarding long-term collaboration.

We are also indebted to four reviewers for Princeton University Press, who provided careful, detailed, and very thoughtful criticisms of an earlier draft of this book: Jeremy Brown, Daniel Leese, Mark Selden, and Yiching Wu. Yang Su provided comments on the penultimate draft, and pushed us to think further about the broader implications of the story that we present here. Geua Boe-Gibson capably designed the maps that accompany the text, and worked hard to reconcile regional boundaries in contemporary geographic databases with the jurisdictions in existence half a century ago. We are grateful to all.

1

Prologue

AFTER THE DEATH of Mao Zedong in 1976 and the subsequent arrest and condemnation of his radical associates known as the "Gang of Four," China moved in a surprising new direction. The new leaders that emerged over the next two years declared that the Cultural Revolution was finally over. The official verdict on this remarkable era of radical communism repudiated it as a decade of "turmoil" (*dongluan*): "The 'Cultural Revolution,' which lasted from May 1966 to October 1976, was responsible for the most severe setback and the heaviest losses suffered by the party, the state, and the people since the founding of the People's Republic."[1]

That the Cultural Revolution lasted for an entire decade initially struck many analysts as odd. An established scholarly literature identified it with the mobilization of Red Guards and rebel organizations that challenged political authority from 1966 to the end of 1968. This freewheeling mobilization ended with the establishment of revolutionary committees. Including the entire decade as one of "turmoil" seemed to obscure sharp differences within a very complex era, hiding clear-cut distinctions between an initial rebellion from below, a subsequent period of harsh repression, and a halting final period of tentative recovery. The new periodization seemed more suitable for propaganda purposes than scholarly analysis.[2]

The post-Mao era brought a wave of new information about political events during the entire decade, and it began to reveal previously hidden continuities

---

1. Zhonggong zhongyang, "Guanyu jianguo yilai dang de ruogan lishi wenti de jueyi" (Resolution on certain problems of party history since the founding of the nation), June 27, 1981.

2. See Anita Chan, "Dispelling Misconceptions about the Red Guard Movement—The Necessity to Re-examine Cultural Revolution Factionalism and Periodization," *Journal of Contemporary China* 1, 1 (September 1992): 61–85.

between the rebellions of the initial period and political events in the years that followed. Some of the first post-Mao studies to examine the entire decade documented protests by workers and others in 1974 and 1975 that turned out to be a continuation of factional struggles from the late 1960s.[3] Chronic factionalism within work units, something that plagued efforts to restore industrial production well into the 1970s, also appeared to be rooted in the political conflicts of the earlier period.[4]

It has gradually become clear that the disruptions of China's social and political order in the decade that began in 1966 showed more lines of continuity than was initially understood. In particular, the designation of the entire decade as one of "turmoil," with its roots in the open factional struggles of the late 1960s, now seems more plausible than it did initially. But our detailed knowledge of this dimension of the decade remains limited to a handful of large cities where the lines of conflict have been traced over the entire decade—Hangzhou, Wuhan, Shanghai, and Nanjing, in particular. Even in this handful of cities there is considerable variation in the extent to which factional antagonisms from the late 1960s survived and continued to drive conflict throughout the decade, and also in the extent to which the local political and social order was disrupted.[5] This makes it even more uncertain how the trends uncovered in these cases were replicated in more than 170 Chinese cities large and small.

While our knowledge of political trends across the decade remains limited to a handful of large cities, we have virtually no comparable knowledge about any of China's more than two thousand counties—largely rural jurisdictions

---

3. The first such evidence, based on post-Mao sources, emerged in studies of decade-long factional conflicts in Hangzhou and Wuhan. See Keith Forster, *Rebellion and Factionalism in a Chinese Province: Zhejiang, 1966–1976* (Armonk, NY: ME Sharpe, 1990); Keith Forster, "Spontaneous and Institutional Rebellion in the Cultural Revolution: The Extraordinary Case of Weng Senhe," *Australian Journal of Chinese Affairs*, no. 27 (1992): 39–75; and Shaoguang Wang, *The Failure of Charisma: The Cultural Revolution in Wuhan* (Oxford: Oxford University Press, 1995).

4. For example, Frederick Teiwes and Warren Sun, *The End of the Maoist Era: Chinese Politics during the Twilight of the Cultural Revolution, 1972–1976.* (Armonk, NY: ME Sharpe, 2007); and Ezra F. Vogel, *Deng Xiaoping and the Transformation of China* (Cambridge, MA: Harvard University Press, 2011), pp. 145–172.

5. Politics across the entire decade have been analyzed in Shanghai by Li Xun, *Geming zaofan niandai: Shanghai wen'ge yundong shi gao* (The decade of revolutionary rebellion: A history of Shanghai's Cultural Revolution), 2 vols. (Hong Kong: Oxford University Press, 2015); and for Nanjing in the series of articles by the present authors that are listed in the bibliography.

where close to 80 percent of China's population lived. There are excellent village-level studies that span the decade, and they frequently devote chapters to the politics of this period. But they reveal conflicts that are intensely local and often personal in nature, making it difficult to characterize the broader lines of conflict at the level of the county government.[6] With an average of more than 350 villages in a Chinese county, it would be foolhardy to try to draw any conclusions about the politics of an entire county even from the most penetrating village-level accounts.[7] The few publications that describe county-level political events during this decade invariably address only the dramatic events of the late 1960s.[8]

Politics at the County Level

This book is the first to focus on county-level factional politics throughout the entire Cultural Revolution. The events that it documents in Feng County, Jiangsu Province, reveal a world of continuous conflict that goes well beyond anything even hinted at in previous studies of this period. Despite its remote location, in a poor and marginal region at the intersection of three provincial

6. The list of relevant village-level studies includes Anita Chan, Richard Madsen, and Jonathan Unger, *Chen Village: The Recent History of a Peasant Community in Mao's China* (Berkeley: University of California Press, 1984); and Edward Friedman, Paul G. Pickowicz, and Mark Selden, *Revolution, Resistance, and Reform in Village China* (New Haven, CT: Yale University Press, 2005). These and other studies have a longer time frame and broader focus than the political conflicts characteristic of the last decade of the Mao era.

7. In the late 1960s, China's 2,066 counties contained some 70,000 townships (communes), and 750,000 villages (production brigades): Jean C. Oi, *State and Peasant in Contemporary China: The Political Economy of Village Government* (Berkeley: University of California Press, 1989), p. 5. This is an average of close to 350 villages per county. The lack of documentary evidence about villages, forcing researchers to rely almost exclusively on oral histories conducted during fieldwork, means that village-level conflicts remain largely unexplored. See Jonathan Unger, "Cultural Revolution Conflict in the Villages," *China Quarterly* 153 (March 1998): 82–106.

8. Ostensibly a village study, William Hinton's *Shenfan: The Continuing Revolution in a Chinese Village* (New York: Random House, 1983), pp. 493–735, contains an extended account of factional warfare over several years that frequently ranges up to the county and even prefecture level. Based exclusively on oral histories, it is perhaps the most extensive narrative of rural factional conflicts in print. Tan Hecheng, *The Killing Wind: A Chinese County's Descent into Madness during the Cultural Revolution* (New York: Oxford University Press, 2017), based on extensive documentary evidence, describes a several-month period of mass killings in late 1967 in one county in Hunan.

borders, the county was deeply disrupted by factional divisions that formed in 1967 and continued to shape local politics until shortly after the death of Mao a decade later. For long periods the county was ungovernable, with different factions in control of their own "liberated zones" and no actors able to enforce their authority over the entire territory. The leading actors in these conflicts were drawn into factional struggles that afflicted other counties and cities in northern Jiangsu. These conflicts came to the attention of figures at the apex of political power, who subjected local actors to prolonged and coercive "study classes" in Beijing that were designed to reconcile adamantly opposed combatants. These antagonisms continued to plague efforts to reestablish stable government in the county up to the year of Mao's death. Anyone familiar with Feng County's history would find little to dispute the notion that the decade of the Cultural Revolution was one of continuous political struggle.

Feng County's history sheds light on a number of aspects of this period that have long remained obscure. Political conflicts at the county level were deeply affected by national political trends to a remarkable degree. Each shift in national politics emanating from Beijing during the 1970s had a major impact on the balance of factional forces in the county, although the impact was often very much at odds with the intentions of national leaders. Across the entire decade, each twist and turn in Beijing's policies reverberated in the county in ways that altered the balance of power between two deeply opposed and clearly defined political factions.

The county's history also reveals in remarkable detail the deep involvement of China's armed forces in the definition and perpetuation of county-level factionalism. Analysts have long known that military intervention was a major axis of factional division across China, with rebel factions that supported military control often becoming known as "moderate" or "conservative" and the opponents of military control becoming labeled as "radical."

Military intervention in Feng County did serve to define the lines of factional conflict, but in ways very different from previous understandings. Military forces that intervened in Feng County in early 1967 came from two different branches of China's armed forces. The local People's Armed Department (PAD), which was subordinate to the Xuzhou Military Subdistrict of the People's Liberation Army (PLA), initially assumed control over the county as its party leadership collapsed in disorder in early 1967. Shortly afterward, regular PLA troops from the Ji'nan Military Region arrived to help stabilize the county's administration. These two branches of the military soon disagreed about how to re-establish local order, and in particular how to treat rival rebel groups. They each became closely aligned with different factions in the county's struggles and actively sought to undercut one another in their efforts to adjudicate local conflicts. Their continued support of different factions kept the conflicts alive well into the 1970s and showed that China's armed forces were themselves beset by the factionalism that divided civilian rebels. Originally conceived as a solution to factionalism among civilian rebels, military intervention served instead to perpetuate it.

Several themes emerge clearly from our reconstruction of political conflicts in this obscure and backward rural county. The first is that a remote location did not insulate the county from national political trends; it only delayed their initial impact. As one might expect, the rebellions of students and workers that affected so many of China's large cities by the summer and early fall of 1966 developed very slowly in Feng County. The local Red Guard and rebel movements were very small, were late in developing, and did not present much of a challenge to local officials until early 1967. Political authority collapsed without any rebel groups attempting to declare a power seizure. It was only after the collapse of the local government and the assertion of political control by the PAD that the conflicts that came to dominate the rest of the decade would emerge. Once these conflicts were locked in, local political developments were closely tied to political shifts in the nation's capital.

The second theme is that the axis of conflict did not, as many analysts once suspected, pit actors aligned with the existing order against their opponents. The conflicts that were common in large cities in late 1966 between the antagonists and defenders of local power structures were barely evident in the county. Military units played an active role in local politics, and indeed they were a dominant force. But they were themselves divided against one another and supported different civilian factions. The local PAD, responding to orders from the central authorities to intervene to support left-wing rebel forces, seized power and pushed aside the county's civilian leadership. This essentially split local authorities against one another, with the PAD moving against almost the entire civilian leadership of the county while aligning itself with rebels within the Public Security Bureau and maintaining control over the PAD's militia forces in most of the county's villages and small towns. Officers from regular PLA units arrived shortly afterward and disputed the actions of the PAD, objecting particularly to its one-sided support for one group of local rebels and its antagonism toward the other. This generated a conflict that divided rebel groups and former party and government functionaries against one another as they aligned with different branches of the military. These conflicts did not pit the forces of order against rebels that sought to overthrow it, but instead expressed divisions within fragmented military and civilian power structures, with students and worker rebels on both sides depending on their sponsors for support.

The third theme is that despite its remote location, the county's conflicts were connected to broader factional disputes in the surrounding prefecture and province, eventually drawing local actors into protracted and coercive negotiations in Beijing designed to reconcile local combatants with one another. These negotiations lasted an entire year and failed spectacularly, despite bringing Feng County's political activists into meetings with Zhou Enlai and a range of other high officials, and despite an appearance by Mao Zedong himself two months before their final session. The end result was the arbitrary imposition of military control under the PAD, an action that led to the harsh suppression of one faction, only to be reversed as national politics shifted in later years, reviving active political contention in the county. What looked like the final repression of factional conflict under a military-run revolutionary committee merely pushed factional animosities into fragile new political structures, only to resurface as civil disorders when the opportunity arose. These political animosities endured through the end of the Mao era.

A fourth theme is the prolonged deterioration of political authority and public order, and in many ways a deep fracturing of the social fabric, public trust, and citizen morale, as this decade of conflict and oppression wore on. Feng County was barely governable for significant parts of the decade and completely ungovernable for brief periods of intense conflict. The failure to re-establish a legitimate political order wore heavily on the factional antagonists, on those who suffered severe oppression, and even on those who were tasked with prosecuting the coercive political campaigns designed to re-establish authority. Unmistakable signs of the fraying of the county's political and social fabric became apparent by the early 1970s.

Given the almost complete absence of comparable accounts from other Chinese counties, the obvious question to ask is how typical or representative are the events detailed in this book. Do the events recounted here seem so dramatic and surprising only because of the extensive sources at our disposal? Would similarly detailed reconstructions of politics in other counties reveal similar patterns? Or was Feng County's experience highly unusual, an outlier relative to other rural regions? In a nation with more than two thousand rural counties, it is unlikely that any one of them exhibited patterns that were closely approximated in more than a minority of localities. It makes more sense to expect that politics across the counties that make up China's vast countryside comprised a wide spectrum of variation, but variation on a common set of themes. At the end of this book we will address this question directly, drawing on recent research by ourselves and others. But such a discussion will be more productive after readers become intimately familiar with what happened in Feng County and why events there developed the way that they did. With this objective in mind, we now turn to the county and its story.

A County at the Margins

Feng County is the least likely of settings for the dramatic and tumultuous saga of political struggle recounted in this book. Despite its location in a famously poor hinterland at the intersection of three northern provinces, the county was drawn deeply into the vortex of national politics during the Cultural Revolution. Its leaders and activists were involved in some of the most consequential political events of the entire decade, at some points connecting them directly with machinations at the top reaches of political power in Beijing. The disruptive impact of the Cultural Revolution was surprisingly deep and long lasting, ending only in the late 1970s, after the death of Mao Zedong and the ascendance of Deng Xiaoping.

Located on the ancient floodplain of the Yellow River, Feng County was far from China's political and economic centers. Wedged into the extreme northwest corner of Jiangsu Province, jutting out between the borders of Anhui Province to the south and Shandong Province to the north and west, it was at the opposite end of Jiangsu from the provincial capital of Nanjing, more than 260 miles away. The closest city, eighty miles distant along a narrow, two-lane road, was the prefectural capital of Xuzhou, a medium-sized city of 450,000, which was important primarily as a railway junction for north-south and east-west lines connecting other parts of China. Another hundred miles to the east of Xuzhou was Lianyungang, a midsize port on the East China Sea in a region known over many imperial Chinese dynasties as Haizhou. Government documents and historical accounts still refer to the region that covers the two cities and the surrounding rural counties as the Xuhai region (*xuhai diqu*), drawing on the first characters of *Xu*zhou and *Hai*zhou. Xuzhou Prefecture was established in 1953 to govern the rural counties in the Xuhai region, including Feng County. The prefecture-level cities of Xuzhou and Lianyungang were placed under the jurisdiction of the provincial government in Nanjing.

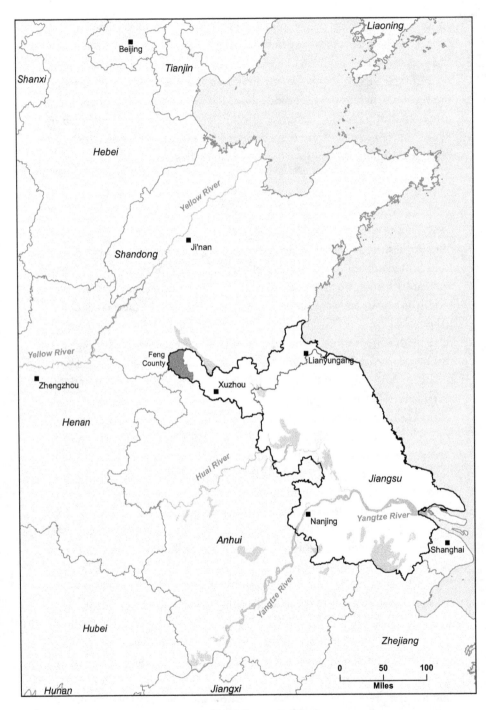

MAP 1. China's Eastern Seaboard

In a recorded history of more than two thousand years that began with its founding during the Qin Dynasty (221–207 BC), Feng County is significant primarily as the reputed birthplace of Liu Bang, the first emperor of the Western Han Dynasty (202 BC–AD 220).[9] During the century that spanned from the 1840s into the 1940s, it was in the middle of what one analyst of the history of banditry and organized violence in the region termed "an exceptionally harsh habitat" in which "[r]epeated ravages of flood and drought created a difficult and insecure milieu in which aggressive survival strategies flourished."[10]

Its harsh environment and remote location at the intersection of three provinces made it an ideal site for guerilla activity during the twentieth century.[11] The Communist Party of China (CCP) first established itself there in 1928, and it grew rapidly during the Sino-Japanese War (1937–1945). At the outset of that conflict the party set up six local district committees that coordinated the activities of almost two thousand party members. By 1940, the CCP had established a provisional government over areas of the county that it controlled, and it competed with two rival governments sponsored by the Nationalist Party and the Japanese occupation forces. After the Japanese surrender in 1945, conflict with the Nationalists continued until the CCP was finally able to take control over the entire county in November 1948.[12] As a battleground between contending forces, the county contained many local residents, including later members of the CCP and government officials, who had complicated prior histories of political involvement with either Japanese or Nationalist forces at some point in time.

Feng County had not always been in a poor and marginal region. Prior to the Song Dynasty (960–1127), flooding due to sedimentation was not yet a problem along the Yellow River, and irrigation from its waters benefited the

---

9. Yu Ruimao, ed., *Jiangsu sheng Feng xian zhi* (Beijing: Zhongguo shehui kexue chubanshe, 1994), p. 2.

10. Elizabeth J. Perry, *Rebels and Revolutionaries in North China, 1845–1945* (Stanford, CA: Stanford University Press, 1980), p. 3.

11. In fact, a fourth province, Henan, is separated from Feng County only by the width of Dangshan County in Anhui.

12. *Jiangsu sheng Feng xian zhi*, pp. 496–497; and Zhonggong Feng xian xianwei zuzhibu, Zhonggong Feng xian dangshi gongzuo weiyuanhui, Feng xian dang'an ju, *Zhongguo gongchandang Jiangsu sheng Feng xian zuzhishi ziliao* (Beijing: Zhonggong dangshi ziliao chubanshe, 1989), pp. 8, 16, and 63–64.

region's prosperous agrarian economy. The temperate climate and seasonal rainfall supported the cultivation of a range of crops and also forestry and the raising of livestock. The county's name, Feng, translates as "rich," "abundant," or "plentiful," reflecting this ancient era of prosperity. After the Song Dynasty the Yellow River shifted from its northern course, bringing it not far to the west of the county. Silting of the riverbed required the building and maintenance of extensive dykes, which frequently failed and led periodically to catastrophic flooding. Less dramatically, soil exhaustion and the disappearance of woodlands marked a deteriorating ecology that brought in its wake severe long-term economic decline.[13]

By the 1950s, Feng County was in a severely underdeveloped agrarian region. With sandy soil and irregular rain, conditions were much less favorable to agriculture than the famously prosperous agricultural regions of southern Jiangsu. Close to 70 percent of precipitation occurred at the height of the growing season in July and August, with almost no rain from October to May.[14] From the 1950s, the new government promoted two plantings per year—almost exclusively wheat in summers and a varied autumn crop primarily of sweet potato, along with soybeans, corn, sorghum, and rice.[15]

Despite the effort to extend two-crop cultivation in the 1950s, the compulsory grain procurement system of collective agriculture, coupled with population growth, ensured that farmers' livelihoods did not improve far above subsistence levels. The famine generated by the Great Leap Forward locked Feng County into a cycle of hunger. The 1966 grain harvests were still smaller than in 1955.[16] The per capita grain quota was 185 kilograms in 1956, but it dropped to 122 kilograms in 1960 (the height of the famine) and recovered only to 148 kilograms by 1965. During these years, wheat flour became a luxury—most of it was shipped off to cities. The staple diet in the villages became dried sweet potato slices, supplemented by corn and other coarse cereals. Before 1970,

---

13. *Jiangsu sheng Feng xian zhi*, p. 128. See also Mark Elvin, *The Retreat of the Elephants: An Ecological History of China* (New Haven, CT: Yale University Press, 2004), pp. 10–26 and 128–140; and Perry, *Rebels and Revolutionaries*, pp. 11–16.

14. Feng xian geming weiyuanhui, "Feng xian 'siwu,' 'wuwu' jingji fazhan guihua (cao'an)" (Feng County's economic development plan for the fourth and fifth five-year plans), March 1973.

15. *Jiangsu sheng Feng xian zhi*, pp. 131–140, and 231–243.

16. Ibid., p. 236. The combined summer and fall grain harvests in 1955 were 161,545 tons; in 1966, they were 157,680 tons, which represented a long slow recovery from the Great Leap famine.

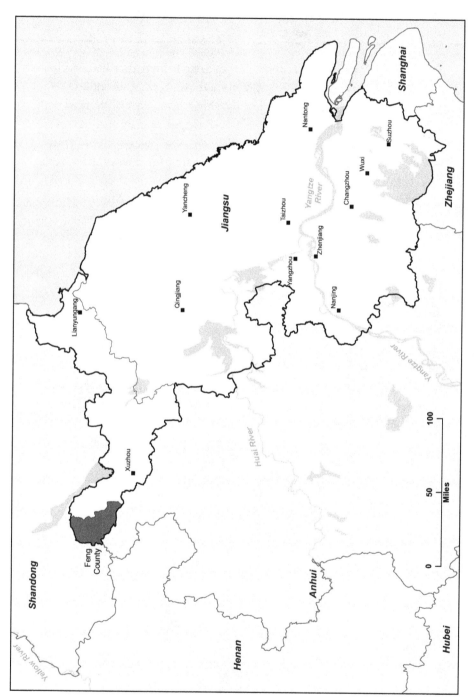

MAP 2. Jiangsu Province and surroundings

most of the rural population wore homespun clothing and lived in houses with earthen walls and a thatched grass roof.[17]

The county was overwhelmingly agrarian, even by the standards of rural China. Only 2.6 percent of its population of 624,000 lived in small towns—an urbanization rate that placed Feng County at the thirteenth percentile of more than two thousand counties nationwide. Only 7,100 adults held salaried non-agricultural jobs.[18] Due to chronic budget shortages, roughly one third of the employees in factories were temporary (*linshi*), seasonal (*jijie*), or contract workers (*hetong gong*). There were only ten state-owned enterprises in the county in 1965, the largest of which were a cotton textile mill and a chemical fertilizer plant, both of which employed several hundred.[19] Much smaller in scale, with workforces that rarely approached one hundred, were small plants that produced hardware, vegetable oils, wheat flour, distilled spirits, and other products, along with a small printing plant and an electric power generation station.[20] Even smaller were collectively owned workshops scattered across rural communes that repaired tractors and other agricultural machinery or produced bricks, furniture, farm tools, and alcoholic beverages.[21]

In the spring of 1966, the county had fifteen middle schools, with a total enrollment of 5,800. Only three of them had a high school division, the largest of which was Feng County Middle School, in the county seat, which recruited students county-wide, with roughly 2,000 enrolled.[22] Small percentages of the county's high school graduates were able to gain acceptance to a university, and a handful were admitted to elite institutions. In the spring of 1966 there were close to 700 post-1962 graduates of the county's high schools who were enrolled in universities across China.[23] Around 100 of them would return to Feng County in 1967 as student rebels and play a briefly influential role in the county's politics.

17. Ibid., pp. 953–954.

18. Ibid., pp. 119 and 675; and the database cited in Andrew G. Walder, *Agents of Disorder: Inside China's Cultural Revolution* (Cambridge, MA: Harvard University Press, 2019).

19. *Jiangsu sheng Feng xian zhi*, p. 271.

20. Ibid., p. 270; and Wang Wensheng, ed., *Feng xian jian zhi* (Brief Annals of Feng County) (Feng xian: Feng xian yinshua chang, 1986), pp. 221–226 and 252–253.

21. *Jiangsu sheng Feng xian zhi*, pp. 292–299.

22. Feng xian jiaoyu ju, *Feng xian jiaoyu dashiji (1903–2016)* (Feng County education chronology [1903–2016]), p. 113; and Zhang Liansheng interview.

23. *Jiangsu sheng Feng xian zhi*, p. 719.

In such an overwhelmingly agrarian county, there were very modest numbers of the students and workers who energized the Red Guard and rebel movements in urban areas during the last half of 1966. This, and Feng County's remote location, makes it somewhat puzzling that the county became so deeply engulfed in prolonged factional strife. This raises two questions. First, by what means would political impulses radiating out from Beijing and other large population centers reach into this impoverished county in the hinterlands? And second, in the absence of large populations of students and workers, who were the local political actors that played a pivotal role in shaping conflicts over the decade to follow? The answers to both questions are the same: the intertwined political and military hierarchies that formed the structure of the Chinese party-state.

The Power Structure

Feng County's economy may have been underdeveloped, but its party and government structures were not. China's party-state was a unitary hierarchy of party committees at the apex of each level of government, which in turn maintained active local networks of smaller party committees and branches. The county's party organization was directly subordinate to that of Xuzhou Prefecture, which in turn was directly subordinate to the Jiangsu Province capital in Nanjing, which in turn was under the central party and government in Beijing. There were 9,181 party members in the county at the end of 1965, in a hierarchy of twenty-one party committees and 581 grassroots party branches covering all workplaces and collective farms.[24]

The county had a well-developed administrative bureaucracy, with separate party and government hierarchies. In May 1966, on the eve of the events recounted in this book, Feng County held its Fifth Party Congress, selecting a county party committee of twenty-six members, nine of whom were at its apex, an executive council known as the standing committee. Gao Ying was the first party secretary, and there were three deputy party secretaries—Qian Xiufu, Teng Zetian, and Zhu Pingfan (see table 1). Except for Teng, all were natives of Feng County and had worked their way up in the hierarchy since the early 1950s.[25] In addition to a general office, the county party headquarters was divided into thirteen administrative departments in charge of

24. *Feng xian zuzhishi ziliao*, p. 5.
25. Ibid., pp. 112–113.

TABLE 1. Standing Committee, Feng County Party Committee
(in rank order), May 1966

Secretary
Gao Ying

Deputy Secretaries
Teng Zetian
Qian Xiufu (County Magistrate)
Zhu Pingfan

Members
Shao Wen (Political Commissar, People's Armed Department)
Dong Hongzhi (Secretary of Discipline Inspection Committee)
Wu Yunxiang (Head, Organization Department)
Meng Qinghua (Deputy County Magistrate)
Yang Zunzhong (Deputy County Magistrate)

Note: There were an additional 17 members of the County Party Committee.

organizational appointments, propaganda, industry, rural work, finance, and other functions.[26]

Alongside this party bureaucracy, and subordinate to it in authority, was the civilian government, the Feng County People's Committee. In mid-January 1966, the county held its Sixth People's Congress, which selected a new county leadership committee. Qian Xiufu, also a deputy party secretary, was appointed county magistrate, along with five deputy magistrates, all of whom were members of the county's party committee.[27] The separate government bureaucracy included a general office and more than thirty bureaucratic departments in charge of public security, the courts, agriculture, personnel, finance, taxation, grain management, transportation, and other functions. These two bureaucracies were by far the largest employers in the county, with more than 1,869 party and government functionaries, or "cadres," serving as full-time administrators.[28]

The party and government hierarchies also extended far outside the county seat. In 1966 there were twenty people's communes and a fruit orchard run as a state farm, each of which had party committees and government administrative

26. Ibid., pp. 116–119.

27. Ibid., pp. 113 and 222; and Zhang Liansheng interview.

28. Zhonggong Feng xian weiyuanhui, "Zhonggong Feng xian weiyuanhui pizhuan xianwei zuzhibu guanyu jiaqiang dang de jianshe wenti de sange baogao" (Feng County party committee transmits organization department's three reports on strengthening party building), May 13, 1966.

offices.[29] Under the rural communes were 441 production brigades (roughly coterminous with villages) and 3,314 production teams.[30] Each of the communes had a party secretary and several deputy secretaries, and cadres in charge of organization (personnel), propaganda, and youth work. In addition, the commune administration had a commune head and several deputy heads, and cadres in charge of civil affairs, finance, grain, production, statistics, accounting, women's issues, and a poor peasants association. These cadres were all on the state payroll, and they oversaw the activity of several administrative units, staffed by a mixture of cadres on the state payroll and rural residents paid out of commune funds: a supply and marketing cooperative, grain purchasing station, credit union, sanitation station, middle school, tractor station, cultural office, veterinary station, and so forth.

The cadres that staffed the bureaucracy were the county's elite. At the village level, the most basic of advantages was escape from manual labor. As a group, cadres had the highest salaries, enjoyed the best benefits and living standards (though very modest by today's standards), and were closely tied to patterns of political communication that radiated downward in the national hierarchy from Beijing to the grass roots. They enjoyed the most extensive personal networks within the county's power structure and had a very large stake in any political campaign, like the Cultural Revolution, which potentially threatened their positions and their vested interests in the system. As we shall see, they were an important political force in Feng County during the decade to come.

Even more consequential than the civilian party and government hierarchy in the conflicts over the next decade, however, were China's armed forces—regular troops serving in regional divisions of the People's Liberation Army, and the local People's Armed Departments and their militia forces. Often neglected in accounts of how China is governed is the military hierarchy that parallels each level in the government hierarchy. As civilian governments collapsed across China in early 1967, military units emerged as the primary instrument of political power and routine administration across vast regions of China. They also became deeply involved in local conflicts, and in Feng County they were at their epicenter.

Regional forces of the PLA were organized into provincial military districts (*sheng jun qu*) and subdistricts (*jun fen qu*) whose structure mirrored that of

---

29. *Feng xian zuzhishi ziliao*, pp. 232–241.

30. Feng xian geming weiyuanhui, "Feng xian 'si wu,' 'wu wu' jingji fazhan guihua."

civilian governments. Military districts were usually coterminous with provinces; military subdistricts with prefectures. They had detachments of troops on local bases. Feng County was under the jurisdiction of PLA units in the Xuzhou subdistrict.

Separate from these regional forces were "main force" combat units not tied to government jurisdictions. There were thirty-six army corps under the command of thirteen large military regions (*da jun qu*). These forces were jointly under the military region headquarters and the Central Military Commission. They included mainline infantry forces, as well as specialized armored, artillery, air, and (along the coasts and inland waterways) naval divisions. Detachments from these forces could be called upon for domestic political tasks as needed, and they were called upon repeatedly in the years to come.[31] In Feng County, a regiment from one of these regular PLA divisions, the 68th Army Corps, which was under the command of the Ji'nan Military Region in adjacent Shandong Province, was assigned to Feng County in 1967. Its officers and troops played a central role in political events as they unfolded across the decade.

At the bottom level of the regional military hierarchy were the garrison commands (*weishu qu*) in large cities, and People's Armed Departments (*renmin wuzhuang bu*) in counties and small cities. At this grass-roots level the military and civilian hierarchies overlapped. The heads of garrison commands and PADs were military officers, but they were under the dual authority of local civilian party committees and the military subdistrict, and were part of local civilian political structures. The heads of PADs, and also their political commissars, were typically members of the local party committee.[32]

People's Armed Departments did not have full-time troops, but they commanded local "people's militias" (*min bing*), which were reserve forces with stockpiles of light weapons. The county seat had one "backbone" (*jigan*) militia regiment, with each commune forming a battalion and each production team or factory a platoon. The militia forces consisted of males from sixteen to thirty years of age and females from sixteen to twenty-five, along with de-

31. Harvey W. Nelsen, "Military Forces in the Cultural Revolution." *China Quarterly* 51 (July–September 1972), pp. 444–474; and Harvey W. Nelsen, *The Chinese Military System: An Organizational Study of the Chinese People's Liberation Army* (Boulder, CO: Westview Press, 1981), pp. 7–9 and 115–123.

32. Wang, ed., *Feng xian jianzhi*, p. 155; *Feng xian zuzhishi ziliao*, pp. 312–313; and *Jiangsu sheng Feng xian zhi*, p. 591.

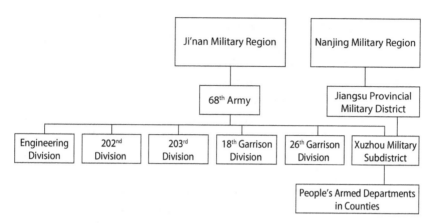

FIGURE 1. Military command structure of the Xuhai region

mobilized PLA soldiers.[33] In the county seat, the PAD had several small administrative offices staffed by about twenty military personnel, and a squadron of around forty military police (*jiefangjun zhongdui*), whose primary responsibility was guarding the county jail. Each commune had several civilian cadres in charge of PAD work.[34]

The Feng County PAD was under the authority of the Xuzhou Military Subdistrict of the PLA, which in turn was under the Jiangsu Military District, which was headquartered in Nanjing. This line of military authority was separate from the mainline PLA troops of the 68th Army Corps, under the command of the Ji'nan Military Region, who were assigned to the county in 1967 and who played an active role in Feng County politics for years thereafter. This division in lines of military authority played a crucial role in the development of Feng County's deep-seated and long-lasting factional conflicts (see figure 1).

On the eve of the Cultural Revolution, Gao Ying, the county's first party secretary, was nominally the PAD's first party secretary and political commissar. However, Shao Wen, one of the nine members of the party's standing committee, actually served as the PAD's full-time commissar and party secretary. Shao was appointed in 1963, having worked previously as head of the Xuzhou Military Subdistrict's propaganda department. The commander of the county PAD was Liu Zongbin, who was one of the twenty-six members of the county's party committee. He had served as the PAD commander since 1961,

33. Wang, ed., *Feng xian jianzhi*, pp. 155–156.

34. Ibid., p. 155; and *Jiangsu sheng Feng xian zhi*, p. 591.

and most of the subordinate PAD officers had long careers in Feng County.[35] Although Liu Zongbin and two subordinates were transferred to other places in early 1969, Shao Wen and most other PAD officers stayed in their positions until end of 1974. These figures in the PAD would play a central role in local political conflicts over the next decade. These conflicts would pit them and their rebel supporters in one of the county's civilian factions, known as Liansi (short for "Allied Headquarters"), in a long struggle against officers from the PLA's 68th Army Corps and the civilian faction aligned with them, known as Paolian (short for "Bombardment Alliance").

The Cultural Revolution developed slowly in Feng County, only after a considerable delay, along with the conflict between these different military forces and the civilian factions allied with them. There was little in the initial months of the campaign that would predict the combustible mix of military and civilian factionalism that eventually destroyed the county's political order for almost a decade. This deceptively slow development of political conflict in the county is the story of the next chapter.

35. *Feng xian zuzhishi ziliao*, pp. 121 and 313; and Zhang Liansheng interview.

2

Factions

THE MAY 16 CIRCULAR, a central party document that launched the Cultural Revolution, was issued on the eve of Feng County's Fifth Party Congress, which met May 18–20, 1966. The county's leaders were unprepared to respond to the flow of directives emanating from the nation's capital, and they were slow to appreciate the significance of this new campaign. Over the next month they focused on consolidating the authority of the new party leadership and making plans for the coming year. The county dutifully responded to Beijing's directives by issuing a notice about the Cultural Revolution on May 25, but it treated the new campaign primarily as an intensified program of political study and education. Mao's works on the Chinese revolution and the political objectives of literature and art, along with editorials in the national newspapers and polemical denunciations of recently purged figures in the nation's capital, were placed on lists of approved study materials.[1]

A Slow Beginning

Two months passed before the county's leaders established a Cultural Revolution committee to conduct the new campaign. When it was finally formed on July 20, it was essentially a subcommittee of the county's top leadership. The first party secretary, Gao Ying, was the head, and the vice-heads were Shao Wen (party standing committee member and commissar of the PAD) and one other party standing committee member. Several other members all held positions in the county's party committee. A special office was set up under the

1. Zhonggong Feng xian xianwei xuanchuan bu, "Guanyu kaizhan wenhua da geming xuexi de tongzhi" (Notice on unfolding the study of the Cultural Revolution), May 25, 1966.

county's propaganda department, and one deputy head of that department was its director.[2]

Like party committees across China, Feng County's leaders initially responded to the Cultural Revolution as if it were yet another in a series of top-down political campaigns. The Cultural Revolution committee's first act, on July 22, was to form a "summer training class" (*shuqi jixun ban*), to be held in the county seat, at Feng County Middle School. The sessions drew together teachers and staff from middle schools across the county, along with all staff of county and commune-level cultural bureaus, the broadcasting station, and the opera and dance troupes. Ostensibly a training class for ideological remolding, the sessions also conducted loyalty investigations, pursued through criticism and denunciation sessions.[3] The sessions began in late July and continued into October. Of the 530 participants, 139 were labeled "counterrevolutionaries" and were subjected to intense denunciation and harsh physical abuse.[4]

The county leadership was able to maintain top-down control of the campaign for almost half a year. Not until the end of December 1966, several months after such events in China's large cities, did Red Guard and rebel groups begin to target Feng County's party leadership. The rebellion of students and others was very slow to develop, but the first stirrings were in the county seat, at Feng County Middle School.

On June 16, the first Cultural Revolution wall poster appeared at Feng County Middle School, in imitation of the nationally celebrated one at Peking University, which appeared near the end of May. The author was a high school senior, son of a commune cadre, and head of his Communist Youth League branch. Due to poor grades, he had been held back one year. This motivated his criticism of the school's leaders for carrying out a "bourgeois educational line" that emphasized academic performance over political commitment. Like

2. Zhonggong Feng xian weiyuanhui, "Guanyu chengli xianwei wuchan jieji wenhua da geming lingdao xiaozu de tongzhi" (Notice on the establishment of county party committee leading small group for the great proletarian Cultural Revolution), July 20, 1966.

3. Zhonggong Feng xian weiyuanhui, "Guanyu shuqi xunlian chuzhong, nongzhong jiaozhi-yuan de tongzhi" (Notice on summer training sessions for junior middle school and agricultural middle school teachers and staff), July 22, 1966.

4. Jiangsu sheng Feng xian paoda silingbu lianhe zongbu, "Mao Zhuxi huishou wo qianjin— Feng xian liangtiao luxian douzheng dashiji (er gao)" (Chairman Mao waves us forward— Chronology of the two-line struggle in Feng County [second draft]), June 5, 1968.

the Peking University wall poster, this was considered the "first shot" of the Cultural Revolution in Feng County.[5]

Immediately afterward, two other seniors in the high school division put up wall posters that expressed similar sentiments. One was Zhang Liansheng, from a poor peasant family. As one of the school's top students, he aspired to continue his education at university. As part of this ambition, Zhang also had an established record of political activism. He was an activist in the Youth League and a representative to the school's student association. Several months earlier, in March 1966, the school's party committee convened a conference of teachers and student representatives, asking for opinions on the school's work. Zhang gave a speech in which he criticized the school administration for not paying sufficient attention to the propagation of Mao Zedong Thought, and for its neglect of political work among the graduating class. Afterward, Zhang wrote out his speech and posted it on school's bulletin board. On June 18, the high school's leaders convened an all-school oath-taking rally to mobilize students to carry out the Cultural Revolution. They selected Zhang Liansheng to give a speech expressing student support for Beijing's decision to launch the Cultural Revolution.[6] In neither of these speeches nor in the three June wall posters did the students directly criticize the school's leaders by name. But the challenge was implied: they were in charge of a school that was allegedly carrying out a "revisionist" educational line, and a confrontation with the school's authorities would follow.

These nascent conflicts with students, however, were overshadowed by preexisting tensions between two informal factions among the school's administrators and faculty, which soon led to an open split in the school's leadership. Feng County Middle School had merged with the former Feng County No. 2 Middle School in 1962, as a budget-cutting measure taken in the wake of the Great Leap Forward. Tensions between the personnel and students from the two schools followed. When the school organized to criticize the school's "revisionist educational line," officials from the two schools tried to place the

5. *Jiangsu sheng Feng xian zhi*, p. 27; "Mao Zhuxi huishou wo qianjin," June 5, 1968; *Feng xian jiaoyu dashiji*, p. 112; and Zhang Liansheng interview. The Peking University wall poster and its consequences are described in Andrew G. Walder, *Fractured Rebellion: The Beijing Red Guard Movement* (Cambridge, MA: Harvard University Press, 2009), pp. 35–38.

6. Zhang Liansheng interview; and Zhang Liansheng, "Gei Mao Zedong zhuxi ji Zhou Enlai zongli, Wang Hongwen fu zhuxi de xin" (Letter to Chairman Mao Zedong, Premier Zhou Enlai and Vice-Chairman Wang Hongwen), October 28, 1973.

blame on each other, and faculty and students connected to the two schools denounced alleged "revisionist cliques" of staff from the other school. At the same time, some militant students denounced *both* leadership cliques. With the school's own leaders turning on one another, the school fell into disorder.[7]

In response, the county's party committee assigned a work team to the school, led by the vice-director of the county's discipline inspection committee.[8] This was in line with a directive from Beijing in early June.[9] The work team's top priority was to reassert control over the politically chaotic situation in the school. They denounced leading officials in both of the two administration factions along with twenty other staff and faculty as members of a "black gang" (*hei bang*), and organized criticism rallies against them. The work team also moved against the three students who had put up wall posters critical of the school administration. Zhang Liansheng and his two classmates were denounced as "obstacles to the healthy development" of the campaign, and faculty, staff, and student activists were mobilized to criticize them as well. The school's director of instruction and its Communist Youth League secretary won the trust of the work team head, and the two became provisional leaders of the school after the school's leaders were forced to step down. Order was temporarily restored.[10]

Two of the students who were attacked for their wall posters were unable to withstand the political pressure and withdrew from the school, claiming illness. Zhang Liansheng, however, decided to tough it out in the school. This decision soon paid off, because news from Beijing turned the tables on the work team. At the end of July, Mao Zedong publicly criticized Liu Shaoqi and Deng Xiaoping for sending work teams to schools and "suppressing revolutionary students." In early August, Mao issued his public support for the "revo-

7. Zhang Liansheng interview; Interview no. 7; and Gao Dalin, *Yu xiu yuan wanji* (An old man's memoirs written in the Yuxiu garden), 2016, pp. 101 and 107–108; and *Feng xian jiaoyu dashiji*, p. 98.

8. *Feng xian jiaoyu dashiji*, p. 112; and Zhonggong Feng xian xianwei dangshi gongzuo weiyuanhui, ed., *Zhonggong Feng xian difangshi dashiji (1928.1–2002.6)* (History of the Chinese Communist Party in Feng County) (Xuzhou, 2002), p. 226.

9. Bu Weihua, *Zalan jiu shijie: Wenhua da geming de dongluan yu haojie* (Smashing the old world: The catastrophic turmoil of the Cultural Revolution) (Hong Kong: Zhongwen daxue chubanshe, 2008), pp. 150–152.

10. Zhang Liansheng interview; and "Mao Zhuxi huishou wo qianjin," June 5, 1968.

lutionary actions" of the Tsinghua University high school students and issued his own wall poster to "bombard the headquarters."[11]

As the political tides shifted, Feng County Middle School's work team convened students and teachers to listen to tape recordings of central leaders' speeches about the political errors of work teams. As soon as the recording ended, Zhang Liansheng stood up shouted "Long live Chairman Mao!" and later that same day, he put up a new wall poster, this time denouncing the work team's "bourgeois reactionary line."[12]

Bowing to these shifting political realities, but only after some delay, the county party committee withdrew the work team near the end of August. As they withdrew, they formed a Cultural Revolution committee for the school, headed by the same two officials that the work team had earlier placed in charge of the school. Student activists demanded that the work team be publicly criticized for suppressing the rebellious students, but the county party committee refused. In response, in mid-September, Zhang Liansheng put up a wall poster criticizing the county party committee, a first in the county.[13]

The conflicts within the school over the work team issue were soon forgotten, however, as students began to take advantage of the new freedom to travel across the country and "exchange revolutionary experiences." Perhaps recognizing the value of sending potentially troublesome students out of the county, the authorities organized and funded delegations of more than one thousand students and teachers to go to Beijing, under the supervision of a county official. By the end of September, most students and teachers headed to Beijing and other cities, individually or in groups. Most of them, and not only political activists, attended the large Tiananmen Square rallies that Mao held for Red Guards in October and November. Zhang Liansheng and some of his classmates attended the last of the Tiananmen rallies, on November 26.[14]

In mid-December, after most of the students and teachers returned to the county, Red Guard organizations were formed for the first time. Red Guard

11. Zhonggong zhongyang, "Zhonggong zhongyang guanyu wuchan jieji wenhua da geming yundong de jueding" (CCP Central Committee decision regarding the great proletarian Cultural Revolution movement), August 8, 1966; and Roderick MacFarquhar and Michael Schoenhals, *Mao's Last Revolution* (Cambridge, MA: Harvard University Press, 2006), pp. 81–92.

12. Zhang Liansheng interview; and "Mao Zhuxi huishou wo qianjin," June 5, 1968.

13. Zhang Liansheng interview; and "Mao Zhuxi huishou wo qianjin," June 5, 1968.

14. Tragically, one female student in the delegation was trampled to death in the crowd at one of the rallies. Zhang Liansheng, "Gei Mao Zedong zhuxi ji Zhou Enlai zongli, Wang Hongwen fu zhuxi de xin," October 28, 1973; and *Jiangsu sheng Feng xian zhi*, p. 28; *Feng xian jiaoyu dashiji*, p. 113.

PHOTOGRAPH 1. Zhang Liansheng as a Paolian leader, in Tiananmen Square, 1968

organizations had appeared in more than 85 percent of China's cities and counties three months before, but this delay was not at all unusual for remote agrarian counties.[15] Six separate Red Guard organizations emerged in the middle
school, three were composed of students, and three of teachers and staff.
Zhang Liansheng was the organizer of one of the student Red Guard organizations. These six organizations would later play a key role in the rebel campaign against the county leadership. In January they would form the first rebel
alliance, the Feng County Middle School Red Guard First Headquarters (*Feng
zhong yisi*). Later that month it would form the nucleus of a broader alliance

15. Walder, *Agents of Disorder*, pp. 30–33.

of student and other rebels, and Zhang Liansheng would emerge as one of its top leaders.[16]

The students and faculty who had supported the school's work team during its brief occupation of the school were unwilling to be shunted aside. The work team, after all, had pursued an energetic campaign against school administrators lacking in loyalty to Mao Zedong Thought. In their view, the fact that they had cooperated with this purge of both factions in the school administration did not disqualify them as left-wing rebels. They formed a rival Red Guard Second Headquarters shortly after the first one appeared. A third Red Guard alliance was formed by yet another group of militant students, led by a student activist who had denounced both factions in the school leadership back in June, and who later put up a wall poster denouncing the county's party secretary in October. Although its stance, like that of the First Headquarters, had been antagonistic to the work team and to the county leaders, members of the third group became rivals in the emerging campaign to confront the county officials over the work team issue. This rivalry led them to form a competing rebel alliance near the end of January, and they absorbed the Second Headquarters into their ranks, despite the fact that they had taken different stances toward the work team.[17] This group would gravitate into the other major faction in the county's subsequent political conflicts. Similar conflicts occurred at the county's other two middle schools, located in Huankou and Songlou Communes, but they did not play such a central role in subsequent events as those in the county seat.[18]

Political activism during the last half of 1966 was not restricted to students. Workers, staff, and even cadres in the county bureaucracy would eventually mobilize rebel groups, but they did so after some delay, and only after students organized rebel groups in December and rebel alliances in January 1967. Workers

16. "Mao Zhuxi huishou wo qianjin," June 5, 1968; Feng xian zhengfa hongse geming zaofan zong silingbu, "Feng xian 'paoda silingbu lianhe zongbu' de qingkuang zonghe" (An overview of the situation regarding Feng County's "Bombard the Headquarters Allied General Headquarters"), March 18, 1967; Zhongguo renmin jiefangjun ji zi 283 budui gongzuozu ji 6174 budui zhu Feng xian sanzhi liangjun budui, "Guanyu 'paolian' wenti de diaocha baogao" (Investigation report on the 'Paolian' question), July 6, 1967; Zhang Liansheng interview; and Interview no. 3.

17. Zhang Liansheng interview; Interview no. 7.

18. These conflicts are detailed in the following sources, but there is little to be gained by detailing them here: Zhang Liansheng interview; "Mao Zhuxi huishou wo qianjin," June 5, 1968; Interview no. 1; Huang Xiuhua interview; and Interview no. 6.

at the largest industrial enterprise in the county, the Feng County cotton textile mill, began to mobilize at the end of January. A major issue motivating workers was the low pay and poor working conditions of the many contract workers hired from the rural communes. Their wall posters criticized the "privileged class" of the shop supervisors and technicians who had higher pay and more comfortable working conditions. These complaints resonated widely with the hundreds of low-paid mill workers, but supervisors and technicians denounced these complaints as "economism," and insisted that the Cultural Revolution should focus on political questions, not on benefits and livelihood.[19]

Workers and staff in the cotton mill formed rebel organizations in late January, under the influence of student activists, based primarily on workshops and work groups. They split into two factions, initially based on the dispute about the legitimacy of complaints focused on living standards. The larger of the two factions included many of the temporary workers, along with some of the permanent employees. It pushed for improvements in pay and working conditions. A second, smaller faction felt that political issues rather than livelihood questions should be the focus of the movement. Unlike the students in the middle school, neither group challenged the county's leaders—there had been no work team in the factory. The factions did not take opposed stances toward their mill's top leaders—both were critical of them. They did disagree with each other over livelihood demands. When two broad political factions formed later in 1967, each faction chose different sides in order to obtain support for their conflicts within the mill.[20]

Far more consequential were internal rebellions by cadres who worked in the county bureaucracy. Roughly half of the county's cadres and staff were sent to carry out the Socialist Education Campaign in nearby counties and did not return to the county seat until late January.[21] This later bred political divisions among the county's cadres. The staff members who had remained in their jobs in the county found it unwise to remain inert in the face of growing challenges to the county leadership by students and others. The first organization of

19. Li Zongzhou interview; and Interview no. 2.

20. Li Zongzhou interview; and Interview no. 2.

21. Interview no. 4. The campaign is described in Roderick MacFarquhar, *The Origins of the Cultural Revolution*, vol. 3: *The Coming of the Cataclysm 1961–1966* (New York: Columbia University Press, 1997), pp. 334–348; and Andrew G. Walder, *China under Mao: A Revolution Derailed* (Cambridge, MA: Harvard University Press, 2015), pp. 189–193.

county cadres and staff, the Party Organs Scarlet Guards (*xianwei jiguan chi-weidui*), was formed shortly after students began their open challenge to the county's leaders. The founder was Li Zhi, an aide in the county propaganda department.

The Scarlet Guards insisted on the "principle of party leadership" and opposed the escalating challenges of student rebels to the county's leaders. The organization, however, was not established in order to defend the county's leaders, whom they soon proved willing to abandon, nor was it organized at their superiors' instigation. According to Li Zhi's retrospective account, he and his colleagues organized on their own initiative only after the party center issued documents in December encouraging workers and staff to form rebel organizations. It seemed wise under the circumstances to conform to the shifting tides of the campaign. An important motivation, Li admitted, was self-protection. He and a number of his colleagues, who worked in the propaganda department, had been active in organizing and running the summer training classes for teachers and staff, and many of those who had been persecuted in the classes were demanding that those responsible be criticized. Li and his colleagues reasoned that they might be able to deflect these demands if they formed a rebel organization of their own. The Scarlet Guards existed only briefly before merging with a broader rebel group in the county government offices, to create a single alliance of cadre rebels in the county organs.[22]

A similar rebel organization, known as the Feng County Politics and Law Red Revolutionary Rebel Headquarters (*Feng xian zhengfa hongse geming zaofan zong silingbu*), was founded in January inside the public security bureau, public prosecutor's office, and court system. It was led by three ordinary staff members, one each from the public security bureau, the public prosecutor's office, and the county court. Its motive also was self-protection for its members. Working in the county's organs of repression, the members feared a backlash from those who had suffered persecution. As a result, they opposed the stance of student rebels who began to attack the county's leaders. But within their corner of the county bureaucracy, they adopted a militant campaign against their own superiors, blaming them for past abuses. Their animus toward their superiors reflected informal antagonisms between Feng County insiders and outsiders who had been transferred in from elsewhere. The directors

22. Li Zhi interview. Similar Scarlet Guard organizations among party and government staff were common across China beginning in September 1966, but they rapidly declined in November. See Walder, *Agents of Disorder*, pp. 40–44.

of each of the three departments in their system had all been transferred in to their posts from outside the county in the past year. Their subordinates were all natives of the county, and they rebelled against their own superiors.[23]

A nationwide rebel campaign to repudiate the "bourgeois reactionary line" of regional and local party committees had been in full swing across China since late October. This was a turning point in the Cultural Revolution. At a three-week conference in Beijing, local leaders were denounced for resisting the rebel campaign by taking measures to block or repress rebel activists.[24] Although this campaign came late to Feng County, where rebel groups were still small and weak, the county's leaders understood the necessity of showing compliance with this national trend. In January, party secretary Gao Ying and other county leaders voluntarily attended several mass rallies sponsored by student rebel groups to "criticize the county party committee's bourgeois re-actionary line." At these rallies, the leaders of high school work teams, the cadres and political activists who ran the summer training classes, and several section chiefs in the county bureaucracy were subjected to mass criticism and denunciation, and several were beaten. The county's leaders did nothing to control the violence.[25]

In a further effort to placate the rebels, on January 25 the county party committee apologized publicly to the victims of their loyalty investigations during 1966. They pledged that the reputations of all victims would be restored, the charges dropped, and that the "black materials" placed in their files would be publicly destroyed.[26] Several days later another rehabilitation notice stated that all individuals who had been criticized, paraded through the streets, or physically abused would have their reputations restored, and that all work unit leaders responsible must convene mass rallies to publicly apologize and de-stroy any "black materials."[27] These concessions appeared to take the energy out of the nascent rebel campaign. Rebel groups held rallies to criticize Gao Ying on January 26 and 31, but they did not move to seize power from the county party committee.

23. Zhang Liansheng interview; and *Feng xian zuzhishi ziliao*, pp. 228–229.

24. See MacFarquhar and Schoenhals, *Mao's Last Revolution*, pp. 136–140.

25. "Feng xian 'paoda silingbu lianhe zongbu' de qingkuang zonghe," March 18, 1967; and "Guanyu 'paolian' wenti de diaocha baogao," July 6, 1967.

26. Zhonggong Feng xian weiyuanhui, "Pingfan tongzhi" (Rehabilitation notice). January 25, 1967.

27. Zhonggong Feng xian weiyuanhui, "Guanyu pingfan wenti de jinji tongzhi" (Urgent directive on the question of rehabilitation), January 30, 1967.

The lack of any move by local rebels to overthrow the county's leaders permitted them to stay in office until the end of February, when the People's Armed Department, under Shao Wen, took over the administration of the county and shunted the civilian party leadership aside. This, however, did nothing to curtail the growing political conflicts in the county, nor did it prevent the emergence of two opposed political factions. To the contrary, the move to exert military control served only to exacerbate and deepen local political divisions.

The Emergence of Factions

Feng County's rebel movement was so small, and so late in developing, that there were no factional divisions of the kind that emerged in China's large cities early in the autumn of 1966. At this point in time there was little disagreement among the disparate mass organizations of students, workers, cadres, and staff that the work teams committed political errors of the kind denounced personally by Mao many months before. There was little disagreement, moreover, that the county leaders had to apologize and make a public self-criticism for their actions.

The opening wedge for disagreements was initially whether additional punishments should be meted out to the heads of work teams, and later, how the county's leaders should be treated, disagreements that emerged in the heat of mass meetings. This initial fissure widened when militant university students returned to their native Feng County to push its politics in a direction that fit more closely with national trends. Resentment against the interference of the returning student "outsiders" helped to create the first factional divisions among the mass organizations that were just beginning to grow after such a long delay in Feng County.

Students and teachers who had clashed with work teams in the county's middle schools made demands about the work teams as early as August and September 1966. At that time the county's leaders stubbornly refused to permit the criticism of work team leaders or to release them to student activists for mass criticism meetings. But these nascent disputes were largely forgotten as student activists went on the road in late September to Beijing and other locations. When these students finally returned home in December, they adopted a more aggressive stance, having been radicalized by their observation of political trends in large cities. They now insisted that their work team's "suppression of the masses" be exposed and criticized on a public stage. These were standard demands of student radicals in cities back in September 1966, and they had the clear approval of Mao and his radical associates in Beijing as early as October.[28] Given the altered circumstances, this time the county's leaders readily agreed. Work team leaders were sent to their respective high schools for public criticism and denunciation.

Problems emerged when students at the Huankou Middle School demanded that their work team head, after undergoing mass criticism, be expelled from the Communist Party. The county party secretary, Gao Ying, refused, arguing that party membership was controlled by the Xuzhou Prefecture Organization Department, and that as a county-level leader, he did not have the authority to expel him.[29] Viewing this as obstruction, the students denounced Gao Ying himself, and the party committee that he headed.

On January 6, 1967, the county party committee convened a conference of county, commune, and production brigade cadres in Shazhuang Commune to discuss agricultural issues. Student activists from Feng County Middle School went to the commune government compound to demonstrate their objections to Gao Ying's alleged obstruction. They viewed this meeting in a remote location outside the county seat as an attempt to avoid student militants. They rushed into the meeting and forced Gao Ying to sign a statement calling a halt to his "secret black meeting." After learning of this planned action, an even larger number of students and faculty from the middle school hurried to Shazhuang and defended the county's leaders, arguing that Gao Ying should not be forced to sign such a statement under duress. They argued that the dissident students were trying to trump up a false charge, "grasping at straws" (lao daocao). Outnumbered and out-argued, the dissident students withdrew.[30]

These nascent fissures were opened wider by the arrival of university students—natives of Feng County and graduates of its middle schools—who returned in January to try to push forward the county's laggard political cam-

28. See Walder, *Fractured Rebellion,* pp. 157–169; and Zhonggong zhongyang zhuanfa zhongyang junwei, zong zheng, "Guanyu jundui yuanxiao wuchan jieji wenhua da geming de jinji tongzhi" (Urgent notice on the great proletarian Cultural Revolution in military academies), October 5, 1966.

29. "Mao Zhuxi huishou wo qianjin," June 5, 1968; "Feng xian 'paoda silingbu lianhe zongbu' de qingkuang zonghe," March 18, 1967; and Zhang Liansheng interview.

30. "Mao Zhuxi huishou wo qianjin," June 5, 1968.

paign against revisionist power holders. The leaders were students at Tsinghua University, Beijing Petroleum Institute, Beijing Medical College, Jilin Industrial Institute, Nanjing University, and Shanghai's East China Normal University. Numbering at their high point close to one hundred, the university students traveled to local schools, factories, and communes to encourage confrontations with "revisionist power-holders." They spurred the formation of new rebel groups at the cotton mill, county power plant, construction company, bus station, and chemical fertilizer plant.[31]

The returned university students strongly supported the dissident students and teachers and pushed them to take a more militant stand against the county's leaders. They helped the students form alliances with workers and staff in other units, and advised them about building rebel organizations. Under their guidance, militant students at the county middle school formed the Feng County Middle School First Headquarters. On January 15, the university students formally organized their own rebel group, the Rebel Brigade of University Red Guards Returning to Feng County (*dazhuan yuanxiao hongweibing fu Feng zaofan tuan*), with more than a hundred members.[32]

The first public confrontation between mass organizations took place on January 17, at a large rally jointly held by all of the county's rebel organizations to "Bombard the County Party Committee." Gao Ying attended, and the plan was that he would apologize to the masses and engage in a self-criticism for carrying out the "bourgeois reactionary line." Trying to prevent violent treatment at the hands of student radicals, Gao wore a PLA uniform. As soon as he appeared and took his place on the stage, the acting chair of the rally, a rebel leader in the county post office, invited Gao to sit down. As he did so, a militant student in the crowd shouted that he should "stand up and hear the criticism of the masses!" The chairman argued that the criticism should be civilized, not harsh and violent. The returned university students loudly supported the demand that Gao Ying stand up. They helped take over the rostrum and then ordered Gao to take off his PLA uniform, saying that as a civilian cadre he had no right to wear it. A majority of the people at the rally opposed this

31. Ibid.; "Feng xian 'paoda silingbu lianhe zongbu' de qingkuang zonghe," March 18, 1967; "Guanyu 'paolian' wenti de diaocha baogao," July 6, 1967; Interview no. 8; and Zhang Liansheng interview.

32. "Mao Zhuxi huishou wo qianjin," June 5, 1968.

and shouted down the militant students, who withdrew. Gao sat through the criticism session without further disruption.[33]

This event drove a wedge between the militant university students, along with the local rebels they supported, and the other rebel groups that had already organized on their own. These included a large and varied collection of recently formed rebel groups: within the county party and government offices, the public security system, the county transportation bureau, the cotton mill, and the hardware factory. It also included high school students who had not clashed with work teams, and more militant high school students who had clashed with their work teams, but who felt a rivalry with the rebels aligned with the university students. On the morning of January 18, these latter groups launched an attack on the university rebels, whom they viewed as interfering outsiders. Several hundred local activists, led by Li Zhi, the aide in the county propaganda department who now headed a rebel group within the county party headquarters, marched to the county government's guesthouse, where the university students were staying, intending to drive them out of the county. Rebels from Feng County Middle School and the county power plant rushed to the scene and argued with them, leading to a stalemate. Later that afternoon, some of the university students and high school rebels invaded the county government compound to search for "black materials" in the county's files. Rebel groups in the county offices blocked them.[34]

The next day, at another mass criticism rally to criticize Gao Ying, conflict ensued. Once again Gao wore a PLA uniform, and once again militant students demanded that he take it off. Gao argued that he had a right to wear the uniform as the nominal political commissar of the county's People's Armed Department. Rebels on the scene phoned the PAD offices and the Xuzhou Military Subdistrict, both of which confirmed Gao's claim. The militant students, unconvinced, began to suspect that these organs were trying to shield Gao.[35] At another rally to "bombard the county party committee" the following day, the dispute over the army uniform broke out once again. When university students jumped onto the stage and demanded that Gao remove his uniform, other students rushed the stage and forcibly dragged the university students away. The mass meeting ended in chaos.[36]

33. Ibid.
34. Ibid.
35. Ibid.
36. "Guanyu 'paolian' wenti de diaocha baogao," July 6, 1967.

The Formation of Paolian

These were the events that sparked the formation of the first broad alliance of local rebels, one that would play a key role in the county's factional conflicts over the next decade. On January 22 the leaders of the Feng County Middle School First Headquarters, joined by rebels from the construction company, the power plant, the chemical fertilizer plant, and Shizhai Commune, along with the returned university students, held a meeting at which they founded a broad rebel alliance, Bombard the County Party Committee United Headquarters (*paohong xianwei lianhe zongbu*). The alliance became one of the county's two large factions, henceforth known by its abbreviated name, Paolian.

Paolian's leading group was organized as a general committee and a standing committee, which included representatives from the Feng County Middle School and more than ten other factories, offices, and communes. The members of the Paolian leadership at this point in time were a cross section of the rebel groups across the county. The most prominent included Shan Shutang, a demobilized soldier and bus driver; Zhang Liansheng, the student activist at Feng County Middle School; a carpenter from the county construction company; and several other worker activists from the power plant, the chemical fertilizer plant, and other units.[37] Like rebel alliances elsewhere in China, Paolian was a loose association of like-minded rebel groups scattered across a large number of schools and workplaces.

Paolian was established only one day after rebels in Xuzhou City seized power, and rebels in the provincial capital in Nanjing seized power from both the provincial and city government four days later, on January 26.[38] This was the point at which militant students from Huankou Middle School demanded that Gao Ying expel their work team head from the Communist Party. Gao had refused, claiming that he had no authority to do so. The students then forcibly escorted Gao and their work team head to Xuzhou to petition the

---

37. "Feng xian 'paoda silingbu lianhe zongbu' de qingkuang zonghe," March 18, 1967; and "Guanyu 'paolian' wenti de diaocha baogao," July 6, 1967.

38. Xuzhou shi shizhi bangongshi bian, *Zhonggong Xuzhou difang shi (1949–1978) (Zhengqiu yijian gao)* (History of the Chinese Communist Party in Xuzhou [1949–1978] [Draft for comments], internal document, Xuzhou, May 2008, p. 159; and Dong Guoqiang and Andrew G. Walder, "Forces of Disorder: The Army in Xuzhou's Factional Warfare, 1967–1969," *Modern China* 44, 2 (March 2018): 139–169.

prefecture party committee, which Gao claimed had the sole authority over such matters. On arriving in the prefecture headquarters, however, the students found that the prefecture party committee no longer existed, having just been deposed by rebels. The Huankou students then checked into a hotel with their two captives to wait for the situation to clear up. A group of Paolian rebels slipped into the hotel that night to kidnap Gao Ying and escort him back to the county, placing him in custody at the county's power plant.[39] With Gao in their custody, the rebels held a mass rally on January 26 to publicly declare the formation of Paolian.[40]

It was at this point in time that the county's leaders withdrew charges against the victims of earlier stages of the Cultural Revolution and voluntarily submitted to mass criticism meetings.[41] These concessions satisfied Paolian's leaders, who made no move to seize power or occupy the county headquarters. The militant university students who returned to Feng County to participate in the rebellion against local leaders urged Zhang Liansheng, now a prominent Paolian leader, to take advantage of the situation and declare a power seizure. Paolian was strongly critical of the county's leaders, but it had no intention of seizing power. Zhang and his colleagues turned aside the advice of the university students, arguing reasonably that they did not have the ability to administer the county.[42] This rationale did not deter rebels in other localities. In response to urgings from Beijing issued in all the national media on January 22, a wave of power seizures over cities and counties spread rapidly across the country. By the end of February, rebel groups had declared power seizures in just over two-thirds of China's rural counties, and by the end of March, just under 80 percent of them. Feng County was among the 20 percent of counties nationwide where rebels did not attempt to seize power over the local government.[43]

39. "Mao Zhuxi huishou wo qianjin," June 5, 1968; and "Feng xian 'paoda silingbu lianhe zongbu' de qingkuang zonghe," March 18, 1967.

40. "Mao Zhuxi huishou wo qianjin," June 5, 1968; and Zhang Liansheng interview.

41. "Pingfan tongzhi," January 25, 1967; and "Guanyu pingfan wenti de jinji tongzhi," January 30, 1967.

42. Zhang Liansheng interview.

43. Calculated from the dataset employed in Walder, *Agents of Disorder*. See the discussion in that book, pp. 79–91, and the analysis of the wave of power seizures in Andrew G. Walder and Qinglian Lu, "The Dynamics of Collapse in an Authoritarian Regime: China in 1967," *American Journal of Sociology* 122, 4 (January 2017): 1144–1182.

How can we explain the lack of a rebel power seizure in Feng County? Paolian's hesitancy is not hard to understand. The primary goal of rebels during this phase of the Cultural Revolution was the withdrawal of charges lodged against individuals in the early months of the campaign. Students who had clashed with their work teams and had been punished as a result, and faculty and staff who had been charged with political offenses during the summer training classes, were motivated primarily to ensure that these charges would not come back to haunt them in the future. Even in major cities with large and militant rebel movements, the primary objective of rebels was an official apology and the destruction of negative materials in their files. One of the top Red Guard leaders in Beijing at the time argued that the rebel movement had achieved all of its aims, and that the further persecution of leading officials was unnecessary.[44] The rebels who led the Jiangsu provincial power seizure in Nanjing near the end of January also initially hesitated to seize power, satisfied that their demands had all been met, and like Zhang Liansheng they reasoned that they did not have the necessary administrative abilities. They seized power only after Zhou Enlai urged them to do so in a telephone call.[45]

Perhaps Paolian would eventually have decided to declare a power seizure, as it became clearer that this was a national trend. The rebel movement in Feng County was late in developing and had not formed a countywide coalition until the very end of January. But the window of opportunity for Paolian to do so would soon close. On January 28, 1967, central authorities ordered the PLA to intervene in the wake of local power seizures to support "the revolutionary masses of the left" and "safeguard production and normal work."[46] If military units intervened before a power seizure, the window would be closed.

The Xuhai region was under an accelerated timetable. The 68th Army, under the Ji'nan Military Region, was moving quickly to consolidate local order after the rapid establishment of the Shandong Province Revolutionary Committee on February 3—the second revolutionary committee in all of China. Military

44. This was Zhu Chengzhao, rebel leader at the Beijing Geology Institute and founder of Beijing's rebel Third Headquarters. Despite being one of the most prominent radical student leaders from September on, he was denounced as a traitor for dissenting from the escalation of rebel demands. See Walder, *Fractured Rebellion*, 201–202.

45. See Dong Guoqiang and Andrew G. Walder, "Nanjing's Failed 'January Revolution' of 1967: The Inner Politics of a Provincial Power Seizure," *China Quarterly* 203 (September 2010): 675–692, at pp. 680–681. Zhou saw a power seizure as the best way to wrap up the rebel campaign and curtail the further deterioration of public order.

46. See Walder, *Agents of Disorder*, p. 117.

intervention occurred in only one-third of China's counties by the end of February, and elsewhere in Jiangsu Province only 20 percent. In Shandong, military units intervened in 60 percent of all counties by the end of February, to prepare for the rapid establishment of local revolutionary committees, and the 68th Army was pushing to accomplish the same thing in the Xuhai region.[47] The opportunity for Paolian to declare a power seizure closed at the end of February, when the PAD stepped in to depose local officials.

Paolian decided to collaborate with local authorities rather than overthrow them. Although *People's Daily* published two editorials to call for power seizures on January 22, Zhou Enlai met in Beijing with rebels from throughout the country the same day, stating that power seizures should permit officials to remain at their posts while working under rebel supervision.[48] This was followed in late February by a central document calling for rebels to "treat cadres correctly."[49] Paolian decided to work together with the now-apologetic county authorities. In mid-February, they set up a Feng County Revolutionary Rebel Provisional Production Monitoring Committee (*Feng xian geming zaofan pai linshi jiandu shengchan weiyuanhui*) to "supervise" the county's leaders.[50] This gave Paolian the appearance of a share in local political power, but it did not constitute a power seizure of the kind spreading rapidly across China.

47. They established a revolutionary committee in Xuzhou City and in three counties in Xuzhou Prefecture (Pei, Pi, and Xinyi) by March, all of which later fell apart.

48. "Zhou Enlai tongzhi daibiao Mao zhuxi, dang zhongyang, guowuyuan, zhongyang junwei, zhongyang wen'ge dui wuchan jieji geming zaofan pai da lianhe, da duoquan wenti zuo zhongyao zhishi" (Comrade Zhou Enlai relays important instructions to proletarian revolutionary rebels about the great alliance and great power seizure on behalf of Chairman Mao, the Party Center, the State Council, the Central Military Commission and the Central Cultural Revolution Group), January 22, 1967.

49. See "Bixu zhengque duidai ganbu" (It is necessary to treat cadres correctly), *Hongqi*, no. 4 (1 March 1967); the editorial was published in advance in *Remin ribao*, February 23, 1967, p. 1.

50. For a brief period, instructions were issued jointly by the county government and the provisional production monitoring committee; Feng xian geming zaofan pai linshi jiandu shengchan weiyuanhui, Feng xian renmin weiyuanhui, "Guanyu fenpei huafei de tongzhi" (Notice on the distribution of chemical fertilizer), February 23, 1967; Feng xian geming zaofanpai linshi jiandu shengchan weiyuanhui, Feng xian renmin weiyuan hui, "Guanyu renzhen zuohao shanyu yumiao yongmei gongying gongzuo de tongzhi" (Notice on carrying out well the distribution of coal for the raising of sweet potato seedlings), February 28, 1967.

The Reaction against Paolian

The formation of Paolian appeared to put the other Feng County rebels, who had pushed back against what they viewed as excessively militant demands by the outside university rebels, in something of a quandary. They responded by adopting a much more militant stance and moved more aggressively against Gao Ying. On February 7 they sent a group to the electric power plant, where Gao was being held by Paolian rebels, and forcibly took him into custody. They subjected him to a mass denunciation meeting and then locked him up, planning to use him in another mass denunciation rally. Frustrated by their loss of control over Gao, Paolian scheduled its own mass denunciation meeting against him for February 9, and demanded that he be released into their custody. The other rebels refused and scheduled their own criticism rally for that same day.[51] More than a thousand Paolian activists stormed their rivals' February 9 rally and seized Gao, injuring several people in the process. The rival rebels retaliated by destroying a Paolian propaganda truck.[52] This became known as the "February 9 Incident"; Paolian and its opponents denounced each other as conservatives who "publicly criticized but secretly protected" Gao Ying.

Having recaptured Gao, Paolian convened its mass rally to denounce him on February 10. The other rebels reacted by summoning several hundred farmers from communes near the county seat to disrupt the event. They later raided a factory controlled by Paolian and took several activists into custody. Paolian's leaders complained to the county public security bureau, asking that the rebels who smashed their propaganda truck and raided the factory be arrested, but their request was denied.[53] At the time, the public security bureau was no longer under the authority of its leaders, who had recently been overthrown by a rebel group within the bureau (as described earlier).

Frustrated by this refusal, Paolian's leaders planned to seize power over the public security bureau themselves, alienating the rebels who already controlled it. In response, the rebels in the bureau arrested two Paolian activists on trumped-up charges of "sabotaging production" and "yelling reactionary slogans."[54] Paolian responded by putting up wall posters that charged that "the

51. "Mao Zhuxi huishou wo qianjin," June 5, 1968.

52. Ibid.

53. Ibid.; and "Guanyu 'paolian' wenti de diaocha baogao," July 6, 1967.

54. "Mao Zhuxi huishou wo qianjin," June 5, 1968; Feng xian zhengfa hongse geming zao-fan zong silingbu, "Feng xian wenhua da geming yundong zhong juliu anjian cheng pibiao"

county public security bureau was a tool of bourgeois dictatorship" and demanded that rebels "bombard the public security bureau."

Seeking support in this emerging conflict, Zhang Liansheng went to the county office of the People's Armed Department. This was in line with the late January orders that the PLA "resolutely support the revolutionary left."[55] In a meeting with two junior officers, he suggested that Paolian enter the public security bureau and seize power, afterward turning over control to the People's Armed Department. The officers declined, claiming a lack of personnel.[56]

This disappointed Paolian's leaders, who began to suspect that the PAD's political commissar, Shao Wen, sympathized with the other side. They recalled that Shao was the deputy director of the Feng County Cultural Revolution Leading Group back at the outset of the Cultural Revolution, and that he was thereby complicit in the summer training classes that left so many aggrieved victims. Perhaps, they thought, he was himself implicated in the bourgeois reactionary line, and preferred the other rebel organizations.[57]

There is at most circumstantial evidence to support Paolian's suspicions about Shao Wen's sympathies. The county PAD did not play any role in political events in the county until mid-February 1967. Shao was not a native of the county and had only been transferred into his current post in 1964. As commissar in charge of the PAD, he was a member of the standing committee of the county's party committee, so he was part of the party establishment. Yet the organization was under the authority of the Xuzhou Military Subdistrict of the PLA, and the PLA was under clear instructions to "resolutely support the revolutionary left." A simpler explanation for the PAD's noncommittal stance is that the PAD could not determine which group of rebels were genu-

---

(Application form for authorizing arrests made during Feng County's Cultural Revolution movement), February 12, 1967; Feng xian gongan ju, "Feng xian gongan ju gonggao" (Public notice of the Feng County public security bureau), February 20, 1967; Feng xian shachang paolian pai "er.san shijian" diaocha zu, "Er yue san ri zhuan'an diaocha baogao" (Investigation report on the 'February 3 incident'), June 3, 1967; and Interview no. 3.

55. Zhonggong zhongyang, guowuyuan, zhongyang junwei, zhongyang wen'ge xiaozu, "Guanyu renmin jiefangjun jianjue zhichi geming zuopai qunzhong de jueding" (Decision regarding the resolute support of the People's Liberation Army for the masses of the revolutionary left), Zhongfa [67], no. 27, January 23, 1967.

56. "Mao Zhuxi huishou wo qianjin," June 5, 1968; "Guanyu 'paolian' wenti de diaocha baogao," July 6, 1967.

57. Zhang Liansheng interview.

ine "revolutionary leftists" and did not want to take a stand prematurely that might later cause them trouble.

The rebels in the public security bureau organized other rebel groups to counterattack against Paolian. They put up wall posters charging that Paolian had violated recent directives issued by Beijing about protecting public security, and that it was a "black organization" filled with "counterrevolutionaries" whose actions would disrupt production and public order. Paolian rebels were attacked in work units where they were in the minority.[58]

The returned university students loudly supported the stance of Paolian, and on February 16 they issued a public statement expressing their determination to carry out the Cultural Revolution alongside Paolian.[59] This spurred a backlash by other rebels. Several of the university students were beaten up over the next few days, and at a Paolian rally at the county party headquarters on February 23 to denounce Gao Ying, some six hundred non-Paolian rebels swarmed into the compound and drove the Paolian members away, separating the university students from locals.[60] The following week, non-Paolian rebels mobilized close to one thousand of their followers to surround the county's Red Guard reception station late at night, where the university students stayed, dragged them out from their beds and verbally abused them almost until dawn.[61] Most of the university students fled the county shortly afterward.[62]

In sum, by the very end of February 1967, factional divisions existed in Feng County in all but name. Paolian's opponents had yet to form a rival alliance with a clear identity, but the foundations for one were well established. These factional divisions began with questions about decorum at mass rallies to denounce the county's party secretary—whether he should be forced to stand up, or whether he had the right to wear an army uniform. They were enlarged by reactions to the militant stance taken by the returned university students, who consistently pushed a hard line and whose actions stimulated a backlash against the perceived outsiders. They grew further by competition between the just-organized Paolian alliance and local rebels who were not included in

58. "Mao Zhuxi huishou wo qianjin," June 5, 1968; "Guanyu 'paolian' wenti de diaocha baogao," July 6, 1967.

59. "Mao Zhuxi huishou wo qianjin," June 5, 1968.

60. Ibid.

61. Ibid.

62. Interview no. 8.

the alliance. The primary issue initially was who would hold Gao Ying in custody and who had the right to organize mass rallies to denounce him. Paolian did not face opposition from those who sought to shield Gao from public censure, or from those who sought to defend the county leaders' record. At no point did Paolian declare its intention to overthrow the county party committee and seize power in its own name. Zhang Liansheng and other Paolian leaders explicitly refused to do so, despite the urgings of the university radicals and the wave of power seizures in Xuzhou, elsewhere in the province, and across China. Perhaps if they had done so, the PAD might have felt obligated to support them in line with directives from Beijing. Instead, Paolian engaged in a distinctly moderate effort to "supervise production" in collaboration with county officials. And Paolian requested help, unsuccessfully, from both the Bureau of Public Security and the People's Armed Department to seek protection from the violent backlash by rival rebels.

At the end of February, the county's factional divisions had yet to be sharply defined, and the conflicts still lacked the political coherence and violence that had become common elsewhere in China by this point in time. This would soon change, as moves by the armed forces to assert control over the county crystallized the lines of factional conflict and raised the stakes for all involved.

3

Enter the Army

IN EARLY MARCH 1967, the Xuzhou Military Subdistrict ordered Feng County's PAD to take over the administration of the county. On March 6, the PAD established the Feng County Production Management Office to ensure the continued operation of the county bureaucracy. This was essential in a planned economy where goods and services moved in response to administrative orders and plans, and not according to the activities of firms and households connected by markets. If the county bureaucracy stopped functioning, supplies would not be delivered, crops would not be planted, harvests would not be taken in and distributed, and household necessities would disappear from the shelves. This would be especially painful in such a poor county, where chronic hunger was still common.

Shao Wen, member of the county's now-defunct party standing committee, and political commissar of the PAD, became the director of the production management office. The deputy directors were Ma Chi, the vice-head of the PAD; Teng Zetian, one of the county's deputy party secretaries; and two other minor county party leaders. The office established subordinate working groups in charge of different administrative functions. The group leaders were PAD officers and cadres in the county bureaucracy.[1]

This production management office was a power seizure in all but name, but not carried out by a rebel alliance. This contrasted with the vast majority of other counties and cities in China, where power seizures by local rebels had

---

1. Zhongguo renmin jiefangjun Jiangsu sheng Feng xian renmin wuzhuangbu shengchan bangongshi, "Guanyu chengli xian shengchan bangongshi bing qiyong yinzhang de tongzhi" (Notice regarding the establishment of the county production office and its use of official seals of government), March 8, 1967.

PHOTOGRAPH 2. Shao Wen, chairman of Feng County Revolutionary Committee,
September 1969

overthrown local governments before the intervention of military units.[2] Feng
County's PAD did not have to decide how to deal with rebel groups that
claimed political power. But it was clear that the old civilian political structures

2. By the end of February 1967, rebel power seizures had occurred in 70 percent of all cities
and counties in China; 80 percent of all cities and counties would experience one by the end of
May. Feng County was among the remaining jurisdictions where military control was implemented in the absence of a rebel power seizure. Walder, *Agents of Disorder*, p. 81.

had been replaced by something new. Gao Ying, the county's party secretary, and Qian Xiufu, the county magistrate, no longer held any leadership positions. One of the deputy secretaries of the county party committee, Teng Zetian, joined the production command office—he had been transferred into the county only in 1965. Very few of the twenty-six members of the county party committee continued to hold any leadership post.[3] The provisional production monitoring committee, which Paolian had formed jointly with the former party committee, was disbanded.[4]

Paolian was the only alliance of rebels that could challenge the new arrangements. The PAD moved immediately to marginalize it, actions that would have long-term consequences.[5] The PAD convinced a number of rebel groups to withdraw from Paolian, and some voluntarily disbanded. By early March, only five of the thirty original rebel groups remained in Paolian—two from Feng County Middle School, and one each from the county power plant, construction company, and bus company.[6] The PAD sought the support of the two main rebel groups within the county bureaucracy, including the one in the public security bureau that had clashed earlier with Paolian.[7] Local allegiances shifted rapidly. The PAD's retention of the outsider Teng Zetian bred resentment among a number of the deposed county cadres, in particular the deputy party secretary Zhu Pingfan.

Some of the remaining leaders of Paolian recommended disbanding in light of new realities—to challenge the PAD risked retribution. Zhang Liansheng

3. Only three of these twenty-six party committee members would survive to hold positions on the revolutionary committee that was eventually founded in 1969: *Feng xian zuzhishi ziliao*, pp. 113, 143, 248–250.

4. "Guanyu chengli xian shengchan bangongshi," March 8, 1967.

5. Paolian zongbu, "Cong zouzipai de zigong kan Feng xian wuzhuangbu Liu Zongbin zhi liu" (The ilk of Liu Zongbin as seen in the confessions of capitalist roaders), p. 6 in Jiangsu sheng Feng xian paoda silingbu lianhe zongbu, "Guanyu Feng xian wuzhuang bu de wenti (di er pi cailiao)" (On the problem of Feng County's People's Armed Department [second batch of materials]), June 1968.

6. "Guanyu 'paolian' wenti de diaocha baogao," July 6, 1967; Feng xian paoda silingbu lianhe zongbu he Feng zhong honglian, "Feng bai hongweidui shi zenyang kuade" (How the Red Guard Brigade of the Feng County department store collapsed), June 1967; Feng xian yinshua chang hongyin zaofan tuan, "Renwu bu shi zenyang yakua women zuzhide" (How the People's Armed Department crushed our organization), June 19, 1967; and Zhang Liansheng interview.

7. Dong Ligui, "Huiyi chouweihui" (Reminiscence about the preparatory committee), April 28, 2016.

insisted that instead of disbanding, Paolian should conduct an "open-door rectification," apologize for some of its "rash" actions, and publicly dispute the unfounded charges made by its opponents. He argued that disbanding would only validate its opponents' accusations and leave it defenseless. His argument prevailed, and the alliance hung together.[8] Paolian publicly declared a stance of nonviolence—a defensive crouch, given their now-weakened state. Paolian's rebel opponents, on the other hand, seized the initiative and went on the attack. They sent large numbers of activists to harass Paolian's assemblies, and set up an investigation group to document the charges that Paolian was a "reactionary organization."[9]

As these trends were getting underway, military personnel in PLA uniforms arrived without fanfare in early March, attending mass rallies, listening to debates, and attending meetings of Paolian and its opponents. No one knew who they were or what their mission was. Paolian leaders treated them politely, hoping to gain support from any quarter possible, and tried to impress them with their nonviolent stance.[10]

The mystery was dispelled one week later. The soldiers were from units under the command of the PLA's 68th Army, a combat division with authority over the Xuzhou Military Subdistrict. The 68th Army was under the Ji'nan Military Region in neighboring Shandong, while the regional forces of the Xuzhou Military Subdistrict were under the command of the Jiangsu Military District and in turn to the Nanjing Military Region, both headquartered in Nanjing. When the Xuzhou Garrison Command was established in the mid-1950s, the 68th Army commander and political commissar were placed in charge of it, while the subdistrict's commander and political commissar were appointed as deputy commander and deputy political commissar.[11] After Beijing ordered the PLA to "support the left" near the end of January 1967, all of these troops became involved in political activities. Because the 68th Army commanders held a higher rank, and the 68th Army had units scattered across the Xuhai region (the cities of Xuzhou and Lianyungang and the eight counties), the Ji'nan and Nanjing military regions agreed that the 68th Army would

8. Zhang Liansheng interview.

9. "Mao Zhuxi huishou wo qianjin," June 5, 1968; "Feng xian 'paoda silingbu lianhe zongbu' de qingkuang zonghe," March 18, 1967.

10. Zhang Liansheng interview.

11. Zhonggong Xuzhou shiwei zuzhibu, zhonggong Xuzhou shiwei dangshi gongzuo weiyuanhui, Xuzhou shi dang'an ju, *Zhongguo gongchandang Jiangsu sheng Xuzhou shi zuzhishi ziliao* (Materials on the organizational history of the Chinese Communist Party in Xuzhou City, Jiangsu) (Beijing: Zhonggong dangshi chubanshe, 1991), pp. 587–588.

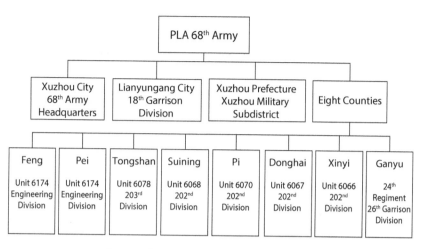

FIGURE 2. Command structure of PLA "support the left" military units

take charge of the mission and establish a "support the left" office in Xuzhou (see fig. 2). The officers and troops from the 68th Army assumed control over key units in Xuzhou in February, and then in early March, they dispatched "support the left" work teams to support local PAD units in the counties. The PLA officers were intended to take the lead in implementing military control.[12]

On March 9, troops from PLA Unit 6174 formally arrived in Feng County.[13] This was a regiment under the 68th Army's engineering division. The unit's regimental commander was Xia Jidao, its political commissar was Zheng Guoxin, and the chief of staff was Guo Fengcai. Zheng Guoxin was assigned to take charge of the overall support mission, while the county PAD was in charge of administering the economy. Essentially, this division of labor meant that the PLA units were in charge of political issues, while the PAD was in charge of routine administration. Xu Fang, deputy commander of the engineering division, accompanied the troops from Unit 6174 and stayed until June. In all, this military contingent formed a work team of roughly four hundred officers and troops. They set up headquarters at the county's rural cadre training school, and its members were sent to local work units and rural communes. The main headquarters of Unit 6174 was in Dahu, a small town in the eastern suburbs of Xuzhou City, where the majority of the regiment's forces were stationed (see map 3).[14]

12. *Zhonggong Xuzhou difang shi,* pp. 160–161; and Dong and Walder, "Forces of Disorder."
13. "Mao Zhuxi huishou wo qianjin," June 5, 1968.
14. Zhang Liansheng interview.

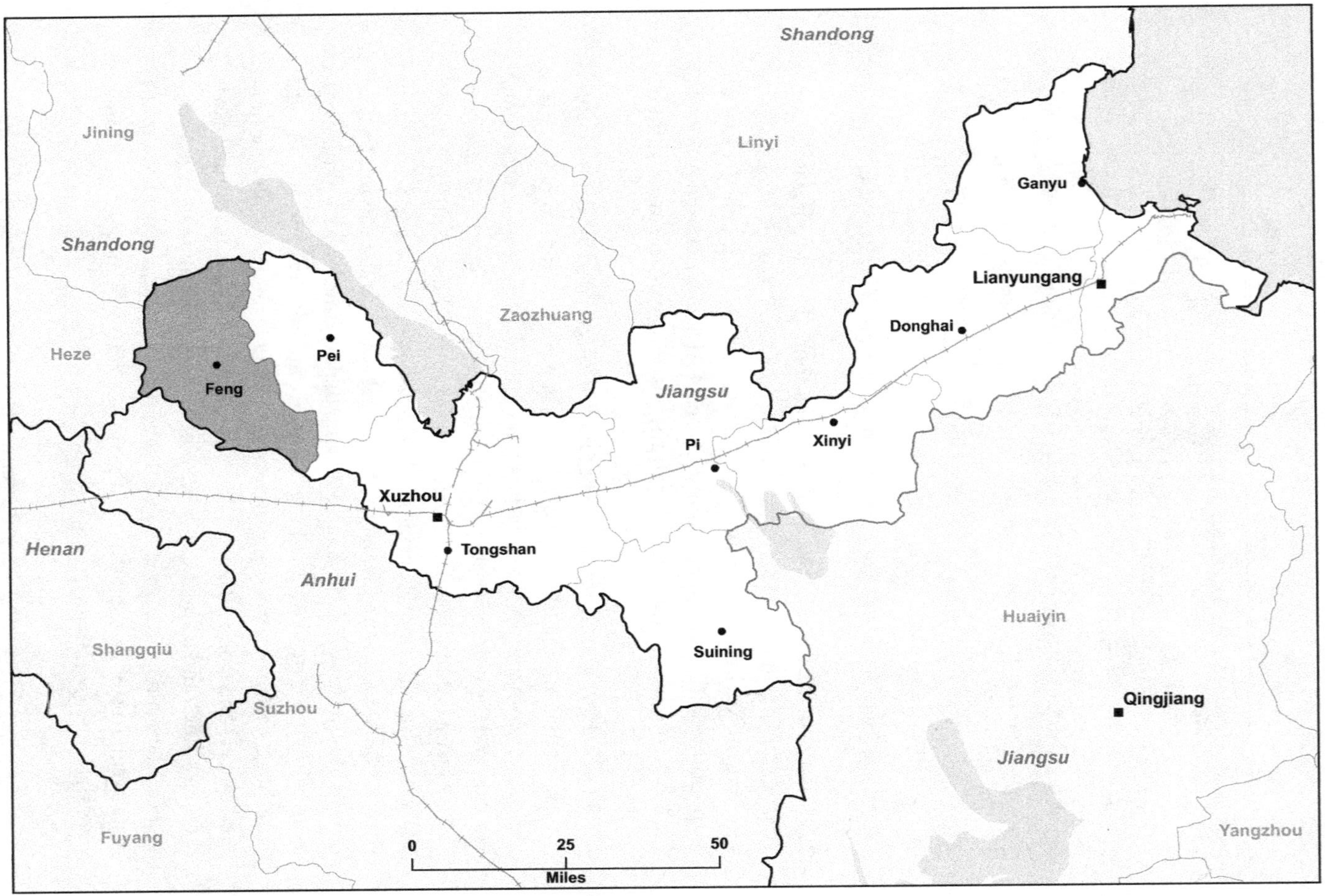

MAP 3. The Xuhai region

Anti-Paolian rebels continued to press their advantage as the PLA troops arrived. The rebel organization that had taken over the public security bureau submitted its investigation materials on Paolian to the PAD. The report charged that some of Paolian's leaders and activists had "impure" family backgrounds and personal histories, and that Paolian had stubbornly defended capitalist power-holders in the county and violated Chairman Mao's directive to grasp revolution and promote production, while pointing the spearhead of their struggle against the PAD. The report concluded that Paolian was definitely a "counterrevolutionary organization." It recommended that Paolian be banned and its leaders punished "according to the law."[15]

The PAD found these charges highly congenial and immediately relayed the report to the PLA work team. But the PLA had a different point of view, based on its earlier investigations in the county. On March 21, they held a meeting with Paolian's leaders and invited PAD officers to attend. The meeting ended acrimoniously, after an angry confrontation between Paolian's leaders and the officers from the PAD.[16]

To block the effort to frame them as a counterrevolutionary organization, Paolian displayed three wall posters in late March that challenged the security bureau rebels to a debate about "whether the old public security bureau was a tool of bourgeois dictatorship during the Cultural Revolution," challenges that the security bureau rebels refused.[17] The hostility between Paolian and the security bureau rebels and the PAD became apparent to the officers leading the PLA work team. The PLA officers hesitated to take sides, however, worrying about discord with the PAD, which was under the Xuzhou Military Subdistrict.

On March 10, Beijing put Jiangsu Province under military control, setting aside disputes between two large rebel factions in the provincial capital of Nanjing.[18] Jiangsu's military control committee consisted of officers from the Nanjing Military Region and Jiangsu Military District. One week later, the Jiangsu military control committee ordered the Xuzhou Military Subdistrict to set up a "Xuzhou Prefecture Grasp Revolution and Promote Production

---

15. "Feng xian 'paoda silingbu lianhe zongbu' de qingkuang zonghe," March 18, 1967.

16. "Guanyu 'paolian' wenti de diaocha baogao," July 6, 1967.

17. "Mao Zhuxi huishou wo qianjin," June 5, 1968.

18. See Dong and Walder, "Nanjing's Failed 'January Revolution' of 1967," p. 690; and Dong Guoqiang and Andrew G. Walder, "Local Politics in the Chinese Cultural Revolution: Nanjing under Military Control," *Journal of Asian Studies* 70, 2 (May 2011): 425–447.

Headquarters" to administer the prefecture. Chai Rongsheng, commander of the military subdistrict, was appointed as its head.[19] This appointment altered previous lines of command among local military units. The relationship between the PLA 68th Army, the military subdistrict, and the subordinate military units in eight counties became a complicated and potentially sensitive matter. The leaders of the engineering division, and its subordinate regiment Unit 6174, now had to consult with military subdistrict leaders when they handled political matters pertaining to Feng County. The views of the military subdistrict commanders about the local situation were shaped by their subordinates in the Feng County PAD, who reported directly to them. Chai Rongsheng reportedly viewed Paolian as a disruptive force that needed to "correct its errors."[20]

The ambiguities in the power relationships between the PLA and the local PAD were ostensibly resolved on April 4, when the 68th Army and the military subdistrict jointly established a military control committee (*junshi guanzhi weiyuanhui*) in Feng County to formally replace the former party committee and county government.[21] The political commissar of PLA Unit 6174, Zheng Guoxin, became the committee's head. The PAD political commissar, Shao Wen; the PAD director, Liu Zongbin; and a deputy commander of PLA Unit 6174 became deputy heads.[22] The officers from PLA Unit 6174 clearly dominated the new power structure.

To replace the old county government, a new production command headquarters was established in early April and housed in the former party and government compound.[23] Shao Wen was appointed its head, while Ma Chi (deputy director of the county PAD) and Guo Fengcai (chief of staff of PLA Unit 6174) became deputy heads.[24]

These moves, ordered from above, would have negative consequences. The PAD officers were now clearly subordinate to the PLA and were only placed

19. *Zhonggong Xuzhou lishi dashiji*, p. 387.

20. "Guanyu 'paolian' wenti de diaocha baogao," July 6, 1967.

21. *Feng xian zuzhishi ziliao*, p. 248.

22. Ibid., p. 142.

23. Its formal name was "Grasp Revolution, Promote Production Frontline Command Headquarters" (*zhua geming cu shengchan di yi xian zhihui bu*).

24. Zhongguo renmin jiefangjun Jiangsu sheng Feng xian junshi guanzhi weiyuanhui, "Guanyu jianli zhua geming cu shengchan di yi xian zhihuibu de tongzhi" (Notice on the establishment of the frontline command post for grasping revolution and promiting production), April 8, 1967.

in charge of routine production and administrative issues. This diminished the authority of the PAD over local political issues in which it had a large stake. Moreover, the new production command headquarters excluded Teng Zetian and a few other local cadres who had only recently been appointed to help lead the PAD's production management office. Their exclusion from formal positions generated resentment, creating an emerging split between insiders and outsiders in the military hierarchy.

Disputes within the Military Control Committee

Taking their direction from the Ji'nan Military Region, the priority for the Feng County Military Control Committee was to promote a great alliance among local mass organizations and establish a county revolutionary committee as soon as possible. The great alliance, of course, could only include groups approved as "revolutionary leftist." Toward this end, in early April the military control committee released lists of thirteen "revolutionary leftist organizations" in the county.[25] The list was a compromise between the PLA and PAD.

Two organizations on this approved list were relatively new, both consisting of junior cadres from the party and government offices. The first, the County Party Office Cadre Red Headquarters (*xianwei jiguan ganbu hongse zongbu*), was led by Shi Hongde, an instructor in the rural cadre training school. The second, the County Government Office Cadre Allied Corps (*xian renwei jiguan ganbu lianhe bingtuan*), was led by Dong Ligui, a cadre in the county personnel bureau. These rebel groups formed after the cadres who had been sent out to conduct the Socialist Education Campaign elsewhere in the prefecture returned to Feng County in January. They were all party members and employees of the county bureaucracy and had not been involved in the disputes between Paolian and the other rebels. They were acceptable to all sides, and both the PLA and the PAD officers sought their support.[26]

25. "Mao Zhuxi huishou wo qianjin," June 5, 1968; Zhongguo renmin jiefangjun Jiangsu sheng Feng xian renmin wuzhuangbu dangwei, "Gei Feng xian renmin de yi feng gongkai xin" (An open letter to the people of Feng County), August 20, 1967; Zhang Liansheng notebooks; and Zhang Ludao notebooks.

26. Feng xian wuchan jieji geming zaofan lianhe silingbu diaocha yanjiu zu, "Touji fenzi de dianfan, chumai linghun de zhuanjia—kan xianwei 'lianhe,' 'hongse' liang bingtuan gebie toutou angzang linghun" (Typical speculators and specialists in betrayal—see the filthy souls of the leaders of the "Lianhe" and "Red" Corps of the county committee), June 22, 1967.

Also included on the list were two rebel alliances that dominated their own work units but had taken opposite sides in the disputes between Paolian and its rivals. A Paolian-affiliated rebel group from the electric power generating plant and an anti-Paolian rebel group from the cotton textile mill were both included on the list. This was a conscious effort to show evenhandedness. It was also thought that if these two opposed groups could compromise, they could set an example for other groups to follow. The others on the list were small rebel groups with ambiguous or neutral stances in the conflict between Paolian and its rivals. To avoid the controversies that would likely follow, neither Paolian nor the anti-Paolian cadre rebel groups in the county administration (including the fiercely anti-Paolian rebels in the public security bureau) were placed on the approved "leftist" list. Their political designation was still pending.

For Paolian's members, this was a small victory—the PAD had been on the verge of designating them as counterrevolutionary. Anti-Paolian rebels, however, resented this decision. They felt that they could have eliminated Paolian if it had not been for the untimely intervention of the PLA, and they were in fact on the verge of doing so with PAD support when the PLA arrived.

Under the direction of the military control committee, the thirteen leftist organizations established the Feng County Proletarian Revolutionary Great Alliance Preparatory Committee (*Feng xian wuchan jieji gemingpai da lianhe chouweihui*) on April 12. Its designated directors were Shi Hongde and Dong Ligui, the heads of the two newly founded rebel groups of county cadres. The preparatory committee was dominated by these junior cadres, who had not been involved in the prior political controversies.[27] While this seemed to be the best way forward, it inevitably drove a wedge between county cadres who had been away from the county in recent months and those who had stayed, and it also alienated rebel groups that had been founded much earlier and had a major stake in existing conflicts.[28]

On April 21, this preparatory committee held a mass rally to criticize Liu Shaoqi and Deng Xiaoping, the highest-ranking national leaders to be purged in Beijing. They made an unfortunate decision when they decided to invite both Paolian and anti-Paolian organizations that were excluded from the list of thirteen leftist organizations. When a Paolian representative started to speak, members of anti-Paolian groups shouted him down. The preparatory

27. Zhang Liansheng interview; and Dong Ligui, "Huiyi chouweihui."
28. "Touji fenzi de dianfan, chumai linghun de zhuanjia," June 22, 1967.

committee convenor ordered the troublemakers to keep quiet. After this, anti-Paolian leaders turned their criticism toward the preparatory committee and began plans to push it aside. Encouraged by news that rebels were mobilizing against the military control committee in Xuzhou, they began active opposition to the PLA troops sent to the county.[29]

This compromise unraveled further as the implications of two new orders to the PLA in early April were felt in Feng County. Two documents from the party center reversed the orders given to PLA "support the left" forces and prohibited the designation of any mass organization as reactionary or counter-revolutionary. Any negative judgments against a rebel organization had to be approved in Beijing, and prior judgments were to be voided and any punishments reversed.[30] At the end of April, the military subdistrict commander Chai Rongsheng came to Feng County and convinced the military control committee to reconsider its attitude toward Paolian. Soon thereafter, Paolian was put on the list of "revolutionary leftist organizations," and the military control committee reversed the verdicts on three small rebel groups it had earlier banned as illegal.[31]

When Commander Chai Rongsheng was in Feng County, the PAD leaders assented to his instructions, but after his departure, they resisted implementation. When the military control committee met on May 3, PAD cadres argued that it was not necessary to rehabilitate Paolian because it had never been labeled reactionary. When the PLA officers pointed out the investigation report on Paolian that the PAD had forwarded to them shortly after their arrival, the PAD responded that it was actually compiled by the rebel group in the public security bureau, which had a right to express their opinions, and that the PAD bore no responsibility for it. When the PLA officers proposed to publicly affirm Paolian's "revolutionary" orientation, the PAD cadres argued that it would only be fair to make the same decision about the anti-Paolian factions. The discussion dragged on late into the night, without resolution. The PAD also

29. "Mao Zhuxi huishou wo qianjin," June 5, 1968; and Dong and Walder, "Forces of Disorder."

30. Zhonggong zhongyang, "Zhonggong zhongyang zhuanfa zhongyang guanyu Anhui wenti de jueding ji fu jian" (CCP Central Committee transmits the Center's decision regarding the Anhui question and attachments), Zhongfa [67], no. 117, April 1, 1967; and Zhongyang junwei, "Zhongyang junwei shitiao mingling" (Ten orders of the Central Military Commission), April 6, 1967.

31. "Mao Zhuxi huishou wo qianjin," June 5, 1968; and "Guanyu 'paolian' wenti de diaocha baogao," July 6, 1967.

vetoed the clearing of former party secretary Gao Ying, even though the PLA officers favored this, in line with recent editorials in *People's Daily* that advocated "correctly treating cadres."[32]

The PAD also sought to undermine the PLA officers' authority. For example, in name of the military control committee, they convened a rural political work conference in Shazhuang Commune on April 26. The participants were all rural cadres and commune PAD heads who supported the county PAD. When local dissidents questioned the legitimacy of the meeting, the PAD officers threatened to label them as conservatives. This conference consolidated an alignment of rural supporters for the county PAD in its growing friction with the PLA. Rural cadres and officers in PAD branches in the communes began to harass PLA work teams in an effort to keep them out of the rural communes.[33]

These moves by the PAD encouraged anti-Paolian rebels, who initiated hostile actions against the preparatory committee. They charged that "the preparatory committee failed to highlight the leadership of the working class, failed to create a leading core based on the main force of workers, peasants, and young revolutionary commanders, and let the leading power fall into the hands of Shi Hongde and a few former government cadres . . . therefore the preparatory committee has become an obstacle" to the Cultural Revolution.[34]

On May 8, anti-Paolian students from Feng County Middle School paraded through the county seat shouting the slogan "Kick Out the Preparatory Committee." A Paolian rally at the school in mid-May was invaded by anti-Paolian students, who beat up several participants. During April, Paolian had held a

32. "Junguanhui huiyi jilu" (Minutes of the Military Control Committee Meeting), May 3, 1967; attachment to "Guanyu Feng xian wuzhuang bu de wenti (di er pi cailiao)," June 1968; and "Bixu zhengque duidai ganbu" (It is necessary to treat cadres correctly), published in *Hongqi* no. 4, March 1, 1967, and *Renmin ribao*, February 23, 1967.

33. Jiangsu sheng Feng xian junguanhui zhua geming cu shengchan di yi xian zhihui bu, "Guanyu zhaokai zhengzhi gongzuo huiyi de tongzhi" (Notice on the convening of the political work conference), April 21, 1967; and Paolian zongbu, "Chaichuan wuzhuangbu 'si.erliu' Shazhuang huiyi de zui'e yinmou" (Expose the People's Armed Department's evil scheme of the April 26 Shazhuang meeting); and "Guanyu shengchan gongzuo zhong de jieji douzheng" (On class struggle in production work), in Jiangsu sheng Feng xian paoda silingbu lianhe zongbu, "Guanyu Feng xian wuzhuang bu de wenti (di er pi cailiao)" June 1968.

34. Chouweihui yibing, "Wei ziji kelian de chouweihui er tanxi" (I heave a sigh for our pathetic preparatory committee), June 23, 1967.

series of mass meetings, consistently taking a defensive stance, avoiding accusations against its opponents, and holding meetings on themes that presumably would appeal to all rebel activists.[35] After the mid-May attack, however, Paolian became more assertive and confronted the leaders of the PAD.

Paolian's decision to counterattack was partly due to encouraging news that its members gathered from their university student allies who had kept in touch with them by mail after their retreat from the county. From them, Paolian learned of a statement by Kang Sheng, a senior official in Beijing who was a radical "advisor" to the Central Cultural Revolution Group, in a meeting with a delegation of rebel leaders from Shandong Province. In the statement, Kang had expressed severe disapproval of the conservative tendencies of local public security bureaus and people's armed departments, and stated that PAD officers should not be accorded the same respect due to the PLA, because they "are nothing but local cadres who wear military garb" and should withdraw from "support the left" work.[36] On May 20, Paolian members from Feng County Middle School put up a wall poster that quoted Kang's statement, and the next day they put up another, titled "expose Shao Wen's crimes to the masses."[37] These two posters had a strong impact on local opinion, which became more supportive of Paolian. Subsequent wall posters denounced the attempt to frame Paolian as a reactionary organization, and called Shao Wen "the big backstage boss behind conservatives in Feng County."[38]

The Formation of Liansi

Paolian's offensive finally spurred the formation on May 25 of an explicitly anti-Paolian alliance, the Feng County Proletarian Revolutionary United Headquarters (*Feng xian wuchan jieji geming pai lianhe silingbu*), known thereafter by the abbreviated name Liansi. Its leaders included Li Zongzhou, a cotton textile mill worker, Li Peng, an aide in the county agricultural work department, Shao Limin, a hardware factory worker, Cheng Yinzhen, a high school

---

35. "Mao Zhuxi huishou wo qianjin," June 5, 1968.

36. "Zhou Enlai Kang Sheng jiejian Shandong daibiao tuan Wang Xiaoyu Yang Dezhi deng ren de jianghua" (Zhou Enlai and Kang Sheng's Speeches in a Meeting with Wang Xiaoyu, Yang Dezhi, and other members of Shandong delegation), April 26, 1967.

37. "Mao Zhuxi huishou wo qianjin," June 5, 1968; and "Guanyu 'paolian' wenti de diaocha baogao," July 6, 1967.

38. "Guanyu 'paolian' wenti de diaocha baogao," July 6, 1967.

student in Feng County Middle School, Zhang Guichun, an employee in the coal mining construction company, and Bai Hexiu, a junior cadre in the county grain management bureau.

The formation of Liansi defined the two factional identities that would drive the county's political conflicts for years to come. The new alliance was pulled together by the two anti-Paolian rebel groups among the county cadres, one of which was the vehemently anti-Paolian rebel group in the public security bureau.[39] The large cotton mill rebel group that previously had been designated as leftist by the military control committee, along with several smaller groups, withdrew from the preparatory committee and joined Liansi. This undermined the preparatory committee that had been carefully constructed by the PLA. One consequence of this rift was that the two rebel alliances of county cadres that headed the preparatory committee (the ones that had returned to the county after a long absence) began to gravitate toward Paolian.[40] This opened a split between these county cadres and their colleagues in anti-Paolian groups.

From this point forward, the PAD and PLA were drawn increasingly into the rivalry between Paolian and Liansi. Paolian decided to take the fight directly to the PAD and asked for a meeting with Shao Wen. The meeting was held on May 31, with Zhang Liansheng and two other Paolian leaders. Dozens of Paolian-affiliated high school students broke into the meeting. Shouting denunciations of Shao Wen, they dragged him off to confess his crimes at a mass meeting to be held later at Paolian's headquarters, at the county construction company.

PLA officers rushed to the scene, criticized the rebels, and forced them to release Shao Wen.[41] This action infuriated Liansi, whose members demonstrated at the PLA headquarters at the rural cadre training school, denouncing the top two PLA commanders and demanding their withdrawal. Paolian-affiliated students repeatedly went to PAD headquarters to confront Shao Wen. In early June, Shao Wen left the county for Xuzhou, ostensibly to attend a conference, but in fact left to escape the wrath of Paolian.[42] In response to a

39. "Mao Zhuxi huishou wo qianjin," June 5, 1968.

40. Dong Ligui, "Huiyi chouweihui."

41. "Mao Zhuxi huishou wo qianjin," June 5, 1968; "Guanyu 'paolian' wenti de diaocha baogao," July 6, 1967; and Zhang Liansheng interview.

42. Ibid.; Hongxin zhanshi, "Jiu Shao Wen shi cuowu de—ping nonggan xiao lianhe zaofandui 'jiu Shao Wen jiu de hao'" (Grabbing Shao Wen is mistaken—an assessment of the ag-

June 6 central document calling for intensified public security work by local military units, Liansi forces began a propaganda campaign denouncing Paolian for attacking the PAD, which they argued was equivalent to attacking the PLA.[43] On June 11 they published a letter from the Xuzhou Military Subdistrict that denounced the kidnapping of Shao Wen. Liansi pledged its undying support for the PAD, and swore to defend it to the end.[44]

Tired of stonewalling by the PAD, the PLA officers on the military control committee unilaterally decided on June 21 to approve the main rebel groups affiliated with Paolian. This further intensified local conflicts, with the PAD openly objecting to the decision. On June 22, members of these newly approved Paolian groups marched to the public security bureau and demanded that evidence collected against them be handed over, but they were refused. The next day Liansi sent more than 150 members to confront the Paolian students occupying the bureau. The students finally left on July 8, after the materials were turned over.[45]

As the split between the PAD and PLA widened, deposed senior officials began to choose sides. The former directors of the public security bureau and county court, who had been stripped of their positions by the anti-Paolian rebels in the security organs, put up a jointly authored wall poster declaring that "Paolian's general orientation is correct."[46] Zhu Pingfan, one of the county's deputy party secretaries, declared that the conflict in Feng County was a class struggle between Paolian "revolutionaries" and Liansi "conservatives," and that county leaders should stand with the former. He also denounced the

ricultural cadre school allied rebel brigade's "The seizing of Shao Wen was done well"), June 17, 1967; and Hanwei 178 hao tongling zhandoudui, "Paolian yi xiaocuo fachule wudou de dongyuan ling" (A handful of people in Paolian issue mobilization order for armed combat), June 27, 1967.

43. "Zhonggong zhongyang, guowuyuan, zhongyang junwei, zhongyang wen'ge xiaozu, tongling" (Notice of the CCP Central Committee, State Council, Central Military Commission, and Central Cultural Revolution Group). Zhongfa [67], no. 178, June 6, 1967; Feng xian wuchan jieji geming zaofan pai lianhe silingbu, "Guanyu xuanchuan, xuexi, zhixing zhongyang liuyue liuri 'tongling' de guanche yijian" (Opinion on carrying out the dissemination, study, and implementation of the Center's June 6 'orders'), June 10, 1967.

44. "Mao Zhuxi huishou wo qianjin," June 5, 1968.

45. Ibid.; Zhang Liansheng interview; Feng xian zhengfa hongse geming zaofan zong silingbu, "Yanzhong shengming" (Grave declaration), June 26, 1967; "Paolian yi xiaocuo fachule wudou de dongyuan ling," June 27, 1967.

46. Paolian yibing, "Paolian de dafangxiang zaojiu cuo ding le" (Paolian's general orientation has long been mistaken), handbill, June 20, 1967.

PAD for its allegedly conservative bias.[47] Under Zhu's influence, many senior cadres in the county became Paolian supporters.

After former officials began to choose sides, Paolian and Liansi targeted different ones in their attacks. Both factions denounced Gao Ying and former county magistrate Qian Xiufu, but they targeted different leading officials. Liansi targeted Zhu Pingfan and Sun Shudian (former director of the public security bureau), both of whom declared support for Paolian. Paolian targeted Teng Zetian and Cai Zhenhong (deputy county magistrate), who had pledged to Liansi.

In late June, the anti-Liansi forces merged into a single alliance—the Feng County Proletarian Revolutionary Alliance Committee (*Feng xian wuchan jieji geming pai lianhe weiyuanhui*), known as the Alliance Committee (*lianweihui*). Zhang Liansheng was the director, and other Paolian leaders were in its leading group. The Alliance Committee, widely viewed as an extension of Paolian, included 129 organizations and more than six thousand members, almost twice the size of Liansi at the time.[48] It depended entirely on the support of PLA Unit 6174.[49]

47. Zhu Pingfan, *Wangshi* (Past events), October 10, 2013, pp. 29–30; and the following materials, which are printed in Feng xian geming weiyuanhui, *Jian bao* 13, August 16, 1970: Jiguan ganbu xuexi ban, "Guangda geming qunzhong gaoju geming da pipan qizhi, hen jie meng pi yexinjia, pantu Zhu Pingfan de taotian zuixing" (Broad revolutionary masses, raising the revolutionary banner of great criticism, fiercely expose and repudiate the monstrous crimes of the scheming traitor Zhu Pingfan); Zhang Liansheng, "Zhichi yipai shi jia, cuan quan fubi shi zhen" (Supporting one faction is fake; usurping to restore power is reality); Li Peng, "Chedi pipan Zhu Pingfan 'ge' yu 'bao' de fangeming miulun" (Thoroughly criticize Zhu Pingfan's absurd theory of "radicals" versus "conservatives"); Li Zongzhou, "Chedi pipan Zhu Pingfan suowei 'renwubu difangxing hen qiang, you baoshou sixiang' de fangeming miulun" (Thoroughly criticize Zhu Pingfan's absurd so-called doctrine that "The PAD is strongly localist and has conservative views"); and Shan Shutang, "Chedi pipan Zhu Pingfan tiaodong qunzhong dou qunzhong de taotian zuixing" (Thoroughly repudiate Zhu Pingfan's monstrous crime of inciting the masses to struggle against one another), August 9, 1970.

48. Paolian's leaders considered all of the mass organizations in the Alliance Committee as Paolian affiliates, but for the purposes of political strategy treated it as a leadership body; Liansi on the other hand treated the Alliance Committee simply as the Paolian faction, and referred to the committee as "Pao chou" (炮筹, Pao Preparatory) or "Pao chou" (炮丑, Pao Ugly).

49. Although it was dominated by Paolian, the Alliance Committee would eventually fall apart, as more radical Paolian groups began to withdraw later that year, dissatisfied with what they considered to be the Alliance Committee's overly moderate line. These developments are described in the next chapter.

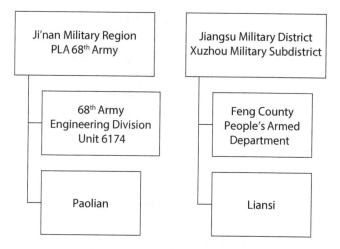

FIGURE 3. Alliances between military units and mass factions

Liansi convened a mass rally in late June that defined the battle lines in the county. The PAD's deputy political commissar Yao Haishu spoke at the rally and declared that the PAD and Liansi would stand side by side in their common struggle. Liansi subsequently put up wall posters denouncing Paolian for destroying the proletarian dictatorship, and vowed to "fight to the death" against anyone who attacked the PAD. Liansi ordered its members to compile information that could be used to denounce PLA officers from Unit 6174 to the Xuzhou Military Subdistrict and Xuzhou Garrison.[50] Most consequential, however, was a conference convened by the county PAD of all security and PAD personnel from rural communes in late June. By consolidating their control of the rural security apparatus, the PAD planned to offset their minority position in the county seat. From this point forward, the rural command structure of the PAD would be mobilized to support Liansi (see fig. 3).[51]

The PLA officers countered these moves by submitting their own investigation report on Paolian to the 68th Army's "support the left" office in Xuzhou. It refuted the report submitted by the security bureau rebels to the PAD and

50. Zhang Liansheng and Zhang Ludao notebooks for the later period covered by the Xuhai Study Class; and Feng xian jiguan ganbu Mao Zedong sixiang xuexi ban, "Li Zongzhou tongzhi daibiao yuan Liansi zongbu xiang quan xian renmin zuo guanyu wuchan jieji wenhua da geming zhong jingyan jiaoxun zongjie huibao" (Comrade Li Zongzhou's summary report to all the people of the county, representing the former Liansi headquarters, regarding the lessons learned during the great proletarian Cultural Revolution), August 27, 1970.

51. "Mao Zhuxi huishou wo qianjin," June 5, 1968.

affirmed Paolian as the first revolutionary alliance in the county. They were the first to put up a wall poster that called for "bombarding" the party committee, the first to criticize party secretary Gao Ying, and the first to challenge the public security bureau. Their report claimed that Paolian's general orientation had always been correct and that their alliance should be supported for faithfully carrying out central policy. The report concluded that "the Paolian issue is one of political standpoint and line; we cannot be equivocal about it."[52]

When the PAD took control of the county in early March, factional rivalries in the county were still ill defined, and rebels competed to be the loudest and most militant in denouncing the party secretary and other top county leaders. After the PAD deposed the county's civilian leaders, local rebels began to align themselves for and against the PAD, sharpening the tensions between Paolian and the PAD. The intervention of the PLA troops dispatched from Xuzhou sharpened and broadened the emerging factional divisions, making them even more difficult to resolve. The PLA's growing support for Paolian and formation of a "great alliance committee" brought two rebel groups of junior county cadres into an alliance while excluding the vociferously anti-Paolian cadre rebels. This drove a wedge between the two groups of county-level cadres, one that deepened when Paolian later merged with supportive cadre rebels in a large new rebel alliance under PLA protection. Senior county officials also split, with most of them forming an affiliation with either Paolian or Liansi. Whatever the personal motives for their choice of factions, it clearly had the effect of offering protection from attacks by the other mass factions. Cadres in rural communes, however, almost uniformly stood on the side of Liansi. The civilian political structures tied to the party organization had collapsed, but the organizational hierarchy that the PAD maintained down into communes and village production brigades was intact, and the county PAD ensured that this structure of authority would bind commune leaders to the PAD and, ultimately, to the Liansi faction.

52. "Guanyu 'paolian' wenti de diaocha baogao," July 6, 1967.

4

Escalation

BY THE END OF JUNE 1967, the lines of factional conflict in Feng County were sharply drawn, with no resolution in sight. Each faction, Paolian and Liansi, had firm backing from different branches of the military hierarchy. Paolian relied heavily on the soldiers from the PLA's 68th Army, while Liansi relied on the PAD and its network of militia that reached into rural communes. As the battle lines were drawn, each side sent delegations to the prefecture capital in Xuzhou, seeking support from either the Xuzhou Garrison, controlled by the 68th Army, or the military subdistrict headquarters, which was in charge of county-level PADs. What these delegations did not initially know was that similar factional conflicts had already developed in Xuzhou City, stimulating rebel defiance of the political order imposed by the 68th Army.[1] This served to deepen the conflicts in Feng County and led to the escalation of violence.

Xuzhou's U-turn and Its Consequences

Events in Xuzhou City unfolded very differently than in Feng County. A large and diverse rebel movement fought briefly in late 1966 against conservative defenders of the party leadership, but the defenders collapsed after the rebel forces seized power on January 21. Rebels in Xuzhou Prefecture carried out a similar power seizure on February 4. Disagreements over power sharing in Xuzhou City led to factional confrontations there. In February, officers and troops from the 68th Army, the 29th Air Force Division, the 2nd Armored Division, and the Xuzhou Military Subdistrict were dispatched to stabilize new structures of power and await instructions from Beijing. They moved quickly

---

1. See Dong and Walder, "Forces of Disorder."

to form an alliance of the city's diverse rebel movement as preparation for the rapid establishment of a revolutionary committee.

With the joint approval of the Ji'nan and Nanjing Military Regions, a Xuzhou Municipal Revolutionary Committee was established on March 18, which included representatives from the major rebel alliances in the city but was dominated by military officers from the 68th Army. Only one deputy commander of the local military subdistrict was placed in the leading body of the revolutionary committee.[2]

Shortly afterward, some of the rebel groups objected to the excessive authority granted the PLA. Several withdrew from the revolutionary committee in protest, but most others remained. This split the rebel movement between groups that supported the new power structure and groups that objected. The revolutionary committee arrested a number of the dissident rebel leaders and suppressed their organizations, only to have these arrests reversed in April by new orders from Beijing that prohibited local troops from banning rebel groups. The reversal permitted the dissidents to regroup and mobilize against the revolutionary committee and its PLA supporters, which in turn made them the enemy of rebels who had remained on the revolutionary committee. The rebels that opposed the revolutionary committee became known as the Kick faction (*ti pai*)—they wanted to "kick aside" the committee. The rebels that remained loyal to the revolutionary committee—and that supported the army's decision to create it—became known as the Support faction (*zhi pai*).[3]

The Kick faction mobilized to challenge the revolutionary committee, and in response the Support faction rebels mobilized to defend it. This split drew the Support faction rebels into a close alliance with the PLA forces, and they enjoyed behind-the-scenes support, especially access to weapons, with which to defeat the Kick faction. At the end of May, the Support forces decisively defeated the Kick faction in a series of violent clashes and were able to drive thousands of Kick activists out of the city. The Kick faction sent protest delegations to Nanjing, Shanghai, Ji'nan, and Beijing, eventually bringing the "Xuzhou Question" to the attention of top officials in the nation's capital.

Concerned that legitimate rebel forces were suffering from suppression at the hands of army-sponsored rebel allies, Mao and the Central Cultural Revo-

---

2. *Zhonggong Xuzhou lishi dashiji*, p. 387.
3. These events are detailed in Dong and Walder, "Forces of Disorder."

lution Group ordered Wang Xiaoyu, the recently appointed head of the Shan-dong Province Revolutionary Committee, and the first secretary and political commissar of the Ji'nan Military Region, to go to Xuzhou and resolve the factional struggles.[4] Wang was a Qingdao city official who had risen suddenly into the leadership of Shandong Province after becoming an early supporter of rebel forces there and leading a provincial power seizure in the provincial capital of Ji'nan.

Wang's interventions in Xuzhou only made matters worse. He declared that the PLA "support the left" forces had made a series of errors and should re-verse their stance. The Kick faction, he argued, was a genuine rebel force, and the armed forces had erred in banning the group. This stance did not go down well with the PLA officers, and many of them deeply resented Wang's inter-vention. Wang pressured officers to accept his claim, cultivated those who came around to his point of view, and reshuffled the leadership of the Xuzhou military, placing agreeable officers into position of power. These officers openly supported the Kick faction, which fought back against the rebels in the Support faction and mounted a large campaign that would ultimately lead to their victory (albeit temporary) by the end of August 1967.

While creating divisions within the military command structure in Xuzhou City, Wang's interventions also served to undermine the PLA in Feng County, and they did so at precisely the time that the two local factions in the county had lined up with support from their respective PLA and PAD backers. The PLA forces and the PAD were subordinate, respectively, to the Xuzhou Gar-rison Command (under the 68th Army) and the Xuzhou Military Subdistrict (regional forces). Both of them were potentially implicated in Wang Xiaoyu's criticisms of the decisions of their military superiors in Xuzhou.

There were no obvious links between events in Feng County and Xuzhou, nor were there parallels in the way that factions developed. There had never been either a rebel power seizure or a revolutionary committee in Feng County,

4. Ibid.; Wang Xiaoyu was a vice-mayor of Qingdao who gained the attention of Mao and the Central Cultural Revolution Group as an early supporter of the rebel movement and as an associate of the son of Kang Sheng. He was later authorized by Beijing to lead a power seizure over Shandong Province, and he became the head of its revolutionary committee. This also made him the party secretary of the Ji'nan Military Region and its first ranking political com-missar. Wang's initial rise is detailed in Bu Weihua, *Zalan jiu shijie: Wenhua da geming de dongluan yu haojie,* pp. 304–308, 386–388, and 525–528. A detailed online biography is available at baike.baidu.com.

and if anything, the stance that the PAD had earlier taken in its effort to crush Paolian most closely paralleled the relationship between the PLA authorities in Xuzhou and the Kick faction. Yet by the time Wang intervened in the Xuzhou mess, it was Liansi's position in Feng County that resembled the Kick faction's oppositional stance in Xuzhou.

Because the different military forces in Feng County had already split by the time of Wang Xiaoyu's intervention, the implications of his intervention for the county were fundamentally ambiguous. When he was in Xuzhou, the PLA officers in Feng County and PAD leaders were summoned to conferences in Xuzhou designed to turn around the orientation of the "support the left" forces. The county PLA and PAD officers both readily agreed with Wang's stance on the Xuzhou issue, but they disagreed about its implications for the situation in Feng County. The PAD argued that the PLA officers had taken the wrong stance (and that Liansi was the equivalent of the Kick faction), while the PLA argued the PAD had taken the wrong stance (and that Paolian was the equivalent of the Kick faction). The net result for both sides in Feng County's emerging factional battles was to encourage each side to believe that it was possible to successfully challenge military authority. Paolian and Liansi both sought to press their advantage, sending delegations to plead their case in Xuzhou, and their respective backers in the PLA and PAD encouraged them to do so because their pleas had obvious implications for political judgments about the correctness of their previous actions.

On the afternoon of July 13, Xu Fang, the deputy commander of the 68th Army's engineering division, met with the leaders of Paolian in Xuzhou to discuss the political situation in the county. The PLA officers had received orders to temporarily withdraw from Feng County in order to attend conferences in Xuzhou organized by Wang Xiaoyu. The officers told the Paolian leaders that there were three possible outcomes to the Feng County problem if the PLA unit was withdrawn: the first was that the PAD would resume its destruction of Paolian by force; the second was to swallow up and absorb the alliance committee, putting Liansi in a dominant position; and the third was that the PAD officers would correct their thinking and treat Paolian with respect. The third, the officers stated, was not a realistic possibility, so Paolian had to prepare itself for a drastically altered situation.

Xu Fang told the Paolian leaders that the PLA command firmly supported Paolian's alliance committee. He advised them to be prepared to defend themselves and not be fooled by PAD efforts to dilute their power on the committee. The next day the Paolian leaders returned to the county, conveyed by army vehicles, and they informed their colleagues of what they had been told.[5] On the morning of July 15, the PLA troops withdrew from the county, and Paolian activists held a large farewell ceremony on the streets of the county seat. Liansi, on the other hand, sent a large delegation to block the road leading out of the county seat toward Xuzhou, and detained and harassed the PLA contingent for two hours. After their departure, Liansi wall posters in the county denounced the troops.[6]

After the departure of the PLA, PAD officers took over the military control committee. Adopting the advice of their PLA backers to remain vigilant, Paolian immediately began to resist. The first occasion was the evening of July 15, when the county broadcasting station relayed a central party document issued July 13, which harshly criticized PAD units in a number of provinces for "instigating peasants, who had no idea of the real situation, to take part in violent clashes in cities, [and] to attack revolutionary mass organizations in factories, government offices and schools."[7] Paolian accused the PAD of delaying the distribution of the document and of deleting passages from the original text. The next day, a group of Paolian students went to the PAD compound to demand an explanation. The officers there refused to answer and called in Liansi activists to drive them out of the compound.[8]

As these local confrontations were intensifying, the events in Wuhan, the provincial capital of Hubei, became known nationwide as the notorious "July 20 Incident." Rebels in the city who were aligned with the PLA forces there captured two prominent officials that Mao had dispatched to negotiate a truce between warring factions (the minister of public security and a member of the Central Cultural Revolution Group), an act that was interpreted as insubordination by the PLA forces. The military commanders were purged and denounced, and a shrill propaganda campaign encouraged rebels across China to "drag out" military officers who suppressed genuine rebel forces.[9] It

5. Zhang Liansheng notebooks.

6. "Mao Zhuxi huishou wo qianjin," June 5, 1968; "Li Zongzhou tongzhi daibiao yuan Liansi," August 27, 1970; and Zhang Liansheng notebooks.

7. "Zhonggong zhongyang guanyu jinzhi tiaodong nongmin jincheng wudou de tongzhi" (Central Committee notice regarding the prohibition of the incitement of farmers to enter the cities for armed combat), Zhongfa [67], no. 218, July 13, 1967.

8. "Mao Zhuxi huishou wo qianjin," June 5, 1968.

9. The events in Wuhan were dramatic. Mao had secretly arrived in Wuhan on July 17 to hammer out a resolution for local factional conflicts. The proposed resolution infuriated one faction in Wuhan, which was unaware of Mao's intervention and arrival in the city. Mao was

was at precisely this point that national events legitimated and in fact encouraged local rebels to challenge local military units. In Feng County, however, the challenge was to the local PAD, not to the recently withdrawn PLA.

Liansi supporters took advantage of this campaign to press *their* grievances against the PLA. They sent a delegation to the Xuzhou Garrison to present their grievances on July 28. They met with the 68th Army's deputy commander, Zheng Tongyi, and argued with him vehemently for several hours. Zheng eventually ducked out of the meeting, saying that he had to take an emergency phone call. He never returned, and the Liansi delegates were asked to come back the next morning. When they returned, the deputy commander did not show up, and the Liansi delegates tried to force their way into the compound but were pushed back by troops. They finally gave up after officers from the military subdistrict rushed to the scene and ordered them to desist.[10]

The Xuzhou Garrison's commanders issued a statement that accused Liansi of defying the CCP Center's order prohibiting attacks on military units.[11] Xuzhou's PLA command had presumably already been rectified by Wang Xiaoyu's intervention, so the incident put Liansi and the county PAD on the defensive.[12] Paolian's members were encouraged by the denunciation of Liansi and intensified their challenge to the PAD. On July 31, they held a mass rally to "resolutely drag out Shao Wen." In a panic, Shao fled to the military subdistrict headquarters.[13]

On August 5, a militant splinter group within Paolian sent two dozen people to Xuzhou to drag Shao Wen back to the county for a struggle session. When they arrived in Xuzhou, Shao was attending a conference inside the military subdistrict compound. Ignoring the pleas of military officers there, they

---

staying in a villa close to where the kidnapping of his representatives took place, and he was rushed out of the city in order to ensure his security. The alarm about Mao's safety explains the extreme reaction in the capital and the emotional denunciation of local PLA forces. See Walder, *China under Mao*, pp. 249–252, for a succinct account of the events. For a more detailed narrative of the background to the event and its political impact, see MacFarquhar and Schoenhals, *Mao's Last Revolution*, pp. 198–216; and Shaoguang Wang, *Failure of Charisma*, pp 149–166.

10. "Li Zongzhou tongzhi daibiao yuan Liansi," August 27, 1970; and *Jiangsu sheng Feng xian zhi*, p. 28.

11. Zhonggong zhongyang, "Zhonggong zhongyang guanyu bude ba douzheng fengmang zhixiang jundui de tongzhi" (CCP Center's notice forbidding turning the spearhead of struggle toward the military), Zhongfa [67], no. 21, January 14, 1967.

12. "Li Zongzhou tongzhi daibiao yuan Liansi," August 27, 1970.

13. "Mao Zhuxi huishou wo qianjin," June 5, 1968.

removed Shao by force, escorted him back to the county, and locked him up in Paolian's headquarters, where he was interrogated and beaten. On the evening of August 6, Paolian held a mass rally to criticize both Shao Wen and Gao Ying.[14]

On August 7, Paolian held another mass rally to denounce Shao and Gao, and afterward paraded them around the county seat. Liansi members tried, unsuccessfully, to stop the procession. In revenge, they sent people to beat up Paolian members in the county's opera troupe, initiating a large brawl, and later sent more than three hundred people to assault a building occupied by Paolian, injuring six people and severely damaging the building.[15]

Paolian held Shao for another two weeks. Two officers, one each from the 68th Army and the military subdistrict, arrived in Feng County to mediate, asking for Shao's release. He had admitted his errors under interrogation and had signed a written confession, so after consulting with his colleagues, Zhang Liansheng agreed to escort Shao back to Xuzhou personally. He did so on August 23, and given Shao's confession, he made a series of demands to the military authorities: the vindication of Paolian's position; the repudiation of the PAD's past actions; and the disarming of Liansi. At a public meeting in Xuzhou with representatives from rebel groups, Shao Wen repeated his confession and called for the rehabilitation of Paolian.[16]

While Zhang was in Xuzhou, Paolian militants broke into the office of the county's military control committee, now dominated by the PAD, and ransacked its files in search of accusations the committee had compiled on Paolian. Afterward they published a statement refusing to recognize the authority of a military control committee headed by Shao Wen. While in the compound, they hung up a sign that read "Japanese Imperial Army," alongside a rising-sun battle flag. They followed with written denunciations and cartoons caricaturing Shao and his PAD officers.[17]

Shao may have confessed to his errors, but his colleagues in Feng County were undeterred, and some resented him for selling them out with his confession.

---

14. Ibid., and Feng xian jiguan ganbu Mao Zedong sixiang xuexi ban, "Zhang Liansheng tongzhi daibiao yuan Paolian zongbu xiang quan xian renmin zuo guanyu wuchan jieji wenhua da geming zhong jingyan jiaoxun zongjie huibao" (Comrade Zhang Liansheng's summary report to all the people of the county, representing the former Paolian headquarters, regarding the lessons learned during the great proletarian Cultural Revolution), August 27, 1970.

15. "Mao Zhuxi huishou wo qianjin," June 5, 1968.

16. Zhang Liansheng notebooks; and Zhang Liansheng interview.

17. "Zhang Liansheng tongzhi daibiao yuan Paolian," August 27, 1970.

They pushed back hard, using the attack on the military control committee office to make their case. The PAD issued two statements stressing its adherence to Wang Xiaoyu's instructions and its sympathy for the Kick faction in Xuzhou. It demanded that Paolian halt attacks on military forces and threatened severe punishment.[18] Three days later, the PAD published a statement detailing the "crimes" of Paolian and warned its members to stop "beating, smashing, and looting" or face severe punishment.[19] Liansi issued statements praising the PAD's support for "genuine revolutionary rebels," while denouncing Paolian and the alliance committee.[20]

Liansi followed up by initiating violent clashes. During the last week of August, it sent several dozen fighters to attack the Paolian liaison office in Xuzhou and sent more than one hundred people to attack the county bus station, which was under Paolian control. It sent factory workers to attack Paolian students at the Feng County Middle School and attacked a Paolian stronghold at the printing plant. Paolian members were beaten up at the hardware factory and cotton mill. And on the last day of August, Liansi sent fighters to lay siege to the Paolian stronghold at the county power plant. The attacks left many injured and caused extensive damage to the facilities.[21]

As violence intensified, deposed county leaders took sides. Zhu Pingfan, one of the county's deputy party secretaries, attended mass rallies sponsored by Paolian to criticize Shao Wen and to celebrate Paolian's attack on the military control committee.[22] Another one of the county's former deputy party secretaries, Teng Zetian, along with former deputy county magistrate Cai Zhenhong and former standing committee member of the county party com-

---

18. Zhongguo renmin jiefangjun Jiangsu sheng Feng xian junshi guanzhi weiyuanhui, Jiangsu sheng Feng xian renmin wuzhuangbu, "Lianhe shengming" (Joint declaration), August 25, 1967.

19. Jiangsu sheng Feng xian renmin wuzhuangbu, "Zhongguo renmin jiefangjun Jiangsu sheng Feng xian junshi guanzhi weiyuanhui yanzheng shengming" (Solemn declaration of the People's Liberation Army Military Control Committee of Feng County, Jiangsu Province), August 28, 1967.

20. Feng xian wuchan jieji geming zaofan pai lianhe silingbu, "Jiu '8·25' lianwei (paochou) qiangza Feng xian junguanhui yi shi zhengzhong shengming" (Solemn declaration concerning the Alliance Committee (Paolian preparatory) looting and smashing of the Feng County Military Control Committee on August 25), August 29, 1967.

21. Zhang Liansheng notebooks; and "Mao Zhuxi huishou wo qianjin," June 5, 1968.

22. See the August 9, 1970, speeches denouncing Zhu Pingfan cited in footnote 47 in the previous chapter.

mittee Dong Hongzhi, declared his affiliation with Liansi.[23] PAD officers also split into groups that remained loyal to Shao, while others denounced him for confessing in a way that implicated them.[24]

As these conflicts intensified, Liansi sent petition delegations to Beijing, Ji'nan, and Nanjing to plead its cause. Paolian responded by sending its own petition delegations to the same cities.[25] Preparing for a difficult fight without the protection of its PLA backers, Paolian tightened discipline over its organization, creating new command structures. Hawkish voices became more influential, strengthened by the return of a number of the university students. Zhang Liansheng and other leaders, however, resisted their calls to withdraw from the alliance committee and re-establish Paolian as a completely independent organization.[26]

On August 31, the Kick faction in Xuzhou decisively defeated the Support faction, driving it out of the city and sending many of its members into exile in other regions. Both Paolian and Liansi were inspired by this victory, because each saw itself as an oppressed rebel force trying to overcome the hostility of military units. Liansi moved to press its advantage with a series of coordinated attacks on Paolian strongholds. During the first week of September, it launched attacks on the county's cotton mill, the Xinhua bookstore, the handicraft industry management offices, the construction company, and the distillery, injuring dozens and kidnapping several Paolian members.[27]

Paolian responded by organizing fighting groups and began to arm them.[28] The groups set up military commands and began to seize weapons where they could find them—spears and two submachine guns from a nearby commune, two handguns from a bank branch, and a dozen small-bore rifles from the county sports commission.[29] The next day they called together the leaders of command posts and ordered them to be prepared for battle.[30] On the morning of September 12, a clash between the rival groups broke out at the cotton textile

---

23. Zhang Liansheng notebooks; Zhang Liansheng interview.

24. Zhang Liansheng notebooks.

25. Ibid.

26. Ibid., and Zhang Liansheng interview.

27. Zhang Liansheng interview; "Mao Zhuxi huishou wo qianjin," June 5, 1968; and "Li Zongzhou tongzhi daibiao yuan Liansi," August 27, 1970.

28. Zhang Liansheng notebooks.

29. "Zhang Liansheng tongzhi daibiao yuan Paolian," August 27, 1970.

30. Zhang Liansheng notebooks; "Mao Zhuxi huishou wo qianjin," June 5, 1968; and "Zhang Liansheng tongzhi daibiao yuan Paolian," August 27, 1970.

mill, and Liansi launched an attack on the Paolian stronghold at the bus station. It occupied the station, capturing all of the vehicles and taking a number
of Paolian captives. Close to four hundred farmers loyal to Liansi took part in
the operation. Paolian withdrew from the station with more than forty members wounded.[31]

When leaders at Paolian's headquarters learned of the battle, they sent an
emergency delegation to the Xuzhou Garrison Command to seek help.[32]
The delegation met with officers at the garrison the same evening and were
informed that PLA troops from Unit 6174 would soon be sent back to Feng
County, but that their mission would be to stop the violence, not to assist
Paolian in wiping out Liansi. The Paolian representatives were deeply disappointed by this response. They had hoped for active assistance from the
army, just as the Xuzhou Kick faction had received support from PLA units
there. They decided that they should launch a counterattack on Liansi to immediately destroy its main force before the army arrived. This, they reasoned,
would strengthen their hand in future negotiations. The delegation immediately returned to the county seat that night and issued orders for an attack on
September 13.[33]

Liansi forces, which were concentrated at the eastern gate to the county
seat, had also heard news of the return of the PLA. They fled in panic as soon
as Paolian began its attack. Encouraged by the rout of Liansi at the eastern gate,
Paolian's forces marched to other Liansi strongholds in the county seat. In the
early morning hours, shortly after these attacks began, a convoy of troops from
PLA Unit 6174 arrived at the east gate and learned that fighting was underway in the western half of the town. They rushed to the scene only to find that
Liansi had already been routed, either surrendering to Paolian fighters or fleeing
to the countryside, to take shelter in communes friendly to Liansi under loyal
PAD units.[34]

31. Zhang Liansheng notebooks; "Mao Zhuxi huishou wo qianjin," June 5, 1968; "Zhang
Liansheng tongzhi daibiao yuan Paolian," August 27, 1970; and Zhang Liansheng interview.

32. Zhang Liansheng notebooks; "Mao Zhuxi huishou wo qianjin," June 5, 1968; and "Zhang
Liansheng tongzhi daibiao yuan Paolian," August 27, 1970; and *Jiangsu sheng Feng xian zhi*, p. 28.

33. "Zhang Liansheng tongzhi daibiao yuan Paolian," August 27, 1970.

34. Zhang Liansheng interview; "Mao Zhuxi huishou wo qianjin," June 5, 1968; and "Zhang
Liansheng tongzhi daibiao yuan Paolian," August 27, 1970.

The county seat was now completely under Paolian control. News of the arrival of PLA troops was enough to destroy Liansi's resolve. The decisive September 13 battle for the county seat lasted less than two hours. Two Liansi fighters were killed, a dozen wounded, and more than three hundred were taken prisoner. The majority of the Liansi forces fled the county seat.[35] On September 14, the Paolian newssheet published a special issue, celebrating the September 13 battle and the support of the contingent from the PLA.[36]

Liansi once again sent out delegations to present petitions pleading its case in Xuzhou, Ji'nan, and Nanjing. In Xuzhou, it set up a refugee camp at a school, providing lodging for several hundred of its members. It would later establish similar camps, each of which accommodated several hundred people, in Dangshan and Xiaoxian, two counties in Anhui Province south of Feng County.[37] The battle of September 13 led to a geographic redistribution of factional forces. Liansi consolidated its hold on friendly communes, relying on the command structure of the commune-level PAD. It prepared to fight a future battle whereby its forces would surround the city from the countryside. It established strongholds in the southeastern region of the county.[38] In all, more than one thousand Liansi activists fled the county seat and adjacent communes still controlled by Paolian. County cadres who sided with Liansi also fled to Liansi-controlled regions. Senior officers of the PAD evacuated the county and took shelter at the military subdistrict headquarters in Xuzhou. Junior officers from outside the county returned home, while those who were natives of the county fled to Liansi-controlled enclaves.[39]

35. Zhang Liansheng interview; Interview no. 5; Interview no. 7; and *Jiangsu sheng Feng xian zhi*, p. 28.

36. Feng xian paoda silingbu lianhe zongbu, "Zhongguo renmin jiefangjun 6174 budui zaici jinzhu Fengcheng, Fengcheng geming xingshi dahao chengnei kaishi huifu xin zhixu" (People's Liberation Army Unit 6174 re-deployed to Feng County Seat, order is being restored), *"Paoda silingbu" haowai*, September 14, 1967.

37. Interview no. 5.

38. "Mao Zhuxi huishou wo qianjin," June 5, 1968; "Li Zongzhou tongzhi daibiao yuan Liansi," August 27, 1970; Zhang Liansheng interview; Huang Xiuhua interview; and Xu Jiashun interview.

39. Zhang Liansheng interview; and "Mao Zhuxi huishou wo qianjin," June 5, 1968. Zhang Liansheng and Zhang Ludao's notebooks also recorded the PAD officers' self-criticism in the Xuhai Study Class on their misconduct during this period.

The Xuzhou Study Class

After the dramatic events of September 13, Paolian appeared to have swept to victory, but in fact it only controlled the county seat and nearby communes. Liansi had dug itself into defensive positions in rural communes that resembled revolutionary base areas. Returning to Feng County in mid-September 1967 after an absence of two months, the PLA forces began to address once again the problem of rebuilding political order. In their absence, factional conflicts had spiraled out of control. The PLA would prove no more successful at the end of 1967 than it had been at the beginning, and factional warfare intensified into the early months of 1968.

The military authorities in Xuzhou were preoccupied with the problem of reconciling the conflict between the Kick and Support factions, who had fought one another since splitting over the first attempt at establishing a revolutionary committee in Xuzhou back in March. They did not have a stake in the outcome of the conflicts in Feng County, and they appeared not to understand them. They simply wanted the fighting to stop. They were told irreconcilable stories by the officers of the PAD and the PLA, and they were bombarded with wholly contradictory claims made by delegations from Liansi and Paolian. Still dealing with the complicated problems of factional conflicts in Xuzhou, and suffering from internal splits in the PLA hierarchy created by the July intervention of Wang Xiaoyu, they could only hope that strict conformity to directives from Beijing would somehow resolve Feng County's problems.

Mao Zedong issued orders on September 5, 1967, that military control must be strengthened at each level in preparation for a great alliance and the accelerating formation of revolutionary committees across China.[40] The municipal revolutionary committee established in Xuzhou back in March had long since fallen apart. Backtracking from the April orders for the military to stand down in conflicts with rebels, the new orders made clear that rebel attacks on armed forces would no longer be tolerated, and the military had a freer hand in deal-

---

40. "Zhonggong zhongyang, guowuyuan, zhongyang junwei, zhongyang wen'ge xiaozu guanyu buzhun qiangduo renmin jiefangjun wuqi, zhuangbei he gezhong junyong wuzi de mingling" (Orders of the CCP Central Committee, State Council, Central Military Commission, and the Central Cultural Revolution Group forbidding the seizure of weapons, materials, and other military supplies from the People's Liberation Army). Zhongfa [67], no. 288, September 5, 1967. See Michael Schoenhals, "'Why Don't We Arm the Left?' Mao's Culpability for the Cultural Revolution's 'Great Chaos' of 1967," *China Quarterly* 182 (June 2005): 277–300; and Walder, *China under Mao* pp. 253–258.

ing with local conflicts. But how to do so in a place like Feng County was manifestly unclear, and the military authorities did not want to take actions that could once again spur reprimands from their superiors.

During September 1967, the Xuzhou military authorities moved once again to address Feng County's conflicts, but their only means for doing so was the military control committee. Unfortunately, that committee consisted of troops from PLA Unit 6174 and officers of the county PAD, and they had clashing preferences regarding factional conflicts. Paolian would only acknowledge the authority of the PLA officers and troops, while Liansi would only acknowledge the authority of the PAD. There was no obvious way to intervene effectively in the county with such a fatally divided military control committee.

The Xuzhou Garrison (dominated by 68th Army commanders) was in charge of imposing political control and, ultimately, for orchestrating a great alliance and revolutionary committee. The only reliable instrument that it had at its disposal were the PLA forces under its direct line of command. So long as this was the case, the viewpoints of these PLA officers would be decisive, and they would inevitably favor Paolian. The officers of that unit had attended study classes in Xuzhou in July and Ji'nan in August to "unify thinking" about the correct way to implement military control, but these sessions spoke to the struggles between the Kick and Support factions in Xuzhou, which had unclear implications for Feng County. The PLA officers in Xuzhou agreed to shift their favor from the Support to the Kick faction, as Wang Xiaoyu insisted, but they insisted on the correctness of their view that Paolian was the Feng County equivalent of the Kick faction and deserved a leading role in a great alliance.[41] The county's PAD leaders were in a difficult position. Their superiors in the military subdistrict did not openly support them in their disagreements with the PLA. They could only cooperate with the PLA publicly while trying covertly to undermine them.

The 68th Army commanders in Xuzhou had hoped that a great alliance would be formed by convincing Paolian to adopt a less hostile attitude toward Liansi. Paolian did comply by toning down its hostile rhetoric, and it halted direct attacks on its opponents. However, it took a series of actions that made Liansi less likely to compromise. It abolished the production command office headed by the PAD and replaced it with a new one dominated by Paolian

41. Guo Chaogang notebooks.

members.[42] Likewise, in the county seat and in communes it controlled, it put Paolian members in charge. Liansi members who had fled to rural bases were denied work points and wages for "leaving work posts without permission." Temporary and contract workers who joined Liansi and left their workplaces were fired. Paolian took over the public security bureau and cracked down on Liansi rebels that had formerly dominated it. It set up study classes in work organizations to educate everyone in the Paolian point of view and to refute Liansi's version of events. In its mass rallies to criticize the former county leaders, it targeted Teng Zetian, who had expressed support for Liansi.[43] None of these actions signaled a willingness to compromise; instead, they signaled a determination to dominate.

For its part, Liansi refused to acknowledge the legitimacy of the PLA work team or Paolian, and it refused to join the proposed great alliance. It focused instead on strengthening its hold over the communes that it controlled, drawing on the structures of the PAD in rural areas. On September 27, it flatly refused an invitation to negotiate with Paolian issued by the Xuzhou Garrison and relented only after pressure. At a meeting the next day, it found the proposed conditions completely unacceptable. On the same day it sent more than four hundred members to a demonstration in the county seat, marching through the streets and shouting slogans that called for the overthrow of the PLA officers.[44]

Because its members were denied wages and grain distributions, Liansi forces exiled in the countryside initiated a series of raids on grain depots, supply and marketing cooperatives, materials shipping stations, and banks to seize food, supplies, and cash. They even attacked PLA personnel who went to rural communes to promote the proposed alliance. In early October, they attacked and destroyed two PLA propaganda trucks sent to Liangzhai Commune, assaulting two dozen PLA soldiers and holding a number of them hostage.[45]

In mid-October, the 68th Army and the military subdistrict leaders in Xuzhou made their first effort to resolve Feng County's problems. They jointly

42. Feng xian shengchan bangongshi, "Guanyu qiyong gongzhang de tongzhi" (Notice regarding the use of official seals of government), November 3, 1967.

43. Zhang Liansheng notebooks; "Mao Zhuxi huishou wo qianjin," June 5, 1968; "Zhang Liansheng tongzhi daibiao yuan Paolian," August 27, 1970.

44. "Mao Zhuxi huishou wo qianjin," June 5, 1968.

45. Ibid.; and "Li Zongzhou tongzhi daibiao yuan Liansi," August 27, 1970.

worked out a "four-point resolution" that demanded an end to all attacks on the PAD and PLA, obedience to the PAD-led production command office, and the return of all activists to their places of work and residence. The resolution was completely ignored by both sides. By the end of October, according to Paolian, more than one hundred members of the PLA work team had been beaten up, and more than seventy were seriously injured. These events only strengthened the 68th Army's sympathy for Paolian.[46]

In late November 1967, the 68th Army commended PLA Unit 6174 for its excellent work in Feng County, where they "had taken a clear-cut stand and made outstanding achievements." Enraged by these announcements, which completely repudiated their position, Liansi supporters responded with a furious offensive. In early December, they distributed handbills charging that the military subdistrict and the Xuzhou Garrison had "suppressed the revolutionary masses." They charged that Paolian members were "conservative dogs" and that Liansi must "fight to the death" to defend themselves.[47] Shortly afterward, they initiated a violent clash at Shunhe Commune in which one Paolian member was killed. They sent fighters to the county seat, vandalizing Paolian outposts and demanding the withdrawal of PLA troops.[48]

Paolian sent a delegation headed by Zhang Liansheng and Shan Shutang to Unit 6174's camp in the Xuzhou suburbs, asking for them to send troops to counterattack, but the PLA officers refused, simply repeating the four-point declaration.[49] Deciding that it was not possible to dislodge PLA troops and Paolian from the county seat, near the end of December Liansi withdrew all members from the county seat and set up armed camps and an independent administration in the rural communes that it controlled. Many PAD personnel in the county seat withdrew also. They planned to organize an armed militia by pulling together all of the weapons scattered across the various communes that they controlled, but they were only able to put together a small squad with two dozen rifles.[50] They supplemented these arms with weapons seized from a PLA radar station at Huashan Commune.[51]

46. Zhang Liansheng notebooks; and "Mao Zhuxi huishou wo qianjin," June 5, 1968.

47. Guo Chaogang notebooks.

48. "Mao Zhuxi huishou wo qianjin," June 5, 1968.

49. Guo Chaogang notebooks.

50. "Mao Zhuxi huishou wo qianjin," June 5, 1968; and "Li Zongzhou tongzhi daibiao yuan Liansi," August 27, 1970.

51. Xu Jiashun interview.

Liansi's move to create armed fighting units panicked Paolian's leaders. They worried that the large stockpile of weapons in the PAD arsenal in the county seat might make their way into the hands of Liansi. After an initial decision to safeguard the arsenal, a militant splinter group in Paolian raided the arsenal and hauled off the entire cache of weapons: more than 1,300 rifles, 100 or so handguns, 40 plus light machine guns, one mortar, more than 700 hand grenades and more than 100,000 rounds of ammunition. The weapons were distributed to various work units in the county seat and rural communes controlled by Paolian.[52]

Relying on this weaponry, Paolian launched several offensives, leading to a general state of armed warfare that lasted until March 1968. In January 1968, Paolian fighters defeated and expelled Liansi members from Shizhai, Shunhe, Huankou, Shouxian, Danlou, and Lizhai Communes.[53] In February, Paolian sent armed fighters to Liangzhai and Wanggou Communes to suppress Liansi, and four dozen armed Liansi members were ambushed by Paolian fighters in Shunhe Commune, resulting in one Paolian death.[54] Liansi staged a series of raids on grain depots and other sites in search of food and other supplies. Small-scale skirmishes in villages resulted in injuries and occasional fatalities; soldiers sent to villages to retrieve arms were fired upon and wounded; battles were fought over arms storerooms. The PLA did little to intervene.[55]

In mid-February, military authorities in Xuzhou realized that they would have to play a more direct role in resolving the spiraling conflicts. Officers from the 68th Army and its Engineering Division met with leaders from both Liansi and Paolian to emphasize a new policy of "supporting the left without supporting one faction." They wanted to isolate the extremists in both factions and bring together the moderate figures. They notified the two factions that the leaders from both factions would soon be brought to Xuzhou to participate in study classes (*xuexi ban*) designed to reconcile the two sides. In meetings with Paolian's leaders, they informed them that the PLA work team in the county

---

52. Zhang Liansheng interview; "Zhang Liansheng tongzhi daibiao yuan Paolian," August 27, 1970; and *Jiangsu sheng Feng xian zhi*, pp. 28–29.

53. "Mao Zhuxi huishou wo qianjin," June 5, 1968; and "Xingfeng xueyu sa Feng nan" (Reign of terror in the south of Feng County), and Shao Liyun "Wode kongsu" (My accusation), reprinted in Feng xian wuchan jieji geming zaofan pai lianhe silingbu, *Jiu.yisan bao*, February 20, 1968.

54. "Mao Zhuxi huishou wo qianjin," June 5, 1968; and Guo Chaogang notebooks.

55. "Li Zongzhou tongzhi daibiao yuan Liansi," August 27, 1970; and "Mao Zhuxi huishou wo qianjin," June 5, 1968.

would be replaced, but that Paolian should not feel threatened by this. They emphasized that the withdrawal of the PLA unit did not signal that they had made mistakes; the PLA commanders in Xuzhou still firmly supported Paolian.[56]

To defuse the hostility that Liansi had developed toward the PLA work team and its commander, the unit would be withdrawn from the county and a new one moved in, with a new set of troops from Unit 6174 and a new commander. The head of the 68th Army's "support the left" office came to Feng County to announce the decision on February 21, 1968. He stated that both factions in the county were revolutionary and encouraged them to reach a great alliance without delay. Several days later, the PLA work team left the county, feeling utterly humiliated, having been sacrificed in an expedient move to defuse local animosities.[57]

The new military propaganda team, headed by commander Xia Jidao, arrived on March 2. It had forty-one officers and one company of three hundred or so soldiers, and a twenty-member performing arts propaganda troupe.[58] Shortly afterward, the county's military control committee was reorganized, with Xia Jidao as its head, and Shao Wen and Guo Fengcai (Unit 6174's chief of staff) as vice-directors. The propaganda team set up military control groups within the public security bureau and the post office, with PLA officers from Unit 6174 in charge of both.[59]

On the day that the new military propaganda team arrived, the 68th Army's leaders met in Xuzhou with the entire leadership of both Paolian and Liansi. Over the next two days, negotiations led to an agreement that called for both sides to disband and disarm their fighting groups, turn over all weapons, cease hostile propaganda, release all captives, compensate the families of the dead, and to halt attacks on the PLA and PAD. The leaders of the two factions signed the agreement in Xuzhou on March 5, 1968.[60] The 68th Army's commander, Zhang Zhixiu, attended the signing ceremony and gave a speech

---

56. Zhang Liansheng notebooks.

57. Ibid.

58. Guo Chaogang notebooks.

59. Ibid.; and "Mao Zhuxi huishou wo qianjin," June 5, 1968.

60. Guo Chaogang notebooks; Feng xian Paolian he Feng xian Liansi daibiao, "Feng xian liang pai guanyu liji zhizhi wudou de shitiao xieyi" (Feng County's two factions on the ten-point agreement to immediately end armed combat), March 5, 1968; and "Mao Zhuxi huishou wo qianjin," June 5, 1968.

urging both sides to stick to the agreement and to not to quarrel with the PLA or the PAD.[61]

Several days after the agreement was announced, large groups of exiled Liansi activists returned to the county seat. The PLA propaganda team sent several officers, along with Paolian leaders Zhang Liansheng and Shan Shu-tang, to welcome the returning Liansi activists at the eastern gate to the county seat. As soon as the two groups met, Liansi activists set upon Zhang and Shan and beat them up, then surrounded and verbally abused the military officers. The welcome delegation quickly withdrew. Liansi then sent out pro-paganda trucks to the county seat and Shunhe Commune, and Liansi members in Shizhai, Huankou, and Shunhe staged armed parades and shouted slogans attacking Paolian and the PLA contingent. Liansi activists in Fanlou Com-mune attacked the Paolian members who occupied the commune government compound, wounding many of them, and carting away two dozen rifles.[62]

These events demonstrated that the leaders of the two factions, who had signed the March 5 agreement, did not exercise control over the dispersed suborganizations affiliated with the two sides. Liansi in particular appeared unable to control its rural affiliates. Violent clashes continued in communes, leading to a number of injuries that required hospitalization.[63] Clashes insti-gated by propaganda trucks broke out in a number of rural communes during March.

In the midst of this highly inauspicious beginning to the new effort to or-chestrate a ceasefire, the Xuzhou military authorities announced a new mea-sure intended to pressure all sides to enforce the agreement. The problems that beset Feng County also plagued military control committees in many of the other counties in Xuzhou Prefecture, and all of them would be dealt with as a single group. The military officers convened in Xuzhou an "Eight County Study Class" in which all of the principal actors across the counties would be isolated for study, thought reform, and self-criticism. The 68th Army com-

61. Zhang Zhixiu, "Zai Feng xian liangpai zhizhi wudou xieyi qianzi yishi shang de jianghua" (Speech at the signing ceremony by two Feng County factions of the agreement to end armed combat), March 5, 1968; and "Paolian zhanshi shizuo geming lianhe de cujin pai" (Paolian fight-ers resolve to promote the revolutionary great alliance), *Paoda silingbu* 35, March 15, 1968, p. 2.

62. Guo Chaogang notebooks; "Mao Zhuxi huishou wo qianjin," June 5, 1968; Zhang Lian-sheng notebooks; and Zhang Liansheng interview.

63. Guo Chaogang notebooks; and "Mao Zhuxi huishou wo qianjin," June 5, 1968.

mander Zhang Zhixiu led the study class, and officers from the 68th Army and the military subdistrict joined its leading group.

The study class was divided into eight groups, one for each county, chaired by PLA officers. The study class members from Feng County included the PLA propaganda team leader Xia Jidao, the PAD's Shao Wen, Paolian leader Zhang Liansheng, Liansi leader Li Zongzhou, and four dozen others from the two factions.[64] Before departing for Xuzhou, the Paolian leaders met to settle on a strategy, and the participants were warned that they represented the interests of the faction and should stand firm and not make too many compromises.[65]

In speeches to all the participants on the first day, the PLA officers laid out the ground rules—participants would study Mao's directives, articles on the great alliance and what it means to support the left but not one faction, and the need to resolutely oppose violence. The leaders of both sides must promote unity and oppose splits. While in Xuzhou, participants must not leave the study class without permission, and they must not bring any weapons with them. Group members must not privately communicate with one another or with their comrades back home. They must not put up wall posters criticizing the other faction. Participants were warned to adhere to these rules. Those who violated them would have "the methods of dictatorship" applied to them. Essentially, the Xuzhou Study Class was an involuntary retreat designed to isolate the principals from local conflicts and pressure them into a compromise.

The Xuzhou Study Class had no immediate impact on the factional warfare still being waged in Feng County. Small-scale clashes continued, especially in rural areas.[66] The PLA propaganda team in the county tried to apply the "study class" method in the county itself. In mid-March, it set up study classes for the leaders of both factions at the cotton mill, chemical fertilizer plant, hardware factory, department store, and a number of other units. Near the end of March, they extended the classes to communes, the security and legal bureaucracy, and the post office. Several of these units and communes announced the formation of great alliances.[67] PAD officers and many Liansi members refused to

64. Zhang Liansheng notebooks; Zhang Liansheng interview.

65. Zhang Liansheng notebooks.

66. Guo Chaogang notebooks; and "Mao Zhuxi huishou wo qianjin," June 5, 1968.

67. Guo Chaogang notebooks.

participate in these local study classes. Clashes broke out in late March when Liansi members initiated confrontations in a number of communes.[68]

To enhance the effectiveness of the study classes, the Xuzhou military authorities went to Feng County to convene a conference of the leaders of the two factions. The PLA propaganda team officers, the PAD officers, and the faction leaders who attended the Xuzhou Study Class all came along with them. Zhang Liansheng and the Liansi leader Cheng Yinzhen both gave conciliatory speeches. Shao Wen made a self-criticism that gave the PAD the main share of the blame for the county's factionalism, and he apologized for his errors. He asked Liansi members to respect the PLA propaganda team. PLA Unit 6174's chief of staff Guo Fengcai also made a self-criticism for failing to "support the left but not one faction" and for failing to support the PAD. Zhang Zhixiu made self-criticism on behalf of the 68th Army party committee for its mistakes and shortcomings in "support the left" work. He asked everyone to learn lessons from their mistakes in order to achieve a great alliance.[69]

Although most leaders of the two factions agreed with this basic direction, there were militant leaders and members of the two factions who shrugged off this show of contrition and reconciliation. The top leaders might comply with the 68th Army's efforts to promote compromise, but the reality was that the factions were loose affiliations of rebel groups from different work organizations and communes, each of which had its own point of view. The subgroups that refused to compromise were able to sabotage any agreements promoted from above by the military authorities. The leaders of Paolian and Liansi were unable to enforce discipline over their more militant members, so violent clashes continued.

In the month after the conference held in the county seat, there were no fewer than twenty-three violent clashes. The largest and most dramatic was a raid by more than one thousand Liansi fighters at Shunhe Commune, in which they looted foodstuffs and other supplies before vandalizing a tractor station and machinery plant. A similar Liansi raid by several hundred in Wanggou Commune attacked a grain management bureau and post office defended by Paolian. Both sides used guns and grenades, leaving dozens wounded and cap-

68. "Mao Zhuxi huishou wo qianjin," June 5, 1968.
69. Zhang Liansheng notebooks.

tured on both sides. In Danlou Commune, Liansi members threw hand grenades into a study class, wounding six participants.[70]

The Xuzhou military authorities were completely helpless in the face of these attacks, and their repeated entreaties to the leaders of the two sides had virtually no effect. Factional subgroups continued to fight over turf and resources as if the study classes and related agreements had never taken place. The alliances announced in a number of work units and communes collapsed, and the effort to implement local study classes was abandoned.

In early May 1968, the March 5 agreement collapsed completely. Liansi members who had returned to their work units in early March moved back to rural communes. Liansi's leaders decided to restore the armed fighting squads that they had disbanded. They manufactured homemade weapons and purchased guns and ammunition from Lianyungang, Nanjing, and other places. They set up bases in Liangzhai, Fanlou, and Jinling communes and, borrowing terminology reminiscent of the anti-Japanese and civil war eras, divided up Feng County into "liberated areas" (*jiefang qu*), "guerrilla areas" (*youji qu*), and "enemy occupied zones" (*di zhan qu*). Liansi also set up bases across the Shandong provincial border in Yutai County and had between two hundred and three hundred armed fighters who threatened Paolian-controlled Shunhe Commune.[71]

Liansi intensified its armed operations. In early May, its forces attacked the Paolian-held Shouxian Commune, and in a raid on Shunhe Commune they beat to death the head of the commune tax office.[72] The next week, they took over a shipping depot in Xiao County, across the border in Anhui Province, seizing over 200,000 yuan in cash and 3.5 million yuan's worth of grain and other products.[73] They later assembled more than one thousand members armed with more than two hundred guns to attack Paolian members in Jinling Commune, wounding five. In mid-May they forcibly occupied the local post office, hospital, and grain management agency in Zhangwulou Commune and

70. Zhang Liansheng interview; Guo Chaogang notebooks; "Mao Zhuxi huishou wo qianjin," June 5, 1968; and *Jiangsu sheng Feng xian zhi*, p. 29.

71. Zhang Liansheng notebooks; and "Li Zongzhou tongzhi daibiao yuan Liansi," August 27, 1970.

72. Guo Chaogang notebooks; "Mao Zhuxi huishou wo qianjin," June 5, 1968.

73. "Mao Zhuxi huishou wo qianjin," June 5, 1968; "Li Zongzhou tongzhi daibiao yuan Liansi," August 27, 1970; and *Jiangsu sheng Feng xian zhi*, p. 29.

looted the supply and marketing cooperative and the grain management bureau in Lizhai Commune. Later that month, more than four hundred Liansi fighters besieged several dozen Paolian members in the Jinling Commune government compound, firing machine guns, rifles, and a 60mm mortar. One Paolian member was killed and eleven wounded, one of whom later died.[74] Xuzhou's intervention in Feng County's conflicts had failed completely, and as the summer of 1968 approached, the county was in a state of low-grade civil war.

74. Zhang Liansheng notebooks; Guo Chaogang notebooks; and "Mao Zhuxi huishou wo qianjin," June 5, 1968.

5

Beijing Intervenes

BY THE LATE SPRING OF 1968, the Xuhai region stood out as particularly problematic. Uncontrolled factional warfare continued despite redoubled efforts by the Xuzhou military authorities to reconcile the warring parties. Jiangsu Province had achieved a ceasefire between its two province-wide factions back in September 1967 and had formed a revolutionary committee in March 1968 under the leadership of General Xu Shiyou, the commander of the Nanjing Military Region. This was achieved only after six months of protracted and contentious negotiations in Beijing by the two major factions in the province.[1] Xuzhou, Lianyungang, and the eight counties in Xuzhou Prefecture were a land apart—the political settlement reached in the rest of Jiangsu did not extend to the province's northernmost district.

The Xuhai problem came to the attention of central authorities, who were engaged in a concerted effort to re-establish some form of stable political order by the end of the year. They would directly intervene in the region in late May 1968, ordering all of the principals involved to attend a Xuhai Study Class (*Xuhai xuexi ban*) in Beijing. The top faction leaders and military officers from the PLA and PAD in Xuzhou, Lianyungang, and the eight counties in Xuzhou Prefecture were summoned to the capital. This was essentially the same mechanism attempted earlier in Xuzhou. Central authorities apparently felt that pressure from higher-ranking officials might be more effective in forging an enduring compromise.

On May 24, ten officers from PLA Unit 6174 were informed that they were required to participate, including Xia Jidao, Zheng Guoxin, and Guo Fengcai.[2]

---

1. See Dong Guoqiang and Andrew G. Walder, "From Truce to Dictatorship: Creating a Revolutionary Committee in Jiangsu," *China Journal* 68 (July 2012), pp. 1–32.
2. Guo Chaogang notebooks.

Shortly afterward, Liansi and Paolian were informed of the plans and were ordered to organize delegations. Paolian convened meetings to work out a delegate list and, at the same time, to fully document what it considered to be the atrocities committed by Liansi, along with an account that illustrated the close cooperation between Liansi and the PAD. It was determined to use the study class in Beijing as an opportunity to present its case directly at the highest levels.[3] Paolian's leaders resolved never to relinquish control over the county seat while the negotiations were still underway. Toward that end, they produced and stockpiled more weapons, hand grenades, and land mines.[4]

Liansi's leaders also convened a meeting to discuss its strategy. They decided to fight two battles simultaneously: a propaganda battle in Beijing and an armed battle in Feng County. Their slogan was "Two Battlefields, One Target, Overwhelm the Opposite Side, Win the Victory."[5] For the propaganda battle, they drew up a list of complaints and compiled evidence of what they considered to be the "crimes" of the PLA work team and Paolian. The list of charges was long and somewhat self-contradictory: on the one hand, Paolian was denounced as "reactionary" because of the reputedly impure historical and class backgrounds of some of its leaders, but on the other hand they were accused of being "conservative" (*baohuang*) because of the presence of large numbers of junior cadres from the county offices.[6]

At end of June and early July 1968, the two delegations headed for Beijing.[7] As it would turn out, the participants' expectations about the upcoming negotiations were completely misguided. Each side anticipated that the study class would be a venue to argue its case against the other side and obtain the approval of higher authorities for a victory at the negotiating table. They did not understand that the upper levels of officialdom were uninterested in adjudicating their competing claims and intended to pressure them to forget about

3. Zhang Liansheng notebooks.

4. Feng xian shizhi bangongshi, Feng xian dangshi di er juan di si bian, ed. *"Wenhua da geming" shinian dongluan (1966.5–1976.10)* (The 'Cultural Revolution' decade of turmoil [May 1966–October 1976]), unpublished book draft, pp. 48–49.

5. "Li Zongzhou tongzhi daibiao yuan Liansi," August 27, 1970.

6. Guo Chaogang notebooks; Zhang Liansheng notebooks; and Xuhai ban Feng xian liansi daibiaotuan, "Wang Xiaoyu, Li Bude jiqi Xu Fang, Zheng Guoxin zai Xuhai diqu tuixing zichan jieji fandong luxian zhi yipai ya yi pai de zui'e" (The crimes of Wang Xiaoyu and Li Bude along with Xu Fang and Zheng Guoxin in carrying out the bourgeois reactionary line of supporting one faction while suppressing another in the Xuhai region), August 6, 1968.

7. Zhang Liansheng notebooks; and Zhang Ludao notebooks.

their factional grievances. The Beijing authorities proved especially uninterested in delving into the complicated cross-accusations of the two sides in an insignificant place like Feng County. The strategies of the two sides suggested from the outset that the Xuhai Study Class would be unlikely to resolve anything and might even have the adverse effect of stimulating a new round of factional violence. This is in fact what happened, remarkably, after a year of fruitless negotiations in the nation's capital.

The Beijing Study Class

The Xuhai region was not the only place in China that suffered from seemingly irreconcilable factional warfare. Military intervention had failed in many regions, as much through indecision and confusion on the part of local military commands as to divisions within PLA commands or between main line PLA forces and local PADs.[8] The problem became acute across much of China in the summer of 1967 and continued to plague most regions well into 1968. Mao Zedong and his radical associates hoped wherever possible to push for negotiation and compromise, somewhat coercively if necessary, by bringing together local military officers and faction leaders to Beijing for re-education, self-criticism, and if needed, denunciation and punishment.[9] Study classes were organized for regions that were placed under military control in the spring of 1967 and still were unable to quell factional warfare to the point that a provincial revolutionary committee could be formed. By September 1967, only seven provincial revolutionary committees had been established; the other twenty-two provinces remained under military control, and most of them suffered from severe and widespread factional warfare of the kind suffered in the Xuhai region. Even some of the seven provinces that already had revolutionary committees still had unresolved local conflicts. In September, Mao Zedong called for an acceleration in the effort and set a target of creating ten new provincial revolutionary committees by February 1968.[10] With the

8. See Shinichi Tanigawa, "The Policy of the Military 'Supporting the Left' and the Spread of Factional Warfare in China's Countryside: Shaanxi, 1967–1968." *Modern China* 44, no. 1 (January 2018): 35–67.

9. This is in fact the procedure used in the six-month Beijing negotiations that preceded the March 1968 formation of the Jiangsu Revolutionary Committee. See Dong and Walder, "From Truce to Dictatorship."

10. Walder, *Agents of Disorder*, p. 152.

formation of Guangdong's revolutionary committee on February 21, only eight had been established, with fourteen provinces still under military control.[11]

The instrument for forging regional compromises was provincial and regional study classes held in Beijing. The Leading Group for the Center's Mao Zedong Thought Study Classes (*Zhongyang ban de Mao Zedong sixiang xuexi ban lingdao xiaozu*) listed Vice-Chairman Lin Biao as nominal director, and three civilian deputy directors—Chen Boda, Kang Sheng, and Jiang Qing, all radical members of the Central Cultural Revolution Group. Most of the members of the leading group were from the office of the Central Military Commission, which was headed by the PLA chief of staff Huang Yongsheng and his deputies Wu Faxian, Li Zuopeng, and Qiu Huizuo. Huang was the deputy director in charge of the daily operation of the study classes. The general office of the leading group administered the study classes under the direction of Nie Jifeng, political commissar of one of the PLA Corps. One of his deputies was Song Weishi, political commissar of the PLA Political Institute.[12]

The primary motivation for organizing the study class for the Xuhai region was the continuing and extraordinarily violent factional conflicts between the Support and Kick factions in Xuzhou.[13] So long as these conflicts were unresolved, factional warfare continued in all of the eight counties in Xuzhou Prefecture. The Xuhai class was not the only one being run in Beijing at that time. In mid-July 1968 there were simultaneous study classes for the provinces of Fujian, Guangxi, Xinjiang, Tibet, and other regions, none of which had yet established provincial revolutionary committees (see fig. 4). Jiangsu Province had formed its revolutionary committee in March 1968, but the Xuhai region was still far from pacified. There were study classes for other subprovincial jurisdictions when the Xuhai class began in mid-1968—among them were classes for the cities of Kunming, Chengdu, and Ji'nan.[14] The effort continued even after the conclusion of the Xuhai Class in July 1969. At that time there

11. Ibid., p 157.

12. Zhang Liansheng notebooks; Zhang Ludao notebooks. When discussing the joint meetings of the entire delegation, the notebooks of Zhang Liansheng and Zhang Ludao overlap and are largely in agreement. However, Zhang Liansheng participated in meetings of faction leaders from which Zhang Ludao was excluded, and Zhang Ludao participated in meetings of party members from which Zhang Liansheng was excluded.

13. Dong and Walder, "Forces of Disorder."

14. Zhang Liansheng notebooks.

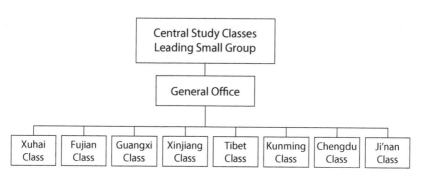

FIGURE 4. Central study classes, 1968–1969

were still study classes underway for the provinces of Shandong, Guizhou, and Tibet, and for the cities of Qingdao and Chengdu.[15]

The classes were held under the general office of the Leading Group for the Center's Mao Zedong Thought Study Classes. Each provincial or regional study class had its own leading small group. The one for the Xuhai class consisted of senior officers from the 68th Army and Xuzhou Military Subdistrict, and it was headed by Zhang Zhixiu, commander of the 68th Army.

The Xuhai class would last for almost a year, a fact that indicated the extreme difficulty of resolving factional animosities through negotiation. The year can be divided into three phases. The first phase, from July to December 1968, was directed by military officers who staffed the office of the Central Military Commission, which focused primarily on the controversies between the Kick and Support factions in Xuzhou, and the problems created by the intervention of Wang Xiaoyu the previous year. Zhou Enlai made an occasional appearance to encourage the two sides to compromise. A second phase ran from late December 1968 to May 1969, when Zhou Enlai split up the delegations, having representatives from the railways, the coal industry, and electric power agencies meet separately in an effort to get them to an agreement first. The third phase ran from May to July 1969, and was heavily influenced by dramatic political developments at the Ninth Party Congress in April. At that meeting, Mao authorized the denunciation and purge of Wang Xiaoyu, including errors that he committed while intervening in Xuzhou. Zhou Enlai, Kang Sheng, Chen Boda, and other central party leaders met with the Xuhai class

15. "Zhongyang shouzhang dui gesheng Mao Zedong sixiang xuexiban chengyuan de jianghua" (Speeches by central leaders to the members of the various Provincial Mao Zedong Thought study classes), October 17, 1969.

participants in late May to announce the new decisions on the Xuzhou issue. The Kick faction was denounced, the 68th Army's commanding officers were forced to make self-criticisms (in particular Zhang Zhixiu), and Zhou Enlai warned the delegates that anyone who defied PLA authority from that point forward would be dealt with by armed force.[16]

The Xuhai class met on the campus of the PLA Political Institute. The delegation was enormous, with close to two thousand participants from the cities of Xuzhou and Lianyungang and the eight counties. They were divided into separate classes by city and county. The delegates reached Beijing in batches in late June and early July. The Feng County delegates registered at the PLA campus on July 14, one day before the opening ceremony was scheduled. Their class was led by the head of the 68th Army's engineering division, Li Gengxin. The military delegates from the PLA and the county PAD met separately from the civilian delegations from Paolian and Liansi.[17] The final Paolian delegation of fifteen was headed by Zhang Liansheng, Shan Shutang, and Shi Hongde. The fifteen Liansi delegates included Li Zongzhou and Cheng Yinzhen.

The Xuhai class was troubled even before it began. A dispute over representation within the Xuzhou Support Faction delegation delayed the proceedings for a month, after a group of delegates walked out in protest.[18] During this initial episode, no delegates from Feng County left the study class, but they continued to pursue their factional activities. The Paolian delegates had arrived in Beijing prepared to argue their case, armed with reports that detailed their own revolutionary activities and denounced the actions of Liansi and the county PAD. Their report claimed that Paolian was an alliance of 142 rebel

16. "Zhou zongli zai jiejian Xuzhou diqu tielu, meikuang xitong, Xuzhou shi liangpai geming qunzhong zuzhi fuzeren he jundui lingdao tongzhi shi de zhongyao zhishi" (Premier Zhou Enlai's important instructions in meetings with leaders of revolutionary mass organizations from the Xuzhou Prefecture railway and coal systems and Xuzhou City, and leading comrades in the military), December 30, 1968; Liushiba jun dangweihui, "Liushiba jun dangweihui guanyu guanche luoshi 'jiuda' jingshen de jige wenti de baogao" (Report of the 68th Army party committee on some questions regarding the thorough implementation of the spirit of the Ninth Party Congress), July 27, 1969; Zhang Liansheng notebooks; and "Fennu jiefa Yang Zhengxiang fandui Mao zhuxi, duikang dang zhongyang de taotian zuixing" (Angrily expose Yang Zhengxiang's monstrous crimes of opposing Chairman Mao and resisting the Party Center), *Xuzhou shi tielu fenju junguanhui, geweihui Mao Zedong sixiang xuexi ban jiefa cailiao zhuanji (shisan)*, October 14, 1970, p. 9. Yang Zhengxiang was leader of the Xuzhou Kick faction.

17. Zhang Liansheng notebooks; Zhang Liansheng interview.

18. Zhang Liansheng notebooks.

groups with more than 6,200 members, and that it had the firm support of the PLA.[19] Zhang Liansheng had Paolian forces back in the county intensify their offensives against Liansi and send more denunciation materials about their enemies to Beijing. They planned to hand the materials to the central leadership and circulate them within the study class.[20]

The Feng County class was handled exclusively by military officers from the study class leadership office. In the early months, central leaders never appeared before the civilian delegates from Feng County and only conferred briefly with some of the military commanders. The leaders of the study class compelled all participants to make self-criticisms and pressured them to sign a great alliance agreement on September 27, 1968, barely more than a month after the class began. Similar agreements were already concluded by the delegates from Xuzhou, Lianyungang, and several other counties. They were signed under political pressure and did not genuinely represent a relaxation of factional animosities.[21] The new agreement simply restated the points agreed to back in March: ending weapons seizures; surrendering all weapons; disbanding all combat units; ending attacks on the PLA or PAD; and ending raids on warehouses, grain depots, and banks. The one difference was that those who violated these points would meet with armed force and arrests.[22]

As was the case with the earlier study class in Xuzhou, an agreement in Beijing had little effect back in Feng County. Second-rank leaders on both sides continued to push for advantage in local struggles. The longer that negotiations in Beijing dragged on, the more local conflicts persisted. After the county delegations left for Beijing in early July, the local PLA propaganda team continued to organize study classes in work units and communes, but to little effect. Violent clashes continued throughout July, with a reported four deaths and dozens wounded.[23] The fighting intensified in August, as Liansi organized

19. Xuhai ban Feng xian 'paolian' daibiao tuan, "Feng xian paoda silingbu lianhe zongbu qingkuang jianjie" (Brief introduction to the situation of the Feng County Bombard the Headquarters Allied General Headquarters), July 1968.

20. Xuhai ban Feng xian paolian daibiao tuan, "Zhi Feng xian paolian zongbu xin" (Letter to the Feng County Paolian headquarters), September 1968; and Zhang Liansheng notebooks.

21. Zhang Liansheng notebooks.

22. Xuhai ban Feng xian daibiao tuan, "Guanyu luoshi 'qisan,' 'qiersi' bugao, liji tingzhi wudou, shoujiao wuqi de xieyi" (Agreement on implementing the "July 3" and "July 24" orders to immediately halt armed battles and surrender weapons), September 27, 1968.

23. Guo Chaogang notebooks; Zhang Liansheng notebooks; and Shao Limin notebooks.

a series of coordinated offensives. There were no fewer than eleven reported violent clashes, eight related deaths, and much larger numbers wounded during August. Raids on storehouses and grain depots continued, and the battles became larger and fighting groups better organized.[24] The combat deaths enraged Paolian leaders who remained behind in the county and spurred them to seek revenge rather than compromise. This began to drive a wedge between them and the leaders of their faction in Beijing, who were willing to compromise, or who were being compelled to do so under pressure and isolation in Beijing. Paolian leaders in the county became increasingly militant, ordered the redoubling of their military preparedness and aggressiveness, and intensified their denunciation of Liansi in handbills and publications, making even more extreme accusations against them.[25]

In early September, the Paolian delegates in the study class submitted reports to central party leaders, detailing the increased violence in Feng County and asking that the 68th Army send troops to punish the perpetrators and disarm Liansi.[26] Much to their disappointment, the officials in charge of the study class showed little interest in what was happening back in the county. They were focused on the much larger problem of the warfare between the Kick and Support factions in Xuzhou. They appeared to assume, erroneously, that Feng County's problems were an extension of those in Xuzhou and would disappear once the Xuzhou problems were solved. Without orders from above, the PLA propaganda team in Feng County remained unwilling to intervene. They continued to issue rambling and cliché-filled directives to the two sides

24. Guo Chaogang notebooks; Zhang Liansheng notebooks; Shao Limin notebooks; and *Jiangsu sheng Feng xian zhi*, p. 29.

25. "Chedi dadao Gao Ying de hei ganjiang Liu Zongbin" (Thoroughly overthrow Gao Ying's reliable tool, Liu Zongbin), *Paoda silingbu*, no. 55, August 15, 1968, p. 2; Guo Chaogang notebooks; "Chedi qingsuan Gao Ying de hei ganjiang Liu Zongbin sanbu 'duo zhongxin lun' de liudu" (Thoroughly liquidate the lingering poison of Gao Ying's reliable tool Liu Zongbin's dissemination of "many centers"), *Fenglei ji*, no. 142, August 21, 1968; Hongweibing Feng xian zhihuibu, "Guanyu Feng xian muqian xingshi de shengming" (Declaration on the current situation in Feng County), handbill, August 25, 1968; and "'Qisan,' 'qiersi' bugao xuanpanle Gao, Qian, Teng, Cai, Liu yihuo de sixing" (The "July 3" and "July 24" proclamations pronounce a death sentence on the Gang of Gao, Qian, Teng, Cai, and Liu), *Fenglei ji*, no. 146, September 1, 1968.

26. Xuhai ban Feng xian paolian daibiao tuan, "Zhi zhongyang ban de Mao Zedong sixiang xuexi ban bangongshi he zhongyang shouzhang de xin" (Letter to the office of the Center-sponsored Mao Zedong Thought study class and to central party leaders). September 2, 1968.

about the proper orientation of class struggle and adherence to Chairman Mao's directives.[27]

Making little real headway in the Paolian-Liansi split, the study class directors concentrated their effort on reconciling the PLA and PAD officers from the county. Officers on each side were to make self-criticisms, but it became clear that there was an underlying animosity between them. The self-criticism sessions frequently disintegrated into quarreling.[28]

The commanders of the 68th Army and the Xuzhou Military Subdistrict wanted to resolve the Feng County issues as soon as possible, but they had little understanding of the problems there. A joint monitoring group was established in the county to administer the new agreement negotiated in Beijing at the end of September, but the PAD and Liansi leaders on the monitoring committee were unwilling to enforce it. The PLA propaganda team reported in early October that they had seized a total of 588 firearms in the county, but only 22 came from Liansi. On October 4, close to four hundred Liansi members held a rally in Fanlou Commune, after which they looted the supply and marketing cooperative and grain management agency, beating up a dozen Paolian members who worked there. In the days to follow, violent clashes broke out in Danlou, Zhangwulou, Malou, Shunhe, Shizhai, Shahe, Liangzhai, and Huankou Communes. On October 10, the county's monitoring group reported back to Beijing that there were so many incidents that it could do little more than investigate them after the fact. In another report submitted days later, it stated that Liansi had ceased turning over weapons per the agreement.[29] Violent clashes continued throughout October.[30]

A subtle shift took place in mid-October, when the delegates from Feng County were ordered to prepare lists of veteran cadres who were acceptable to them as part of a great alliance. They learned that the PLA would be in charge of "support the left" work in the county, but that the PAD would be in charge of the "three-in-one combination" of former party leaders, rebel leaders, and military officers who were to be included on a new revolutionary committee.[31]

27. Guo Chaogang notebooks.

28. Ibid.

29. Ibid., and Zhang Liansheng notebooks.

30. Guo Chaogang notebooks; Zhang Liansheng notebooks; and Xuhai ban Feng xian paolian daibiao tuan, "'Jiu.erqi' zhizhi wudou cuoshi qianding yilai, Feng xian Liansi dazaqiang shao zhua jianlun" (Brief statement about the beating, smashing, looting, arson and kidnapping by Liansi since the signing of the "September 27" measures to curtail armed conflicts), January 1969.

31. Zhang Liansheng notebooks; Zhang Ludao notebooks.

MAP 4. Feng County and surroundings

This shift in the division of labor had the important consequence of elevating the PAD's role in composing a new government. It now became clear that the PLA's presence in the county was temporary, and that the soldiers would eventually leave. Handing primary authority over the selection of a new county government to the PAD had ominous implications for Paolian.

Arguments arose immediately when the two factions were asked to recommend former senior party officials for inclusion in the new government. Paolian nominated former deputy party secretary Zhu Pingfan, but Liansi delegates charged that Zhu was a traitor, a Japanese spy, and a capitalist roader. Zhu, of course, had openly declared his allegiance to Paolian in 1967. When Liansi delegates nominated another former deputy party secretary, Teng Zetian, Paolian delegates immediately objected, charging that he was a fake CCP member, and that his father was a landlord executed during the revolution. Teng, of course, had earlier pledged his support to Liansi. The military officers were helpless in the face of such furious disagreements, and the nomination meetings were postponed.[32]

Just as the two delegations began discussions about a new government, a series of violent clashes broke out in Feng County. During the last week of October, Liansi mobilized farmers to besiege the Liangzhai Commune government compound and loot the local supply and marketing cooperative. They met with resistance from local Paolian members and many were wounded.[33] Paolian sent two trucks to Xiao County, Anhui, to transport exiled Liansi members back to the county seat: the exiles refused the return trip and detained the trucks. Later that day, Liansi attacked and looted the warehouses of Shunhe Commune's electrical relay station.[34] Farmers affiliated with Liansi invaded and looted buildings that housed a local headquarters of Paolian.[35]

News about these incidents made negotiations in Beijing even more difficult. Paolian demanded that the Xuzhou PLA restrain Liansi and enforce the September agreement, but the military officers in charge of the study classes would only counsel Paolian to "correctly treat Liansi" and "correctly treat the

32. Zhang Liansheng notebooks; Zhang Ludao notebooks.

33. Guo Chaogang notebooks; and Xuhai ban Feng xian paolian daibiao tuan, "'Jiu.erqi' zhizhi wudou cuoshi qianding yilai," January 1969.

34. Guo Chaogang notebooks; and "'Jiu.erqi' zhizhi wudou cuoshi qianding yilai," January 1969.

35. Zhang Liansheng notebooks; and "'Jiu.erqi' zhizhi wudou cuoshi qianding yilai," January 1969.

PAD."[36] In early November, Zheng Guoxin, political commissar of PLA Unit 6174 and former head of the county's military control committee, met with angry and frustrated Paolian delegates. He said, "it's understandable that you are frustrated about recent events in Feng County, but we are now in Beijing and can do nothing about it. We must trust our comrades back home. They will resolve the problems in the appropriate way." He emphasized that Paolian delegates should not be distracted by events back home. He promised them that PLA troops would deal with the problems and move immediately to curtail violence.[37]

But the factional fighting continued through November. Paolian delegates continued to receive reports of Liansi offensives. Liansi mobilized farmers in several communes to raid commune and brigade offices and loot local grain management agencies, supply and marketing cooperatives, and post offices. Paolian activists were ambushed, kidnapped, tortured, and killed, and their homes searched and looted. Pitched battles broke out in rural communes. More than thirty armed Liansi fighters in Jinling Commune kidnapped a Paolian member and tortured him for two days. Armed Liansi members in Huankou Commune kidnaped and tortured a Paolian leader. In one attack, Liansi-affiliated farmers attacked a Paolian mass rally armed with two machine guns and several rifles.[38] Our sources are limited to reports received by the Paolian delegates, but we can reasonably assume that Liansi's delegates received similarly one-sided reports of Paolian transgressions back in the county.

The effort to establish a county revolutionary committee pushed ahead, but now with Shao Wen chairing the meetings. This did not bode well for Paolian. At a meeting on November 18, Shao announced that a plan for the composition of the Feng County Revolutionary Committee had already been worked out and awaited approval by the upper levels. There would be fifty-nine members of the revolutionary committee in all, with slots allotted to civilian cadres, military officers, workers, farmers, and students. There would be a fifteen-member standing committee, consisting of five civilian cadres, four military officers, and six mass representatives from the two factions. At the apex of the new government would be one head and six deputy heads.

36. Zhang Liansheng notebooks; and Zhang Liansheng interview.

37. Zhang Liansheng notebooks; and Zhang Ludao notebooks.

38. Zhang Liansheng notebooks; Guo Chaogang notebooks; Zhang Ludao notebooks; and "'Jiu.erqi' zhizhi wudou cuoshi qianding yilai," January 1969.

Predictably, sharp disagreements arose over the factional balance of representatives and, in particular, the balance of military and civilian cadres. For Paolian, the biggest sticking point was the proposal that Shao Wen himself would head the new revolutionary committee. Paolian's protests were bluntly rejected by the army officers leading the study class. In early December, the county delegation was urged to reach a consensus as soon as possible and warned that the party center would not permit this to be dragged out beyond the end of 1968.[39]

Paolian delegates were frustrated by the rigidity of the military officers running the study class, and they resented the military subdistrict leaders, especially Chai Rongsheng, who was part of the Xuhai class. He had not shown up at mass meetings. Instead, only one deputy chief of staff attended several sessions on behalf of the subdistrict leaders. When Chai's deputy chief of staff did make a self-criticism, he only admitted that military subdistrict and the PAD "made some mistakes," but emphasized that they "had a consistent attitude on the Feng County problem." The Paolian delegates felt that the military subdistrict officers had never really changed their supportive attitude toward the PAD and their antagonism toward Paolian.

The top priority for the PLA officers running the study class seemed to be simply to wrap up matters as quickly as possible, without adjudicating substantive political issues. It was as if their patience had come to an end, or perhaps pressures from above were forcing them to ignore political issues. None of them appeared interested in the origins of factional conflicts in the county, and they appeared not to care whether Liansi had turned in their weapons and ceased hostilities. The PLA officers dispatched to the county had supported Paolian over the past eighteen months, but in the study class they were evidently caving in to their superiors' demands to wrap things up without delay. They now pushed Paolian's delegates to compromise, leaving them to the mercy of the military subdistrict and the PAD.[40]

As the end-of-year deadline approached, the delegates worked separately to select their candidates for the revolutionary committee. Back in Feng County, Paolian and Liansi constantly made phone calls or sent messengers to Beijing to report on local clashes, which rekindled animosities in the delegation. On December 26, Mao's seventy-fifth birthday, huge celebrations were held in Beijing. On December 28, the explosion of China's first hydrogen bomb

39. Zhang Liansheng notebooks; Guo Chaogang notebooks; Zhang Ludao notebooks; and "'Jiu.erqi' zhizhi wudou cuoshi qianding yilai," January 1969.

40. Zhang Liansheng interview.

was celebrated as a great victory of Mao Zedong Thought and a great achievement of the Cultural Revolution. The entire Xuhai class held a celebration rally that lasted until the early morning hours.[41]

None of this pageantry had any effect on the delegates' willingness to compromise. The fighting in the county had, if anything, gotten worse. There were no fewer than thirteen major incidents during December, some involving hundreds of fighters, and each resulting in deaths or severe injuries. Commune headquarters, government compounds, and grain storage depots continued to be looted. In some incidents, Liansi relied on its control of rural areas to mobilize more than a thousand farmers for demonstrations, and hundreds for armed battles.[42]

Reversal of Fortune

At the end of December, there was a decisive shift in the balance of power back in the county. On December 28, the PLA propaganda team negotiated an agreement between the two factions that would permit members of Liansi who had jobs in the county seat to return to the town.[43] This marked a major shift in Liansi's stance: it had previously refused to send its members back into a county seat that was controlled by Paolian. But the Liansi mobilization of farmers in rural communes over the previous several months, relying on the PAD hierarchy and its network of militia forces in communes and production brigades, had strengthened its hand in local conflicts. Several thousand farmers under Liansi's direction were moving into the county seat and nearby communes, and the forces of the two sides were evenly matched for the first time since the dramatic Liansi exodus more than a year earlier. The longstanding refusal of Liansi fighters in rural areas to turn over their weapons also helped to shift the balance of power. From Paolian's perspective, what was billed as a "peaceful return" of Liansi to the county seat began to look more like an "armed takeover," as Liansi forces moved to occupy a series of installations and factories in the county seat.[44]

41. Zhang Liansheng notebooks; Zhang Ludao notebooks.

42. Zhang Liansheng notebooks; Zhang Ludao notebooks; and "'Jiu.erqi' zhizhi wudou cuoshi qianding yilai," January 1969.

43. "Li Zongzhou tongzhi daibiao yuan Liansi," August 27, 1970.

44. Ibid.; Guo Chaogang notebooks; and "'Jiu.erqi' zhizhi wudou cuoshi qianding yilai," January 1969.

The most dramatic of these clashes took place at Paolian's headquarters at the county's general services company on December 29. Paolian had built a four-story defensive tower in the company compound. When close to a thousand Liansi fighters besieged the compound, Paolian fighters in the tower shot and wounded five attackers. A platoon of PLA soldiers rushed to the scene. Most Paolian fighters surrendered and were allowed to leave. But four Paolian fighters on the top of the defensive tower refused, fearing reprisal. By this point, the number of Liansi members on the scene had increased to several thousand. They set a fire at the base of the tower, while others tried to scale it with a block and tackle and began ramming it with a large log. The four Paolian fighters, panicked, came down to surrender. The Liansi fighters surrounded and beat them. The troops tried to protect them but they were pushed away, punched, and hit with stones. After some Liansi fighters forcibly took away the four Paolian captives, the soldiers searched the tower and found seventy hand grenades, seven handguns, 150 bullets and some spears, a stockpile that the defenders had not dared to use. Liansi demolished the tower. In the incident, five Liansi fighters were wounded, one Paolian member was killed, and two dozen were wounded. Paolian's headquarters were destroyed.[45]

After this incident, Paolian's leaders and members fled to communes in the northern part of the county. Some fled to the Dahu barracks in the Xuzhou suburbs, seeking protection from the PLA troops in Unit 6174. Others fled to Xuzhou, staying in the compound of the Xuzhou Prefecture headquarters.[46] The county seat was now under the control of Liansi, a dramatic reversal in the balance of forces. The PLA propaganda team had no idea what to do, and it withdrew in stages to the unit's permanent barracks in Dahu. Many of the defeated Paolian members followed them. More than half of PLA Unit 6174's top officers were attending the Xuhai study class in Beijing, and those who remained in the county were panicked. They received little by way of useful instructions from their comrades in Beijing, who told them to "act correctly." The Xuhai study class directors told exiled Paolian forces that they could not stay at the unit's base in Dahu, but that they also must not return to Feng County to fight and should avoid contact with Liansi.[47]

45. Guo Chaogang notebooks; and "'Jiu.erqi' zhizhi wudou cuoshi qianding yilai," January 1969.

46. "Wenhua da geming" shinian dongluan, pp. 55–56 and 64.

47. Guo Chaogang notebooks.

On the evening of New Year's Eve, two haggard Paolian leaders appeared at the residence of the Feng County delegation in Beijing. At an urgent meeting of the Paolian delegation, they reported on the catastrophic events in the county. They said that Liansi's control of the county was so complete that they had to cross the Anhui border into Dangshan County before they could make their way to Beijing.[48] Most of the Paolian delegates were outraged and demanded that they should issue an order for Paolian to re-arm and retake the county by force. Zhang Liansheng disagreed, and an argument ensued, almost leading to a fistfight. Military officers rushed in and broke up the argument, criticizing the more hotheaded Paolian delegates.[49]

These dramatic developments caught the military officers in charge of the Xuhai class by surprise. They suspended further meetings and instead focused on how to prevent further violence. On January 4, 1969, PLA Unit 6174's chief of staff, Guo Fengcai, rushed to meet Zhang Liansheng, in a panic, with sweat streaming down his forehead. He reported that many Paolian activists had swarmed into his unit's barracks in Dahu, trying to loot weapons and launch an offensive to retake the county. He added that a large shipment of weapons had recently arrived at the base and that if these weapons fell into the hands of Paolian, the consequences could be disastrous. He asked Zhang to go to Dahu immediately and dissuade them from rash action.[50] Zhang rushed back to Xuzhou by train that evening with one other Paolian delegate.[51]

Back in Dahu, the engineering division's chief of staff convened a meeting of Paolian leaders on the evening of January 5, to relay three instructions from the 68th Army leaders in Beijing: Paolian must evacuate the Dahu compound and return to Feng County to "grasp revolution and promote production"; they should avoid violence; and they should not contact members of their faction in other localities. The Paolian participants agreed to persuade members of their faction to comply.

When Zhang Liansheng traveled from Beijing to Dahu to persuade the Paolian refugees to accept the PLA's orders, Shan Shutang, a militant Paolian delegate who arrived from Beijing a few days later, instead insisted that Paolian had to fight back. Shan's views were shared by the vast majority of the refugees.

48. Zhang Liansheng notebooks.

49. Zhang Liansheng, "Gei Mao Zedong zhuxi ji Zhou Enlai zongli, Wang Hongwen fu zhuxi de xin," October 28, 1973.

50. Ibid.

51. Zhang Liansheng interview.

Zhang called a meeting of Paolian leaders, counseling restraint. Those who agreed with him were in the majority, and they outvoted the militants, but a deep division emerged among the Paolian leaders. The more militant leaders denounced Zhang for "capitulationism." In debates over the following days, the militants demanded a revote on the proposal to fight and a change in Paolian's leadership. They subjected Zhang to withering criticism and locked him in a room for an entire day, denying him food and water. He was eventually freed by army officers, who escorted him to the 68th Army's guesthouse in Xuzhou.[52]

After Zhang's departure, the militant leaders sprang into action and mounted counterattacks on Liansi. On January 16, Paolian fighters looted weapons from troops in the county seat, and others initiated a violent clash in Shunhe Commune when they returned from Dahu and the next day beat up a PAD officer in Shunhe.[53] The local leaders of both factions tried to enlist support from the Paolian delegates in Beijing. As a result, almost all of the Paolian delegates quit the study class and came to Dahu, where there were still around one thousand Paolian activists at the barracks.[54] PLA officers in Xuzhou relayed orders from Beijing for the Paolian delegates to return to the study class and refrain from further assaults. The more militant Paolian leaders ignored the orders, vowing to "fight to the death" with Liansi. Since the PLA refused to support them, Shan Shutang and his supporters left Dahu to seek weapons.[55]

On the morning of January 23, the moderate Paolian leaders left Dahu for Xuzhou, after trying unsuccessfully to dissuade the refugees from further action. Zhang Liansheng and other delegates returned to Beijing, while the other Paolian leaders returned to temporary shelters within the county. The more militant leaders left with followers in search of weapons. Three to four hundred Paolian members remained in Dahu. A major counterattack was prevented, but the split within Paolian's leadership hardened. Five militant Paolian leaders in the Beijing delegation, headed by Shan Shutang, did not return to Beijing.[56] As it turned out, this made it easier for the military officers running the study class to orchestrate a compromise between the two factions.

52. Ibid.; and Zhang Liansheng, "Gei Mao Zedong zhuxi ji Zhou Enlai zongli, Wang Hongwen fu zhuxi de xin," October 28, 1973.

53. Zhang Liansheng notebooks.

54. Zhang Ludao notebooks.

55. Zhang Liansheng notebooks.

56. Zhang Liansheng, "Gei Mao Zedong zhuxi ji Zhou Enlai zongli, Wang Hongwen fu zhuxi de xin," October 28, 1973.

Feng County's factional warfare in the second half of 1968 was emblematic of the political situation throughout the Xuhai region. In Beijing, the Xuhai class had failed utterly to curtail factional conflicts in the cities of Xuzhou and Lianyungang and most of the eight counties in the prefecture. The fighting only intensified as pressure was applied in Beijing for the leaders of the factions to reach a final accord. A key development, in late December 1968, was the outbreak of warfare in Xuzhou's railway system, as a militant splinter group within the Kick faction called a strike that paralyzed transportation across eastern China for seven days.

These events forced central leaders to shift tactics. The first step was to divide the Xuhai class according to bureaucratic systems and occupational specialties. On December 30, 1968, Zhou Enlai and other central leaders met personally with the delegates to read out a new decision by the central authorities. Zhou and Wen Yucheng, Deputy Chief of Staff of the PLA, would take charge of negotiations among factions in the railway system, the coal industry, and electric power generation system in Xuzhou. The second new measure was to send the celebrated Capital Workers Propaganda Team to the Xuhai class in mid-January 1969 to advocate more forcefully for obedience to Mao Zedong Thought and an end to factional strife. This was intended to pressure participants by bringing a nationally celebrated model unit into the effort. The third new measure was to enlarge the Xuhai class by bringing more factional leaders to take part.[57]

After weathering the Dahu crisis, Zhang Liansheng and the other moderate Paolian delegates arrived back in Beijing on January 26, 1969.[58] In the absence of the more militant Paolian leaders, who would not return to Beijing for more than two weeks, the meetings went smoothly, with leaders of both factions making self-criticisms in the presence of officers from all of the military units active in the county. The delegates were urged to cease fighting, disarm, and disband their factional organizations. On January 31, the two sides signed an agreement that was essentially the same as the March 5 and September 27 accords the previous year. They drafted an "Open Letter to the People of Feng County" that announced the terms.[59]

---

57. "Zhou zongli zai jiejian Xuzhou diqu tielu, meikuang xitong," December 30, 1968; Zhang Liansheng notebooks; Zhang Ludao notebooks; and *Zhonggong Xuzhou lishi dashiji*, p. 395.

58. Zhang Liansheng notebooks.

59. Zhang Ludao notebooks.

Back in Feng County, the PLA struggled to control the factions. During the dramatic events of December 29, Liansi had taken control of the county seat, but violent clashes between the factions continued to generate a steady stream of casualties in rural communes.[60] Most of the PLA personnel who staffed the propaganda team had withdrawn to their base in Dahu, and only a few remained in the county as observers. They had little ability to intervene.[61]

Violent clashes in neighboring provinces also undermined public order in the county. In January, defeated rebels from Heze County, west of Chengwu County across the Shandong border, fled to Feng County and were afforded protection by Liansi. Some branches of Liansi helped the Shandong rebels raid a weapons storehouse in Shan County, across the border in Shandong, seizing weapons in the PAD headquarters and beating up the officers inside.[62]

Tens of thousands of copies of the January 31 Agreement were printed and distributed throughout Feng County. Military officers convened a meeting of faction leaders to discuss how to implement its terms. But subgroups in both factions, especially in rural villages, totally ignored the agreement. Defeated Paolian fighters wanted to recoup their recent losses, while many in Liansi wanted to seize the opportunity to finally eliminate Paolian. On February 7, one of the standing committee members of Liansi's headquarters personally led an armed group to attack the Huankou Commune government compound. Meeting resistance from armed Paolian forces who controlled the building, three of the attackers were wounded.[63] In response, militant Paolian activists planned an attack on the headquarters of Malou Commune the next day. During a furious gun battle two were killed, after which Paolian set fire to a building to dislodge the thirty-five Liansi fighters defending it. After their forced surrender, one Liansi fighter was beaten to death.[64] Six similar incidents took place over the next two weeks.[65]

Despite the agreement forged in Beijing, the rural communes in Feng County descended into a state of anarchy in March and early April 1969. In March and April, there were ten reported violent clashes in rural communes that generated more injuries and deaths, and the violence was becoming

---

60. Ibid.; and Guo Chaogang notebooks.
61. Guo Chaogang notebooks.
62. Shao Limin notebooks.
63. "Zhang Liansheng tongzhi daibiao yuan Paolian," August 27, 1970.
64. Guo Chaogang notebooks; and *Jiangsu sheng Feng xian zhi*, p. 29.
65. Guo Chaogang notebooks.

increasingly vicious and personal. On April 1, several Paolian members were hung up by their arms and beaten by Liansi members in Huankou Commune, and another Paolian member was kidnapped and tortured three days later, shortly before the corpses of two Paolian members killed in earlier fighting were disinterred and burned publicly.[66]

Tensions between the Feng County PAD and the PLA troops there perpetuated the conflicts. Ever since the PLA Unit 6174 troops were sent to the county in March 1967, a PLA officer, either Zheng Guoxin or Xia Jidao, was nominally the top military leader. The Xuhai class tipped the balance of power toward the PAD. The commanding officers of the PLA unit were summoned to Beijing for the study class, leaving junior PLA officers in charge. After Liansi fighters occupied the county seat by force at the end of the year, many PAD personnel returned to the county seat with them. Active tensions between the two military branches resumed. The PAD personnel used every opportunity to undermine the PLA officers. Liansi's leaders were aware of this attitude and as a result did not take the PLA propaganda team seriously, ignoring most of its orders with impunity. This, in turn, frustrated the PLA officers and heightened their hostility toward the PAD.[67]

It was at this point in time that Zhang Liansheng was informed in Beijing that Shao Wen was slated to become the head of the county's revolutionary committee. The leaders of the study class told Zhang that Paolian had nothing to fear, and Shao Wen would not be able to exact revenge on Paolian.[68] Zhang now understood that the 68th Army's commanders had accepted the views of the Feng County PAD and Xuzhou Military District. He did not yet know the reason why—this was yet another example of how political shifts in the capital affected politics at the local level. Paolian's protectors in the 68th Army command structure had become collateral damage in the latest twist in Beijing's factional politics. Wang Xiaoyu had intervened in Xuzhou back in July 1967 to force PLA commanders to shift their allegiance from the Support to the Kick faction. This split the 68th Army command structure, and the officers of the military subdistrict also dissented from Wang's intervention.

Wang Xiaoyu was now in severe political trouble that would lead to his disgrace and purge during the Communist Party's Ninth Congress in

66. Ibid.
67. Ibid.
68. Zhang Liansheng notebooks.

April 1969.[69] With the shifting of the political tides, Paolian lost its support in the PLA. The 68th Army's commanders, the commanders of the engineering division, and the officers of PLA Unit 6174 had all gone along with Wang's decisions on the Xuzhou factional strife between the Support and Kick factions. It was of little consequence to them, because that conflict had no bearing on their area of responsibility in Feng County. They nonetheless became identified as "followers" of Wang Xiaoyu. Now they were weakened as the chips fell in the wake of Wang's disgrace.

In April 1969, the leaders of the Xuhai class increased the number of cadre representatives for both factions—they presumably would be more moderate and amenable to compromise, and as state cadres and party members presumably more amenable to the reassertion of discipline. On April 10 and 11 each faction was directed to send an additional six cadre delegates to Beijing.[70] A large telephone conference was then planned for April 12.[71] In Beijing, delegates met at the Third Municipal Post Office Branch—the military officers Li Gengxin, Xia Jidao, and Shao Wen, along with Li Zongzhou and Li Peng, who represented Liansi, and Shan Shutang and Zhang Liansheng, who represented Paolian. At the other end of the line, the Feng County participants assembled at the post office in the county seat. There were more than fifty Paolian representatives and more than eighty from Liansi.[72]

The conference call ended in disarray. When the discussions began, the venue was disrupted by more than two hundred Liansi-affiliated farmers, who broke into the conference room. They abducted several Paolian delegates who would later be abandoned with head wounds and broken legs. The victims were located later that night, but doctors in the local hospital refused to treat them for fear of Liansi retribution. The wounded were sent in an army truck to a nearby county in Shandong Province.[73]

The PLA contingent did not come down hard on the Liansi leaders responsible for this incident, for fear of further exacerbating factional animosities and tensions with the PAD. Leaders of the Xuhai class in Beijing were similarly unconcerned, because the addition of six cadre delegates from each faction

69. See Dong and Walder, "Forces of Disorder," pp. 156–159.

70. Guo Chaogang notebooks; Zhang Ludao notebooks.

71. "Li Zongzhou tongzhi daibiao yuan Liansi," August 27, 1970.

72. Zhang Liansheng notebooks.

73. Guo Chaogang notebooks; and "Li Zongzhou tongzhi daibiao yuan Liansi," August 27, 1970.

was helping to reach agreements in Beijing.[74] They quickly established a new accord in the days after the telephone conference fiasco. They agreed to stop denouncing one another, to disband factional organizations among county cadres and staff, to cut off contact with the headquarters of each faction, and to accept only the authority of military personnel. On April 25, the CCP's Ninth National Congress concluded, and the Feng County signing ceremony took place that day. Three days later, at the first plenary session of the congress, Feng County delegates presented their agreement as a model of success.[75]

Mao Zedong himself granted a seven-minute audience to the entire Xuhai class members in the Great Hall of the People on May 19, accompanied by Zhou Enlai and other central leaders. Mao said nothing; he slowly waved his hand and walked along the rostrum, basking in cheers from the excited audience.[76] The political theatrics in Beijing, however, did nothing to alter the situation in Feng County. The disastrous telephone conference of April 12 further undermined the authority of the PLA troops. Violent clashes in rural communes continued, and rebel factions from neighboring Shandong counties were involved in some of them.[77]

The PLA unit was finding it increasingly impossible to carry out its mission in the county. Although it was ultimately in charge of political decisions, the PAD personnel were ignoring its authority. Local Liansi leaders, following the lead from the PAD, were behaving in the same fashion. Some of the PAD officers now openly argued that the outside PLA unit had no business running things in their county.[78] News of Shao Wen's imminent appointment as head of the new revolutionary committee meant that they could ignore the PLA with impunity.

Encouraged by the PAD's openly contemptuous attitude toward the PLA, Liansi intensified its attacks. In mid-May, armed Liansi members in Shunhe Commune attacked a local village. Two Paolian members were abducted and many others wounded. Liansi forces from neighboring communes attacked Paolian in Huankou Commune, and in a battle fought over three days, six combatants from the two sides were killed.[79] At the beginning of June, more

74. Zhang Ludao notebooks.

75. Guo Chaogang notebooks; and Zhang Ludao notebooks.

76. Zhang Liansheng notebooks; and Zhang Ludao notebooks.

77. Guo Chaogang notebooks.

78. Ibid.

79. Ibid.; Shao Limin notebooks; "Li Zongzhou tongzhi daibiao yuan Liansi," August 27, 1970; and *Jiangsu sheng Feng xian zhi,* p. 29.

Paolian members evacuated the county seat. Liansi then sent armed combat teams to attack them in the communes, driving them out.[80] Days later, Liansi fighters, helped by allies from nearby Shandong Province, broke into the public security bureau and took fifty-three guns from the PLA troops, who made no attempt to resist.[81]

Military authorities in Beijing had more urgent matters to attend to than the troubles in Feng County. Shortly before midnight on May 26, Zhou Enlai and other central leaders met with Xuhai class delegates, accompanied by Wang Xiaoyu, Ji'nan Military Region commander Yang Dezhi, 68th Army Commander Zhang Zhixiu, and a rebel leader from Shandong province. Wang Xiaoyu and the rebel leader gave self-criticisms at the session for errors they had committed in Shandong Province and the Xuhai region. Mao Zedong had decided that Wang Xiaoyu had committed serious errors that created the seemingly irresolvable conflicts in the Xuhai region. Wang and his delegation from Shandong were being held behind after the Ninth Party Congress to submit to criticism. The center's attitude toward Xuzhou's political problems had changed.[82]

The long-delayed planning for the county's revolutionary committee accelerated. On June 10, the two factions reached an agreement for proportional membership on the committee. Civilian cadres and military officers would hold 40 percent of the sixty-three seats, while "revolutionary masses" would hold 60 percent. Real power would be concentrated in a standing committee of fifteen persons, and within that body it would be further concentrated in the head and six deputy heads. A military officer would serve as head, and the six deputies would consist of two civilian cadres, two military officers, and two mass representatives. The head and all of the deputy heads would be members of the Communist Party—a requirement that effectively excluded the main leaders of both Liansi and Paolian from real positions of power.[83]

Disagreements continued over the individuals to be named to these top positions, with both sides nominating cadres who had sided with them in prior

80. Shao Limin notebooks.

81. Guo Chaogang notebooks.

82. Zhang Liansheng notebooks; Zhang Ludao notebooks; and "Zhongyang shouzhang jiejian Mao Zedong sixiang xuexi ban Xuhai ban de jianghua" (Talks by central leaders when meeting with the Xuhai group in the Mao Zedong Thought study class), May 26, 1969.

83. Xuhai ban Feng xian daibiao tuan, "Guanyu choujian Feng xian geming weiyuanhui de shishi fang'an" (On preparations for the establishment of the Feng County revolutionary committee), June 10, 1969.

disputes. Paolian nominated as leading civilian cadres Zhu Pingfan (former deputy party secretary) and Meng Qinghua (former deputy county magistrate). Liansi nominated Teng Zetian (former deputy party secretary) and Dong Hongzhi (former party secretary in charge of the discipline inspection committee). Each side made serious political allegations against the cadres nominated by the other side. Paolian charged that Dong was the son of a capitalist who worked for the Nationalist government before the anti-Japanese war, and during the 1957 Anti-Rightist Campaign he had been sanctioned for anti-party statements. It charged that Teng was from a landlord family and that his father was a local thug who had been executed by revolutionary peasants.[84] Liansi charged Zhu with collaborating with Japanese occupation forces and accused Meng of desertion during the anti-Japanese war.[85] During the group discussions with Paolian delegates in late June and early July, representatives of the Central Study Classes General Office and the 68th Army leadership expressed their approval of Liansi's nominees and doubts about Paolian's.[86]

On July 9, the Feng County delegation attended a rally of the entire Xuhai class. From leaders' speeches at the rally, they learned of the massive overall scope of the bureaucratic effort to resolve factional warfare in different regions. They were told that as of July 1969, study classes had been conducted in Beijing for twenty-two months. There had been sixty different classes for civilians from twenty-five different provinces and cities, and a total of thirty for military officers from various regions. Each class lasted around two months. The Xuhai class was unique in lasting more than one year.

After the conclusion of the CCP's Ninth Party Congress, the center decreed that the remaining study classes would focus on rebuilding regional party organizations. The thirteen party members in the Feng County delegation met separately. They were told that Shao Wen had made no major political errors and had no historical problems. If they had reservations about him, they must set them aside.[87] While party members in the delegation were open to such appeals, the Paolian delegation was united in its opposition to Shao Wen. In a letter addressed to central leaders, they detailed a long series of his alleged

---

84. Zhang Liansheng notebooks.
85. Zhang Ludao notebooks.
86. Zhang Liansheng notebooks; and Zhang Ludao notebooks.
87. Zhang Ludao notebooks.

errors dating back to early 1967, amounting chiefly to his consistent practice of "supporting one faction" in local disputes.[88]

This time the leaders of the study class responded immediately. On July 11, the same day that the letter was handed over, Wu Huaicai, deputy commander of the 68th Army, called a meeting for the party members in the Paolian delegation. Wu told them: "Shao Wen's appointment is a collective decision made by the Xuzhou Military Subdistrict party committee, the 68th Corps party committee, and the Central Study Classes General Office. This decision is a result of a long and thorough discussion. You should consider this matter carefully. If you get involved in factional activities now, you will be exposed by the masses and be punished in the future. Shao Wen did make mistakes. We will ask him to correct them, and to win forgiveness and trust from the masses by making a self-criticism. Paolian comrades should believe that he can correct his mistakes."[89]

Over the following week, Wu chaired several meetings to reconcile the Paolian delegation to Shao's appointment. In attendance were military delegates from both the PLA and the PAD, including Shao himself. The Paolian delegates reiterated their objections to Shao. Wu told them that the errors were the responsibility of the top officers in the 68th Army, not of the soldiers of PLA Unit 6174 or the local PAD. He said there was no real difference between the PLA and the PAD, and both should be treated with trust and respect. On July 18, all of the top military officers involved in the county made long self-criticisms of their past actions. Wu insisted that the PAD and PLA Unit 6174 treat both factions equally after their return to the county.[90]

On July 23, 1969, the party center issued a central document on "the Shanxi Problem," which denounced as criminal behavior continued factional battles, attacks on military units, the destruction of public property, and the looting of banks and storehouses—all activities that were still prevalent in Feng County. The document warned that harsh measures would be applied if such

88. Xuhai ban Feng xian paolian daibiao tuan, "Zhi Xuhai ban lingdao xiaozu he zhongyang ban de Mao Zedong sixiang xuexi ban zong bangongshi de xin" (Letter to the Leading Group of the Xuhai Study Class and the General Office of the Center-Sponsored Mao Zedong Thought Study Class), July 11, 1969.

89. Zhang Ludao notebooks.

90. Zhang Liansheng notebooks; and Zhang Ludao notebooks.

activities persisted.[91] It was highlighted in the final appeals to the Feng County delegates as the Beijing authorities prepared to wrap up the Xuhai class.

Shortly before midnight on July 24, Zhou Enlai, generals Huang Yongsheng and Li Zuopeng, and other central leaders met with the top leaders of the 68th Army. Zhou told them that the Xuhai region had fallen behind and needed to catch up. The directives about Shanxi, he argued, were a warning that harsh measures would be employed if matters did not improve soon.[92] Three days later, meeting with a delegation from Lianyungang City and Feng, Ganyu, and Pei Counties, Zhou acknowledged that the problems in Feng and neighboring Pei Counties had yet to be resolved: "I won't say too much on the Feng County and Pei County problems. You can discuss and resolve their problems after you get back home. I believe that under the leadership of the comrades from the 68th Army, the Ji'nan Military Region, the Jiangsu provincial military district, and the Xuzhou Military Subdistrict, you absolutely can resolve these problems."[93] Essentially, Beijing was washing its hands of Feng County.

The final meeting of the Xuhai class was late in the evening of July 30, with Zhou Enlai and other central leaders in attendance. Zhou and the other leaders all made speeches, and Li Zuopeng (PLA deputy chief of staff) read out the central authorities' approval of the written self-criticism submitted by the 68th Army. Attached to this document was the plan for restructuring the Xuzhou Municipal Revolutionary Committee. Zhou and the other leaders threatened the factions with punishment if they refused to adhere to the agreements reached in Beijing. To drive home the point, they singled out several leaders from each faction in Xuzhou by name and forced them to pledge to adhere to the agreements.[94]

The meeting lasted into the early morning hours, and the Xuhai class was immediately disbanded at its conclusion. Almost all of the delegates left Beijing by train the same day.[95] A tentative resolution had been reached about Xuzhou, but Feng County's problems were now turned over to the Xuzhou

91. Zhonggong zhongyang, "Zhongguo gongchandang zhongyang weiyuanhui bugao" (Proclamation of the Central Committee of the Chinese Communist Party), Zhongfa [69], no. 41, July 23, 1969.

92. Zhang Liansheng notebooks; and Zhang Ludao notebooks.

93. Zhang Liansheng notebooks.

94. Ibid.

95. The only exception was the delegation from Lianyungang, which was held back to continue negotiations that lasted until mid-September: Zhonggong liushiba jun weiyuanhui, "Guanyu chengli Jiangsu sheng Lianyungang shi geming weiyuanhui de qingshi baogao" (Re-

military authorities. The Feng County delegates reached Xuzhou the next evening, but they were not allowed to return to the county. Instead, they were sent in military trucks to a cadre training school in Jiawang, a small town in Xuzhou's eastern suburbs.[96] They could not return to Feng County because the situation there was out of control. The agreements signed in Beijing were worthless scraps of paper. They had only served to intensify local factional warfare as each side tried to strengthen its hand in anticipation of the final settlement. Clashes and ambushes in several villages in Huankou Commune on July 11 set off a chain reaction in neighboring communes. The next day, clashes erupted in nearby Shizhai Commune, where armed fighters from Shunhe, Shouxian, and Liangzhai Communes responded to pleas from besieged Liansi supporters. The two sides clashed on July 13 in a battle that left four dead. The battles had resulted in six deaths, and neither the PLA troops nor PAD forces had intervened.[97] On July 24, militant Paolian leaders decided to launch counterattacks in a number of communes, and after several days they brought several of them under their control.[98]

Liansi countered with an effort to retake Shouxian commune. On July 30, several Liansi leaders went to a village near the county's northern border with Shandong, intending to solicit help from allies in Yutai County, but they learned that an armed band from another Shandong rebel group had moved into a nearby village to help in the fight against Paolian. They assembled their forces and worked out a battle plan. Armed with three heavy machine guns, two dozen light machine guns, more than three hundred rifles, and one mortar launcher, they set out on the next day to attack the Shouxian Commune government compound. Paolian defenders were forced to retreat. After negotiations, they were permitted to surrender and leave the commune without their weapons. Afterward the fighters from Shandong Province robbed the local bank.[99]

In response, Paolian mobilized more than a thousand fighters to raid a weapons stockpile in Xuecheng County, in Zaozhuang Prefecture, north of

port on the request for instructions regarding the establishment of the Lianyungang City revolutionary committee), September 12, 1969.

96. Zhang Liansheng notebooks.

97. Shao Limin notebooks; "Li Zongzhou tongzhi daibiao yuan Liansi," August 27, 1970; "Zhang Liansheng tongzhi daibiao yuan Paolian," August 27, 1970; and *Jiangsu sheng Feng xian zhi*, p. 29.

98. "Zhang Liansheng tongzhi daibiao yuan Paolian," August 27, 1970.

99. Shao Limin notebooks; "Li Zongzhou tongzhi daibiao yuan Liansi," August 27, 1970; and *Jiangsu sheng Feng xian zhi*, p. 29.

Xuzhou. Taking a train to Xuecheng from Xuzhou, they raided the local PAD arsenal late at night, taking away more than one thousand rifles. On the way home, they were intercepted by local Shandong troops, and in an exchange of gunfire two Paolian fighters were killed and about eighty were captured. The rest escaped and returned to Feng County with more than three hundred rifles.[100] The fighting across the provincial border continued well into August. Near the end of the month Paolian fighters raided Yutai County, Shandong, seized thirty-two guns from the local militia, and brought them back home.[101]

Given the intensity of the fighting, Feng County's delegation could not be permitted to return home. The army officers in charge concluded that the fighting there would destroy the fragile unity that had been achieved in Beijing. The delegates were held in Jiawang, far from Feng County, for yet another study class sponsored by military officers, this time to plan how to implement a preliminary ceasefire.[102] The Xuhai Study Class, as far as Feng County was concerned, had been an utter failure.

100. "Zhang Liansheng tongzhi daibiao yuan Paolian," August 27, 1970; and *Jiangsu sheng Feng xian zhi,* p. 29.

101. "Zhang Liansheng tongzhi daibiao yuan Paolian," August 27, 1970; and Zhang Liansheng interview.

102. Zhang Liansheng notebooks.

6

Forging Order

IN THE WAKE of the Xuhai Study Class, on August 1, 1969, the Xuhzou Municipal Revolutionary Committee was restructured yet again. The city's first revolutionary committee was established back on March 18, 1967, but it fell apart as factional warfare broke out between the Support and Kick factions. That revolutionary committee was reorganized on March 1, 1968, under pressure from Wang Xiaoyu. Now that Wang was purged in disgrace in the wake of the Ninth Party Congress, the revolutionary committee was reorganized once again, with the 68th Army's Commander, Zhang Zhixiu, becoming its head.[1] On the same day, a revolutionary committee for Xuzhou Prefecture was established, headed by Chai Rongsheng, commander of the Xuzhou Military Subdistrict.[2] These revolutionary committees were a complete victory for the military officers who had dissented from the changes forced by Wang Xiaoyu in 1967.

The Xuzhou authorities adopted several measures to deal with Feng County's continuing violence. First, they moved aggressively against the militant leaders in Paolian who had declared independence from the moderate Paolian leadership. This group styled itself "New Paolian" in June 1969 and had been responsible for many of the recent armed attacks in the county. The group's leaders and a number of their followers were arrested and disarmed soon after returning from a raid on an arms depot in Shandong.[3]

Second, they carried out a campaign in PLA Unit 6174 to correct errors allegedly committed under the "Wang Xiaoyu line."[4] This weakened the unit

---

1. *Zhonggong Xuzhou lishi dashiji*, p. 398.
2. *Xuzhou shi zuzhishi ziliao*, p. 487.
3. "Zhang Liansheng tongzhi daibiao yuan Paolian," August 27, 1970.
4. Guo Chaogang notebooks.

in its rivalry with the PAD. Zheng Guoxin and Xia Jidao, the unit's two top officers, would eventually be dismissed from all of their posts in 1970 as alleged followers of Wang Xiaoyu, and as punishment they were sentenced to hard labor on a military farm.[5] Their political error had been to incorrectly designate Paolian as *the* revolutionary faction, thereby breeding factional warfare.

Third, they replaced the entire top leadership of the county PAD. Liu Zongbin, PAD head, traded places with Zhao Guanghou, the head of Donghai County's PAD; and PAD deputy director Ma Chi and deputy political commissar Yao Haishu were also transferred elsewhere. These moves were intended to help reconcile Paolian to the shift in power toward the PAD on the revolutionary committee.[6] The new PAD leader had no history of conflict with Paolian, but he did come from another county in Xuzhou prefecture.

Fourth, they intensified pressure on the leaders of both factions to accept the new power structure, focusing especially on Paolian's reluctant leaders. On August 19, the military commanders convened a meeting with the Feng County delegates to the Xuhai class, who were still being held at the Cadre Training School in Jiawang. Shao Wen chaired the meeting, accompanied by Xia Jidao and officers from the engineering division of the 68th Army. The military forces, they promised, would no longer continue the error of supporting only one faction. However, continued resistance would no longer be tolerated, and defiance of authority would be met with force.[7] On August 28, the delegation was told to return to Feng County and help the army implement the agreements reached in Beijing. They were threatened with punishment if they continued factional activities.[8]

Despite these moves, Paolian's leaders were still not reconciled to Shao Wen. They held a closed-door meeting in early September to discuss the problem. Due to the recent arrest of the militant Paolian leaders, the meeting was dominated by moderates, but they nonetheless all agreed that Shao was unacceptable.[9] To pressure Paolian to accept Shao, the Xuzhou military authorities called the faction leaders to Xuzhou on September 10 for yet another "study

5. Ibid., and Zhang Liansheng interview. They would be released and exonerated in 1974, after another shift in Beijing's factional politics, and retired from military service.

6. Zhang Liansheng interview.

7. Ibid.; and Zhongguo renmin jiefang jun liushiba jun, "Gei Feng xian, Pei xian guangda geming qunzhong de yi feng xin" (Letter to the broad revolutionary masses of Feng and Pei Counties), August 19, 1969.

8. Zhang Liansheng notebooks.

9. Ibid.; and "Zhang Liansheng tongzhi daibiao yuan Paolian," August 27, 1970.

class." Paolian leaders were put under additional pressure to accept Shao, and they were assured that he would not be in a position to take revenge. Paolian's leaders realized that they could no longer depend on officers in the 68th Army or military subdistrict to protect their interests. The officers were forced under pressure to withdraw their support of Paolian, and their superiors no longer seemed to care about the outcome of the factional disputes. Because Shao's appointment was inevitable, Paolian could only hope that sympathetic PLA officers remained in the county.[10]

Building the New Order

On September 20, 1969, the Feng County Revolutionary Committee was finally established. This was one of the last to be established in the entire country.[11] Shao Wen became its chairman, and PLA Unit 6174 commander Xia Jidao became the first ranking vice-chairman. The newly appointed PAD head Zhao Guanghou was the other vice-chairman. Officers from the PAD and PLA Unit 6174 were appointed as committee members (see table 2).[12]

The power was now in hands of the PAD officers. But to maintain the illusion that there was a "great alliance," leaders and activists from both factions were named to the revolutionary committee. Some of the veteran cadres nominated by each side were denied a seat. Of Liansi's nominees, only Dong Hongzhi was included. Teng Zetian had to wait for a year to get a significant post.

10. Zhang Liansheng interview.

11. According to the database employed in Walder, *Agents of Disorder*, there were only twenty-seven counties and cities in the entire country that had not established revolutionary committees by September 1969.

12. Zhonggong liushiba jun gongqu weiyuanhui, "Guanyu chengli Jiangsu sheng Feng xian geming weiyuanhui de qingshi baogao" (Report on the request for instructions on establishing a revolutionary committee in Feng County, Jiangsu), September 16, 1969; and Zhonggong liushiba jun weiyuanhui, "Dui liushiba jun gongqu dangwei 'Guanyu chengli Jiangsu sheng Feng xian geming weiyuanhui de qingshi baogao' de pishi" (Comments on the report from the party committee of engineering unit of the 68th Army on establishing a revolutionary committee in Feng County, Jiangsu), September 17, 1969. The latter document provides unusual detail about the composition of the forty-two-member revolutionary committee: twenty-six were party members, six were Communist Youth League members; and ten were neither. The members ranged in age from twenty-two (Zhang Liansheng and two other students) to fifty-two (Dong Hongzhi). Reflecting the poverty of the region, thirty-one members had a family origin of "poor peasant," five were "lower middle peasant," five were "middle peasant," and one "rich peasant" (Zhao Guanghou of the PAD).

PHOTOGRAPH 3. Rally to celebrate Feng County Revolutionary Committee, September 1969

TABLE 2. Standing Committee, Feng County Revolutionary Committee (in rank order), September 1969

Chairman
Shao Wen

Vice Chairmen
Xia Jidao, Vice-Chairman (Commander, PLA Unit 6174)
Zhao Guanghou, Vice-Chairman (Head, People's Armed Department)

Members
Yao Haishu (Deputy Political Commissar, People's Armed Department)
Chen Changxin (Deputy Head, PLA Unit 6174 Political Department)
Dong Hongzhi (Veteran Senior Cadre, Liansi)
Zhu Guangren (Veteran Senior Cadre, Paolian*)
Li Zongzhou (Cotton Mill Worker, Liansi)
Shan Shutang (Driver, Long Distance Bus Company, Paolian)
Zhang Liansheng (High School Student, Paolian)
Li Peng (Staff Worker in Agriculture Department, Liansi)

*Zhu Guangren did not have a clear factional alignment when the Revolutionary Committee was formed, but he later became associated with Paolian.

Paolian's nominees, Zhu Pingfan and Meng Qinghua, were flatly refused. Instead, Zhu Guangren, former head of the county finance department, who previously had no obvious factional affiliation, was included. Paolian leaders thought his appointment somewhat offset Liansi influence and consented to his inclusion on the standing committee.

As difficult as it was to create this committee, this was only the first step in re-establishing political order. The county revolutionary committee had yet to establish authority at lower levels of political organization. It now faced the complex and arduous task of building revolutionary committees within each of the enterprises and offices under the county government and, more difficult still, in each of the rural communes that had been the sites of the most severe factional violence. This would take up most of the next year.

Shao Wen laid out ground rules for setting up these committees, which decisively shifted power away from rebel leaders and toward former cadres and PAD personnel in the communes. Most cadres, he decreed, were to be trusted, and the rural revolutionary committees should consist of members of the militia (under the PAD). If "revolutionary cadres" could not be found in communes, then commune PAD personnel should be appointed as heads.[13] Shortly after taking over, Shao appointed the heads of two departments that would carry out the county revolutionary committee's work. Both were headed by the county PAD officers, with PLA officers as deputies, further illustrating the PLA's loss of authority.[14]

Over the next four months, the county revolutionary committee struggled to rebuild order in work units and communes. Factional animosities proved very difficult to dispel, and there were scores of work units and rural jurisdictions to pacify, each with its own complex history of factional strife. In the factories and communes, meetings to select revolutionary committees were plagued by stubborn arguments, protests, and even occasional violence.[15] Study classes convened to promote alliances in the communes were ridden with factional animosities; many could not reach any agreement, while some reached tentative agreements that soon collapsed.[16]

Power shifted further toward the PAD when a central document was issued on November 6, 1969, which placed the Xuzhou Municipal and Prefecture revolutionary committees directly under the Jiangsu Province Revolutionary

13. Shao Limin notebooks.
14. Zhang Liansheng notebooks.
15. Shao Limin notebooks; and Zhang Liansheng notebooks.
16. Zhang Liansheng notebooks; Qi Zhongmin interview; Hou Xianli interview.

PHOTOGRAPH 4. Parade to celebrate founding of Feng County Revolutionary Committee, September 1969. Holding the placard are Zhu Guangren (*left*) and Dong Hongzhi (*right*). Shao Wen is to the left of Zhu Guangren, looking over his shoulder.

Committee.[17] The local PLA contingent had been under the Ji'nan Military Region in Shandong, while the PAD was under the Xuzhou Military Subdistrict, the Jiangsu Military District, and ultimately the Nanjing Military Region.

17. *Zhonggong Xuzhou lishi dashiji*, p. 400.

This change of jurisdiction unified the military command structure over the county. General Xu Shiyou, formerly in charge of military control in Jiangsu and now the head of the Jiangsu Revolutionary Committee, had strenuously opposed Wang Xiaoyu's intervention in Xuzhou from the outset.[18] This shift strengthened the authority of the anti–Wang Xiaoyu officers within the Xuzhou military command, further strengthening the PAD. Under orders from the Jiangsu Revolutionary Committee, Xuzhou launched a campaign known as the "Cleansing of the Class Ranks" (*qingli jieji duiwu*), which spread across the country in the summer of 1968 in order to consolidate political order. The Xuzhou military authorities also tightened military discipline in response to recent border clashes with the Soviet Union.[19] The county's PAD took advantage of these orders to tighten its control and to stamp out resistance from Paolian.

On November 15, a prefecture work team, headed by the engineering division leader Li Gengxin and the military subdistrict leader Wang Ruzhen, held a meeting with a large number of former Paolian leaders, only some of whom had been selected to serve on the revolutionary committee. The assembled Paolian leaders vented their frustrations over the actions of Liansi and the PAD. They pointed out that a large number of Liansi members from the communes were still in the county seat, and many of those in the communes had not surrendered their arms. The PAD and Liansi were manipulating appointments to commune leadership posts to favor their side. The commercial system was under Liansi's control and discriminated against Paolian-held units and villages. The "mass dictatorship headquarters" that were being formed to enforce order at various levels of government were composed of former Liansi fighting squads, and they were now using their positions to detain and beat Paolian members. When PLA troops tried to intervene, they were met with resistance. Paolian members who left their jobs for factional activity were finding that they had been fired and replaced by temporary workers. Those who left their production brigades for political activity were being denied grain rations and work points as punishment. Under these circumstances, they said, Paolian leaders were being "punished economically," "suppressed politically," and "subjected to an armed crackdown." All of this was being done with the active support of PAD units in villages, and Shao Wen was doing nothing to intervene. Wang conceded that there were still serious problems, and that it was his fault for not sufficiently "educating" the PAD officers. He ended the

18. Dong and Walder, "Forces of Disorder."

19. *Zhonggong Xuzhou lishi dashiji*, p. 400; and Zhang Liansheng notebooks.

meeting by asking Paolian leaders to "unite with the PAD and fight against common enemies."[20]

Not surprisingly, the problems reported by the former Paolian leaders persisted. The result was often violence. In mid-November, a month after the county revolutionary committee was established, Liansi members in Huashan Commune were still denying jobs and rations to returning Paolian activists. The Paolian activists complained to a squad leader in PLA Unit 6174, who ruled that they were entitled to their jobs and rations. This angered the Liansi members, and a violent clash broke out between the two sides. The fighting lasted several days and left many wounded. Eventually the Paolian activists were besieged in the commune purchasing station, outnumbered by Liansi fighters. Armed PLA troops arrived to stop the fighting, and they detained one member of Liansi and confiscated two guns. More Liansi members arrived on the scene and freed their comrade by force, and seized a gun from one of the soldiers.[21]

The county revolutionary committee responded with meetings to "promote ideological revolution," transcend factional loyalties, and build "party spirit." The leaders of the prefecture work team gave self-criticisms, as did PLA troops from Unit 6174 and PAD personnel, including Shao Wen. But when Paolian and Liansi leaders made speeches, they inevitably circled back to accusations against the other side. Paolian again complained that the PAD favored Liansi and that it continued to suffer discrimination.[22]

The prefecture work team left a few weeks later without accomplishing anything. County leaders continued to struggle for months to reconstitute authority in factories and communes. It was one thing to make self-criticisms in meetings but quite another to resolve disputes in workplaces and villages. Although the PAD controlled power in the county, and although it had long favored Liansi, Paolian adherents were in the majority in many locations, and they continued their resistance. They continued to complain about discrimination in the treatment of temporary and contract workers, back pay, restoration of jobs and salaries, grain coupons, and work points; and they protested the appointment of commune PAD personnel as commune leaders.

Recognizing that the current approach was ineffective, the Xuzhou authorities decided to rotate the PLA units stationed in the county and place a new

20. Zhang Liansheng notebooks.
21. Ibid.
22. Ibid.; and Shao Limin notebooks.

PLA unit in charge. In February 1970, the contingent from PLA Unit 6174 was withdrawn and replaced by a "PLA Unit 6063 Mao Zedong Thought Propaganda Team" (another unit from the 68th Army). The new contingent was composed of personnel from the 202nd Division of the 68th Army, and headed by its deputy division commander Wei Xianlai.[23] This PLA propaganda team was given authority over the county revolutionary committee. Shao Wen was now subordinated once again to a PLA contingent—at least temporarily. This was a move to placate Paolian and restrain Shao. The new PLA contingent had no history of involvement in local conflicts and could be viewed as a more neutral arbiter of ongoing disputes. To further reduce the influence of the PAD, a temporary party committee was formed within the propaganda team, with Wei as its head. Shao was not included as a deputy head for several months.[24] This was a subtle but clear signal that Shao had failed to pacify the county, and it was also a signal to Paolian that their complaints had been heard.

The arrival of the new PLA propaganda team finally began to break down local resistance. The withdrawal of Unit 6174 removed Paolian's longstanding supporters, and the demotion of Shao Wen and the PAD to a subordinate position was a blow to Liansi. The 202nd Division officers on the propaganda team sped up the restoration of the county's former party leaders to responsible positions and further marginalized the leaders of rebel factions. The veteran cadres were more amenable to party discipline and easier to control. Paolian could no longer refuse to accept the authority of the county revolutionary committee by claiming that it was controlled by the PAD. This PLA unit had no history in the county and was an outside third party. The soldiers disbanded the controversial "mass dictatorship headquarters" in the communes that were dominated by PAD officers and their Liansi supporters. They enforced equal quotas for factional memberships on workplace and commune leadership committees. They more aggressively disarmed members of both factions. And when they rehabilitated former civilian cadres, they restored the jobs of more of Paolian's followers than before.[25]

Even more effective were several threatening campaigns unleashed in Xuzhou Prefecture to investigate and punish those who had committed acts of violence and continued to resist the restoration of order. In addition to the "Cleansing of the Class Ranks," the "One Strike, Three Anti" (*yida sanfan*) and

23. *Jiangsu sheng Feng xian zhi*, p. 29; and Zhang Liansheng interview.
24. *Feng xian zuzhishi ziliao*, p. 143; and Zhang Liansheng interview.
25. Zhang Liansheng notebooks; Shao Limin notebooks.

the "Investigation of May 16 Elements" (*qingcha wuyaoliu fenzi*) were carried out, more or less at the same time. Each had a different focus, but they all made clear that a harsh crackdown was underway. In Xuzhou, these campaigns focused heavily on the Kick faction, many of whose members were subjected to mass criticism sessions, arrested, imprisoned, and in some cases executed. This had the effect of frightening the leaders of both Liansi and Paolian, although neither group had been tied to the Xuzhou Kick faction. Neither of them could be certain that their past actions might not make them targets of one of these campaigns.[26]

On March 1, 1970, Wei Xianlai read out the central documents about the "One Strike, Three Anti" campaign at a conference of the county revolutionary committee.[27] They called for a severe crackdown on all "active counterrevolutionaries," whose activities included privately communicating and plotting disorders, undermining the socialist economy, committing murder and arson, trying to reverse verdicts, attacking party leadership, robbing state property, and undermining social order.[28] The documents called for the sentencing and execution of those who committed the most serious offenses. The announced targets must have sent chills down the spines of activists on both sides of the county's factional divide, because many of their past activities could be characterized in a way that made them vulnerable to punishment.

Perhaps to drive home this point, the county revolutionary committee called a meeting of the leaders of both factions in mid-March and detailed the massive economic cost of factional warfare in the county, focusing specifically on the repeated theft of grain and grain coupons, cotton cloth for clothing, and coal for heating and cooking.[29] Those who engaged in past factional activities surely recognized that their looting of storehouses and their participation in armed battles might drag them into the jaws of this campaign.

26. Dong and Walder, "Forces of Disorder."

27. Zhonggong zhongyang, "Guanyu daji fangeming pohuai huodong de zhishi" (Instructions regarding striking against counterrevolutionary sabotage activities), Zhongfa [70], no. 3, January 31, 1970; Zhonggong zhongyang, "Guanyu fandui tanwu, touji daoba de zhishi" (Instructions regarding opposing corruption and speculation), Zhongfa [70], no. 5, February 5, 1970; Zhonggong zhongyang, "Guanyu fandui puzhang langfei de tongzhi" (Notice regarding extravagance and waste), Zhongfa [70], no. 6, February 5, 1970.

28. Zhang Liansheng notebooks; and Shao Limin notebooks.

29. Shao Limin notebooks.

Three weeks later, the propaganda team rehabilitated a number of the county's leaders who had lost their positions when the PAD seized power in early 1967. The eventual list of leading cadres to be "liberated" in this fashion included fairly balanced representation of those who supported Liansi and Paolian, and also some officials targeted by both, such as former county party secretary Gao Ying and former county magistrate Qian Xiufu. The forceful intervention by the 202nd Division's propaganda team returned a number of veteran cadres and government staff to their former jobs, a first step in restoring administrative order. The propaganda team also put the leaders of both factions into yet another round of study classes that made them the primary targets of ideological remolding and rectification. Once again, they were to confess and criticize their own past conduct and renounce all factional activities. It was no longer possible to fight for factional advantage. At this point, the main concern for both Liansi and Paolian was to escape becoming targets in the "Class Cleansing" and "One Strike, Three Anti" campaigns, which loomed in the background of these increasingly threatening study classes.[30]

In late April, a mass rally was held at the county theater to introduce the "Cleansing of the Class Ranks." Family members were encouraged to show their loyalty by denouncing the crimes of relatives. Historical problems and past crimes would be treated leniently if they were revealed by voluntary confession, but failure to confess to crimes uncovered by other means would be treated harshly. The campaign would distinguish between those with good attitudes and bad attitudes; between severe and ordinary problems; between the chief criminals and reluctant followers; between genuine counterrevolutionaries and those who were politically backward; between those who intentionally disrupted production and those who did so accidentally; between those who engaged in illegal trading and petty thieves; and between good people who made mistakes and bad people who purposefully acted with malice. Voluntary confession would be the only way to obtain lenient treatment. Otherwise, severe punishment would follow.[31]

Under this concerted pressure, the resistance of factional leaders collapsed. Many were deeply distressed by the study classes, finding it difficult to sleep, and others were listless and despondent. Some of the lesser leaders exposed and criticized the past actions of their superiors. Others confessed their involvement

---

30. *Feng xian zuzhishi ziliao,* p. 249; Zhang Liansheng interview.
31. Shao Limin notebooks.

in armed fighting and in raids on state property and grain depots.[32] All participants were ordered to confess or to expose others' involvement in factional
activities, including fighting, theft of state property or funds, corruption, and
instigating or participating in violent clashes. This would eventually provide
considerable detail about the violent incidents in the county in past years.[33]
At one point, a Paolian leader from one of the communes escaped from the
study class, running off in the middle of the night. He had been accused of
corruption and murder, and his flight condemned him as a criminal.

The first wave of study classes for Paolian and Liansi activists concluded
near the end of May. The 579 participants were isolated for thirty-five days.
Among them were 30 military personnel, 78 veteran cadres, 357 faction leaders,
and around 100 members of the county's revolutionary committee or office
staff. More than 1,400 written accusations were submitted, and more than 300
people were subjected to prolonged interrogations. Descriptions of some 180
violent incidents were compiled: 26 in the county seat and 154 in various communes. These confessions revealed that more than 80 people had been killed
in violent clashes and that more than 500 were wounded. More than 300
people were found guilty of theft or corruption.[34]

With the conclusion of these study classes, the officers from the 202nd Division of the PLA apparently felt that their mission had been accomplished, and
that they had finally broken the back of factional animosities in the county. In
late May 1970, Wei Xianlai left the county along with several other officers
from his unit. Shao Wen resumed his position as the county's top leader. The
PLA propaganda team no longer restrained the PAD, and Paolian would soon
pay the price as a second round of study classes, this time under the PAD,
began at the end of May.[35]

The PAD immediately reverted to its favoritism toward Liansi, and the new
suppression campaigns meant that Paolian would suffer unbridled retribution.
This new round of study classes included only the top leaders of the two factions. Also included were former government staff who had yet to be restored
to their original posts. Shao steered the study classes through his PAD deputies who were placed in charge. In their opening speeches to the study class,

32. Ibid.
33. Zhang Liansheng notebooks; and Shao Limin notebooks.
34. Zhang Liansheng notebooks; and Shao Limin notebooks.
35. Zhang Liansheng interview.

they announced that Paolian had made many mistakes and that its actions were manipulated by class enemies. Ominously, the goal was now to unmask the class enemies hidden within Paolian.[36]

The PAD also initiated a denunciation campaign against Zhu Pingfan and Sun Shudian, two former county leaders who had supported Paolian. The charges brought against them were severe. They were accused of being "capitalist roaders," "renegades," and "black hands" behind mass organizations. These charges had ominous implications for Paolian, because the new authorities had earlier stated a policy of leniency toward veteran cadres. Now the two most prominent supporters of Paolian were accused of political crimes and of manipulating a mass organization—signaling trouble to come for Paolian. The Paolian leaders had no choice but to go along with the criticisms lodged against the two officials. On August 9, the county revolutionary committee held a mass rally at the county's theater to criticize Zhu Pingfan, and the top leaders of both factions gave speeches denouncing his alleged crimes.[37]

At one session in the study class for faction leaders, the objectives of the "One Strike, Three Anti" campaign were announced. Individuals were now responsible for the grain, cash, and property that was lost or misappropriated during the past struggles. Faction members would be required to return one *jin* of grain ration coupon and 0.35 yuan in cash for each day they were absent from work. Illegally seized property must be returned; if it was damaged or destroyed, full cash value must be provided to compensate the rightful owners. Those who bought watches, bicycles, sewing machines and radios or built houses with stolen funds would be punished. Cash and grain collected as taxes by factions in charge of communes must be repaid to the state. Grain and cash provided to factional fighters must be returned.[38] These measures all attested to the extent that the planned economy had deteriorated during the years of factional warfare.

36. Ibid.

37. See the August 9, 1970, speeches denouncing Zhu Pingfan cited in footnote 47 in chapter 3.

38. Feng xian geming weiyuanhui, "Guanyu wuchan jieji wenhua da geming zhong liang, qian, wu qingli de yijian (huiyi taolun gao)" (Suggestions regarding the problem of grain, funds, and supplies during the great proletarian Cultural Revolution [meeting discussion draft]), July 21, 1970. The document detailed back wages, work points, grain rations, and compensation for individuals who were displaced from their jobs and homes, who left work as part of combat teams, and who were injured, hospitalized, or killed.

Near the end of August, this second study class concluded with reports by each of the factions confessing to violations over the past three years. Zhang Liansheng gave the main report on behalf of Paolian. He admitted responsibility for a series of violent events and for raiding arms stockpiles in Shandong Province. He admitted that it was wrong to subject Shao Wen to struggle sessions, to oppose the PAD-dominated military control committee, and to break into the PAD storehouse to seize arms. He also confessed to having plotted to oppose Shao's appointment as revolutionary committee head during the Xuhai Study Class. Finally, he confessed that Paolian had illegally squandered 270,400 yuan in cash and 800,000 *jin* of grain.[39] Li Zongzhou gave the main report on behalf of Liansi. He confessed to its role in a number of violent events in the county and admitted to a series of actions against the 68th Army and PLA Unit 6174. He also confessed to a series of raids on commune grain storage depots and storehouses.[40]

While on the surface both factions apologized for the same types of errors, Paolian's leaders felt that the treatment of the two seemed imbalanced. Liansi's self-criticism was only twenty pages, while Paolian's was thirty-four pages. A number of problems exposed about Liansi in the first round of study classes— its refusal to turn over weapons, its opposition to the preparatory committee, its seizure of state property and refusal initially to hand it over—all were passed over in their final report. In the investigations of violent events, there were eighty-three deaths attributable to violent factional clashes, and more than sixty of them were members of Paolian. Yet the Liansi report passed over this issue lightly, mentioning only a handful of cases. Unlike Paolian, Liansi did not provide a full accounting of the state property that they had seized. Eight people who had committed various crimes and had been labeled in an earlier draft of the report as "bad elements within Liansi's mass organizations" went unmentioned in the final version.[41]

As the Paolian leaders feared, the reports provided a basis for the further persecution of their faction. Liansi leaders escaped with light punishments, and the veteran cadres aligned with Liansi were restored to office after light

39. "Zhang Liansheng tongzhi daibiao yuan Paolian," August 27, 1970.

40. "Li Zongzhou tongzhi daibiao yuan Liansi," August 27, 1970.

41. Yuan liansi zongbu, "Yuan liansi zongbu guanyu jige zhongda wenti de jiancha baogao" (Self-criticism of former Liansi headquarters regarding some major issues), May 20, 1970; Zhang Liansheng interview; and the speeches cited in the previous two footnotes.

criticism.[42] Another troubling sign was the fact that Zhang Liansheng had become a primary target in the second study class. During the first, the 202nd Division officers in charge had shown him high regard, appointing him as the leader of one of the groups in the study class. In the second study class, the PAD officers steered criticism toward Zhang, offering other leaders in Paolian the opportunity to escape punishment by denouncing Zhang, which they did. Zhang's efforts to rebut the accusations were treated as showing a bad attitude and unwillingness to reform.[43]

Shao Wen's domination of the new county government became even more pronounced when the county party committee was re-established in June 1971, and he became the county's first party secretary.[44] Only three PLA officers remained on the county party committee as placeholders, and they were vastly outnumbered by the county's PAD and its civilian cadre allies.[45] In the months to follow, party committees were formed in communes and other work units. Paolian members of the commune revolutionary committees formed in the fall of 1969 were generally excluded from positions as party secretaries or vice-secretaries. Liansi-affiliated individuals dominated the new party organizations at the lower levels.[46] In short, the authority of Shao and the PAD was consolidated by the end of 1971. Paolian members, and their supporters among the county's cadres, became targets for further persecution.

Exercising Dictatorship over Paolian

During this period of extreme political disruption, a series of political suppression campaigns were waged across China in order to consolidate political order. These began shortly after the establishment of city and county revolutionary committees. Across China, the median date for establishing city and county revolutionary committees was April 1968. The first such campaign was

42. Zhang Liansheng interview.

43. Jiangsu sheng Feng xian geming weiyuanhui zhenggong zu, "Guanyu zhaokai Zhongguo gongchandang Feng xian di liuci dahui de xuanchuan tigang" (Propaganda outline regarding the opening of the Sixth Feng County Communist Party Congress), April 20, 1971; Zhang Liansheng notebooks; and Zhang Liansheng interview.

44. *Zhonggong Feng xian difangshi dashiji*, pp. 241–242; *Feng xian zuzhishi ziliao*, pp. 144–145.

45. They would eventually leave the county in 1974. *Feng xian zuzhishi ziliao*, pp. 143 and 145; and Zhang Liansheng interview.

46. *Feng xian zuzhishi ziliao*, pp. 149–152.

known in almost all regions as the "Cleansing of the Class Ranks," which typically began roughly four months later (median date, August 1968). Two campaigns followed in subsequent years. The median date for the onset of the "One Strike, Three Anti" campaign was February 1970, and for the "Investigation of May 16 Elements," April 1971.[47] These campaigns were instruments in a prolonged effort to re-create stable social and political order in localities that were deeply disrupted by factional conflict.

Jiangsu Province as a whole did not deviate from the national pattern. In the seventy-five counties and cities in the province, the class-cleansing campaign began earlier (median date July 1968), as did the May 16 elements campaign (median date February 1971). The deeply disrupted Xuhai region, however, lagged well behind the rest of its province and the nation as a whole. The counties and cities in the region did not generally establish their revolutionary committees until one year after the rest of Jiangsu (median date July 1969), so they initiated the first and second of these suppression campaigns well after the rest of the country. The region's median date for the onset of the class-cleansing campaign was eighteen months later than the rest of the province (December 1969), and for the "One Strike, Three Anti" campaign, eight months later (October 1970).[48]

With a revolutionary committee that was delayed until September 1969, Feng County was part of this general pattern, but as a result it conducted the three suppression campaigns more or less simultaneously, often mixing together their presumably distinct objectives. The documents from the county during this period reflect this: the three campaigns were generally folded into a single "Criticism and Cleansing Campaign" (*piqing yundong*).

As the suppression campaigns unfolded across the county, they took on an especially broad scope. Almost all of our interviewees agreed that the factional battles in rural communes and production brigades often mapped onto power rivalries between different village clans, or purely personal political rivalries that did not map onto clan loyalties. These conflicts are impossible to document with evidence about county-level factions, and they make it hard to characterize factional struggle at the village level in terms of political categories that make sense at the county level. An additional source of fuel for these campaigns was the fact that the county was occupied by Nationalist, Japanese, and Communist forces during the decade that began with the Japanese inva-

47. Based on the dataset employed in Walder, *Agents of Disorder*.
48. Ibid.

sion in 1937. Local elites often collaborated in order to survive, and quite a few local residents switched sides over time, serving first in posts appointed by Nationalist or Japanese forces before defecting to the Communists. These people had "problematic histories" and were all vulnerable to political charges of betrayal or espionage during these campaigns.

Moreover, many local party cadres and others still followed the rural custom of taking on nominal kinship with others (*ren ganqin*), or swearing oaths of brotherhood (*bai bazi*), and still others formed master-disciple relationships (*shitu guanxi*) as part of training in martial arts. All of these people were vulnerable to denunciation for forming potentially subversive groups. Finally, recent involvement in factional violence could support a charge that someone was an "active counterrevolutionary" or a radical "May 16 element." With more than one hundred violent clashes in the county and more than eighty documented deaths, thousands of participants in these events were vulnerable to accusation and punishment.

These campaigns therefore potentially targeted a broad and diverse swath of the population, and the victims defied easy characterization in terms of factional alignments in the county. However, the clearest designation of targets for any of these campaigns was for the "Investigation of May 16 Elements." This campaign was targeted at individuals who were leaders of factions that had defied efforts to re-establish political order, who had engaged in factional violence, and especially those who led resistance to military units. With PAD-affiliated officials now firmly in charge of Feng County, these definitions would be interpreted in ways that turned Paolian's leaders and activists into targets during this campaign.[49]

A county Cleansing of the Class Ranks office was formally established in March 1970. Its leaders and staff were drawn primarily from the PAD.[50] A separate department, the Second Office for the Cleansing of the Class Ranks (*qingdui di er bangongshi*) was established in February 1971, in response to central documents mandating the "Investigation of May 16 Elements." Initially led by PLA officers, it was later taken over by a commune leader affiliated with Liansi, and the investigators on the staff, which eventually grew to ninety people, were

49. The nationwide campaign to investigate "May 16 elements" was turned against the most disruptive rebel leaders, usually long after they were politically active. Its political background and impact are described in MacFarquhar and Schoenhals, *Mao's Last Revolution*, pp. 221–238.

50. *Zhonggong Feng xian difangshi dashiji*, p. 236; and Shao Limin notebooks.

dominated by either former Liansi members or cadres who had sympathized with them.[51]

During this period, the county also established a May 7 Cadre School (*wu qi ganxiao*) in the spring of 1971. This was a rural camp for cadres who had yet to be reassigned to new jobs or who were still under investigation. Initially, close to one hundred cadres were sent to this camp for reeducation and manual labor; the number grew to close to four hundred as the campaign expanded. The majority of the participants were cadres who had sided with Paolian at some point in time, and in the later phases of the campaign, Paolian leaders who initially had been appointed to positions on the revolutionary committee were sent there as well.

After establishing the class-cleansing office on March 16, 1970, the investigators started by conducting the campaign in grassroots social organizations.[52] Shao Wen was in charge of the office, with one of the remaining PLA officers and the PAD deputy director as his deputies.[53] This was a massive bureaucratic effort. Over the next month, they held 5,829 class-cleansing study classes across the county.[54] A month later, they reported that they had trained more than 13,000 grassroots investigators for cleansing work. The campaign was being conducted in fifty units under the county government, in all twenty-one communes, and in 295 production brigades.[55]

After two months, the county authorities announced that 1,526 individuals in twelve communes had confessed: 687 of them for political behavior, and 839 for misallocation of property and other economic offenses.[56] At Feng County Middle School, one teacher committed suicide while under pressure to confess.[57] One production brigade in Wanggou Commune compelled thirty-two targets of their investigation to confess their crimes. In the county

51. Qi He notebooks; and Shao Limin notebooks.

52. *Zhonggong Feng xian difangshi dashiji*, p. 236.

53. Shao Limin notebooks.

54. *Zhonggong Feng xian difangshi dashiji*, pp. 236–237.

55. Ibid.; Liulingliusan budui zhu Feng junxuandui linshi dangwei, Feng xian geming weiyuan hui, "Guanyu guanche zhixing Xuzhou zhuanqu geming weiyuanhui 'Yingjie weida lingxiu Mao zhuxi 'qi.erjiu' guanghui pishi yizhou nian tongzhi' de baogao" (Report on thoroughly carrying out the Xuzhou Prefecture revolutionary committee's 'notice on welcoming the first anniversary of the great leader Chairman Mao's glorious 'July 29' comment'), May 14, 1970.

56. *Zhonggong Feng xian difangshi dashiji*, p. 238.

57. Ibid. p. 238; Gao Dalin, *Yu xiu yuan wanji*, pp. 108–109; and Zhang Liansheng interview.

seat, 116 individuals were designated as prime suspects. Among them were seven "spies," two "traitors" to the Communist Party, eleven "murderers," twenty former Nationalist military personnel, and one "reactionary" Daoist master.[58] By the end of 1970, the campaign uncovered a total of 2,494 "class enemies."[59] Shunhe Commune uncovered a "reactionary" Daoist sect. Among its three senior masters, one was a convicted "rightist" in 1957, one was a former landlord and Nationalist army officer. They had a reported three hundred followers engaged in "counterrevolutionary activities."[60]

Many of the victims were framed by false charges. Six Paolian leaders from Shunhe Commune who stubbornly resisted the imposition of PAD military control in 1969 were sentenced for an alleged gang rape in early 1970; the false charges were eventually overturned in 1975.[61] Shahe Commune claimed to uncover an "underground anti-Communist brigade" in April 1970. Several implicated Paolian members were sent to a study class by the case investigators, where they were subjected to severe torture to compel confessions—ten of them died, and six suffered permanent disabilites. The case was partially overturned in 1975.[62]

Shao Wen turned the new campaign against Paolian. A study class was formed in September 1970 to investigate the group and it continued to year's end. Veteran cadres who had supported Liansi (and who were consequently targeted by Paolian) led the class, along with PAD officers.[63] When the Second Class-Cleansing Office was established in February 1971 to lead the May 16

58. Feng xian geming weiyuanhui qingdui bangongshi, "Guanyu dangqian qingdui gongzuo de jidian yijian" (Opinions on current class-cleansing works), June 25, 1970.

59. *"Wenhua da geming" shinian dongluan*, p. 31.

60. Feng xian daji daohui men linshi bangongshi, *Qingkuang jianbao*, no. 4, January 7, 1971.

61. Feng xian renmin fayuan, "Jiangsu sheng Xuzhou diqu zhongji renmin fayuan xingshi panjue shu" (Criminal judgment passed by the People's Court of Xuzhou Prefecture, Jiangsu Province), September 24, 1975.

62. *Jiangsu sheng Feng xian zhi*, p. 30; *Zhonggong Feng xian difangshi dashiji*, pp. 236–237. A few of the lower-ranking investigators were punished when the case was reinvestigated in 1975 and 1979. In 1987 more local cadres and case investigators were punished, including the former commune head. Feng xian hecha bangongshi, "Guanyu 'Shahe fangong tuan' jia'an de diaocha ziliao" (Investigation materials on the false case of the "Shahe Anti-Communist Group"), January 1, 1987.

63. Zhang Liansheng notebooks.

elements investigation, it was staffed by PAD personnel from the communes. Most of the top Paolian leaders, and the cadres who stood with them, were sent to a special study class.[64]

The campaign spread panic among former Paolian leaders and followers. In Shunhe Commune's Wanghai Production Brigade, more than four hundred former Paolian members fled their village when the local authorities set up their first class-cleansing study class in 1970. They had good reason to do so. The local case investigators used torture to extract confessions, and seven people died under interrogation.[65] Two Paolian members who worked in the Shunhe Commune grain management station committed suicide while they were detained in the study class.[66] According to one summary account, the class-cleansing campaign identified 393 "renegades," 48 "spies," 492 "historical counterrevolutionaries," 159 "bad elements," 109 "active counterrevolutionaries," and 55 others who had earlier avoided classification as landlords, rich peasants, rightists, or bad elements. The total number labeled and punished in the cleansing campaign was 1,256; 129 committed suicide, and 255 were fired from their jobs.[67]

The investigation of alleged May 16 elements took place during the last half of 1971, shortly after the new county party committee was established. At a speech to kick off the campaign, one of the leaders stated that there were several major violent events in the county that required close investigation. Many of the events he mentioned were attacks by Paolian on Liansi or on caches of weapons. He stated that the main purpose of the campaign was to capture perpetrators and identify their backstage supporters. In August, the revolutionary committee held a series of meetings of their representatives and staff. In the meetings, they charged that May 16 elements were scheming to seize power, and that there were undoubtedly May 16 elements on the revolutionary committee and hidden among its staff, so everyone should maintain vigilance.[68] In early September, Xu Shiyou, head of the Jiangsu Province Revolutionary Committee, came to Xuzhou on an inspection tour and urged local

64. Shao Limin notebooks.

65. Zhang Liansheng notebooks.

66. Xu Zuolun, "Xu Zuolun shensu xin" (Xu Zuolun's petition), November 20, 1977; and Xu Zuolun, "Xu Zuolun shensu xin" (Xu Zuolun's petition), June 19, 1978.

67. Shao Limin notebooks.

68. Ibid.; and Anonymous, work notebooks.

leaders to energetically carry out the campaign against May 16 elements. This greatly intensified the campaign in Feng County.[69]

In mid-October 1971, the county authorities held a mass rally to denounce one of the targets of the campaign, a demobilized soldier who worked as the head of the Huankou Commune Health Center in the early 1960s. Prior to the Cultural Revolution, he charged that the party secretary of his commune had raped his wife. After his complaint was ignored by the authorities, he quit his job and moved with his wife back to his hometown in Shandong. When the Cultural Revolution began, he returned to Feng County to join in the rebellion against the county party committee, and he became a zealous supporter of Paolian. When Paolian was suppressed in the spring of 1967, he disappeared from the county without a trace. He was tracked down and arrested by personnel from the Xuzhou Military Subdistrict in the summer of 1968 and brought back to Feng County. At the mass rally, he was denounced for collaborating with Paolian, for fabricating false charges, and for attacking anti-Paolian mass organizations. He was executed in April 1972 as an "active counterrevolutionary" and "May 16 element."[70]

In early January 1972, a county party committee document reported that by the end of 1971, the May 16 elements investigations had exposed another 132 "renegades, spies, and other class enemies," uncovered "historical problems" for 1,020 individuals, closed 66 cases of "counterrevolutionary activity," and identified 2,079 criminals who had engaged in economic crimes. Depending on the severity of the crimes, some were sent back to their communities to be put under "mass surveillance," some were put in prison, and some were executed.[71] As the campaign began to wane in March 1973, most of these suspects were released to return to their jobs, but around two dozen "prime suspects" were sent to a study class at Feng County Middle School for further investigation, where they remained until the end of 1973.[72]

---

69. Zhonggong Xuzhou diwei, "Xuzhou diwei dianhua huiyi jilu" (Minutes of the telephone conference of the Xuzhou Prefecture party committee), September 7, 1971.

70. Shao Limin notebooks; Zhang Liansheng interview.

71. Zhonggong Feng xian xianwei, "Guanyu yijiuqiyi nian geming, shengchan de jiben qingkuang he jindong mingchun gongzuo anpai yijian" (Regarding the basic situation in revolution and production in 1971, and suggestions about arranging work this winter and next spring), January 3, 1972.

72. Zhang Liansheng interview; Qi He notebooks.

Zhang Liansheng's Ordeal

Zhang Liansheng's notebooks illustrate the way that these suppression campaigns were turned against Paolian. After the arrival of the 202nd Division work team in February 1970, Zhang participated in that unit's study class and gave Paolian's self-criticism report along with the leaders of Liansi. In early January 1971, he asked for permission from the study class leaders to return to his family's production team in Danlou Commune, engage in agricultural work, and receive "education" from poor peasants. He worked as a pig breeder and married a local woman. He was uninvolved in factional activity and satisfied with a peaceful rural life.

As the May 16 investigations accelerated near the end of 1971, Zhang was summoned to a conference in the county seat. He did not find the summons worrisome, because he had been selected as a standing committee member of the county revolutionary committee in 1969. When he arrived, however, he was told that he would be sent to a study class at the May 7 Cadre School, where he was held in isolation and interrogated continuously over the next twenty months.[73] In March 1972, Zhang became a "prime suspect" in the study class and was repeatedly subjected to struggle sessions, mass denunciation rallies, and small group criticism sessions. Under pressure, former Paolian leaders, both militants and moderates, turned on him and denounced him for links with "capitalist roaders," opposition to the PAD, promotion of "bad elements" within Paolian, "anti-army" activities, and instigation of violent clashes. They charged that Zhang was the "chief leader of the May 16 conspiracy in the county," that his reactionary stance had never changed, and that his self-criticisms were false and deceptive. The leaders of the study class brought Zhang's pregnant wife to convince him to confess his crimes. Under pressure, she wrote him a letter saying that she would divorce him if he refused to make a thorough confession.[74]

When Zhang first heard news about the May 16 elements investigations, he anticipated that the PAD officers in charge of the county would use it as a tool to wreak revenge on Paolian, but he never thought the campaign would be taken to such extremes. While incarcerated at the May 7 Cadre School he discovered that almost all of the suspects were Paolian members or cadres who

73. Zhang Liansheng interview.

74. Ibid.; and Zhang Liansheng, "Gei Mao Zedong zhuxi ji Zhou Enlai zongli, Wang Hongwen fu zhuxi de xin," October 28, 1973.

had sided with them. They were being charged not simply with mistakes in the course of the movement, but as "counterrevolutionaries" and "class enemies," normally treated as capital crimes. He was put under twenty-four-hour surveillance by case investigators and became a virtual prisoner. While in custody, he learned that two former Paolian activists from the county government offices had committed suicide in the study class, but he suspected that "suicide" was actually a cover for death under torture. He knew that in past political campaigns organized by the central authorities, party cadres and political activists who had tortured or killed people were almost never punished. At most, they would be criticized for "an error of political line."

As a strategy of survival, he concluded that the best line of action would be to confess to all charges and not resist, but hope for a reversal of false charges at a later point in time. Considering his predicament, Zhang acknowledged the charges against him, confessed fully, and showed contrition and willingness to reform. But he refused to confess to membership in an underground conspiracy of May 16 elements, since he had never heard of such a thing. The case investigators were frustrated by this and frequently beat him during late night interrogations. But in the end the county leaders seemed satisfied. They did not really care whether he confessed to a May 16 elements conspiracy. They wanted his submission to their authority.[75]

From the time he was sent to the study class at the end of 1971, Zhang thought about escaping in order to present a petition about this abuse in Beijing. But the twenty-four-hour surveillance at the study class made this impossible. During the twenty months that he was isolated for interrogation, he had six different investigators in charge of his case. He observed that as the rank of his investigators declined, their propensity for violence increased. In July 1973, however, the interrogations and surveillance seemed to relax. He was allowed to read newspapers, where he learned about the Tenth National Congress of the Communist Party. He was encouraged because the news about the congress did not denounce the rebels' actions in earlier years and instead emphasized the positive role of rebellion during the Cultural Revolution. He resolved to escape from the study class and present a petition to protest his treatment and seek redress in Beijing.[76]

75. Zhang Liansheng interview; and Zhang Liansheng, "Gei Mao Zedong zhuxi ji Zhou Enlai zongli, Wang Hongwen fu zhuxi de xin," October 28, 1973.

76. Zhang Liansheng interview; and Zhang Liansheng, "Gei Mao Zedong zhuxi ji Zhou Enlai zongli, Wang Hongwen fu zhuxi de xin," October 28, 1973.

Anticipations of Change

As these campaigns wore on, the leaders of the Second Office expressed frustration about the many individuals who refused to confess. They also complained that the investigators who worked under them in these seemingly endless interrogations were beginning to suffer from poor morale. Case investigators "ignored discipline and regulations," returned home often, and stayed away from their work as much as possible.[77]

These complaints reflected a number of underlying problems with the campaign. First of all, the definition of "May 16 elements" was unclear from the start, and in fact it was subsequently shown that no such underground organization ever existed.[78] So as the investigations unfolded, more and more innocent people fell under suspicion—even, as it turned out, some of the case investigators themselves. This created a pervasive sense of apprehension and fear. Second, the authorities expected the case investigators to eat and sleep together in the study class twenty-four hours a day and to continue until the campaign reached an overall conclusion. This made many case investigators feel as if they were prisoners themselves. Third, the webs of personal relationships in this agrarian county were dense, including ties of clan, marriage, neighborhood, work units, and the party hierarchy, making it hard for case investigators to decide which connections to pursue. Also weighing on the minds of many case investigators, many of whom had Liansi connections, was the possibility that a future shift in party policy might open them up to revenge.

To address these problems, the county authorities instructed the Second Office to carry out a rectification of the case groups to correct the situation. They should curtail further absences without approved leaves; they should not reveal anything about their work to others; they should not secretly express sympathy toward suspects; and they should not seek higher wages or other benefits for their work. They called for investigators to keep up their morale, maintain a correct political standpoint, observe discipline, and implement policy properly.[79]

In retrospect, it seems clear that these grassroots persecution campaigns took a toll on people other than their victims. But victims there were. Various

---

77. Qi He notebooks.
78. MacFarquhar and Schoenhals, *Mao's Last Revolution*, pp. 221–238.
79. Qi He notebooks.

sources indicate that by the middle of 1972, the May 16 elements campaign had sent more than seven hundred suspects to coercive study classes, and at least thirty-five of them died under interrogation in the May 7 Cadre School.[80]

The investigations that were combined under the label "Criticize and Cleanse" had a wide range of negative social consequences. The first was illegal flight from the county. An internal document issued by the county Public Security Bureau in July 1972 stated that 1,120 county residents had fled in the face of these campaigns, and called for measures to stem the tide. Local authorities were admonished not to curse, beat, or use firearms to dissuade people who try to leave—an admonition that suggests that such actions were already common.[81]

Second, an underground spirit of resistance seemed to be spreading. Several "counterrevolutionary wall posters" had been torn down, and a number of individuals had petitioned to have their cases reviewed by higher authorities.[82] A person from Songlou Commune had written to Hong Kong to ask to join a Nationalist spy organization, asking for weapons and funds.[83] In early 1973, local cadres and other residents were discovered listening illicitly to foreign broadcasts by "enemy" countries. In Sunlou Commune there were 207 radios with this capability, and 157 people were involved.[84]

80. Shao Limin notebooks; Xuzhou diqu fu ning shangfang tuan, "Jiefa pipan Xuzhou diqu wenti huiyi jiyao zhier" (Minutes of the exposure and criticism meeting about the Xuzhou Prefecture problem, no. 2), pamphlet, May 14, 1974; Xuzhou diqu fu ning shangfang tuan, "Jiefa pipan Xuzhou diqu wenti huiyi jiyao zhisan" (Minutes of the exposure and criticism meeting about the Xuzhou Prefecture problem, no. 3), pamphlet, May 14, 1974; Zhang Liansheng notebooks; and Zhang Liansheng interview.

81. Feng xian gongan jiguan junguanhui, "Dangqian gongzuo de jidian yijian" (Several suggestions regarding current work), July 7, 1972.

82. Feng xian gongan jiguan junguanhui, "Qingkuang jianbao, disanqi, sanyue fen di, she qingkuang" (Situation report, no. 3, Enemy's activities and social situation in March), March 28, 1972. Some other issues of the situation report also reflect these problems.

83. Feng xian gongan jiguan junguanhui, "Qingkuang jianbao, dijiuqi, jiuyue fen di, she qingkuang" (Situation report, no. 9, Enemy's activities and social situation in September), September 28, 1972.

84. Feng xian gongan jiguan junguanhui, Feng xian geweihui zhengfa zu, "Guanyu Sunlou gongshe fanxinzhan douzheng shidian gongzuo de zongjie baogao" (Summary report on the provisional methods practiced in Sunlou Commune to fight against the enemy's psychological warfare), April 10, 1973. Some other issues of the situation report and other official documents also reflected similar problems.

Third was the spread of political rumors. Some veteran cadres who had sympathized with Paolian were telling people that Beijing had criticized the local campaigns for going too far.[85] In several cases, it was rumored that Wang Xiaoyu would soon make a political comeback, and that the party center had criticized the excessive scope of the May 16 elements investigations. Another rumor was that Shao Wen would soon be transferred to another county.[86]

As it turned out, many of these rumors were based in fact. Beijing did issue instructions in early 1972 to avoid carrying the May 16 elements campaign to extremes, and also not to carry it out at all in rural areas.[87] The death of Lin Biao, the head of the PLA, designated as Mao Zedong's "closest comrade in arms and successor" at the outset of the Cultural Revolution, would soon lead to a decisive shift in national political trends. Lin died under mysterious circumstances when his jet crashed in Mongolia in September 1971, allegedly after a failed attempt to assassinate Mao as part of a military coup. Beijing subsequently indicated in August 1972 that military control of local governments would soon end, meaning that Shao Wen's removal was only a matter of time.[88]

In response to these troubling trends, Shao Wen doubled down on meetings to stress the importance of the suppression campaigns and defended their accomplishments. At a cadre conference in May 1973, he denounced those who were presenting petitions about alleged injustices in Xuzhou, Nanjing, and Beijing, blaming them for "circulating false charges" and "causing trouble." He called for forbidding these activities. He insisted that those who failed to fully confess deserved to be placed in isolation; that investigators should maintain discipline, overcome disturbances, and insist on the correctness of the

85. Qi He notebooks.

86. Feng xian gongan jiguan junguanhui, "Qingkuang jianbao, disiqi, siyue fen di, she qing-kuang" (Situation report, no. 4, Enemy's activities and social situation in April), April 28, 1973. Some other issues of the situation report and internal documents reflected similar problems.

87. Wu De, "Wu De guanyu qingcha 'wu.yiliu' de jianghua" (Wu De's speech on the "May 16" investigations), December 20, 1971; Ji Dengkui, "Ji Dengkui zai guowuyuan huibao ganbu huiyi shi de jianghua jingshen" (The essence of Ji Dengkui's speech at the cadre reporting meeting of the State Council), March 31, 1972; and Wu De, "Wu De guanyu qingcha 'wu.yiliu' de jianghua" (Wu De's speech about the "May 16" investigations), April 1972.

88. Zhonggong zhongyang, "Zhonggong zhongyang, zhongyang junwei guanyu zhengxun dui sanzhi liangjun wenti de yijian tongzhi" (Notice of the CCP Central Committee and Central Military Commission on questions about the three supports and two militaries), Zhongfa [72], no. 32, August 21, 1972.

struggle; and that people should not believe rumors and repeat them.[89] None-theless, in response to the growing sense of public resentment, the county authorities removed a few local cadres who had committed some of the worst outrages.[90]

Near the end of May 1973, the county authorities finally began to wind down the May 16 elements investigations. The Second Office held a meeting of case investigators, telling them that most suspects would soon be sent back to their work units. Only a handful would remain in detention, but the inves-tigators should continue to be vigilant. They should not permit any commu-nication with the outside, and they should not permit the few remaining sus-pects to escape.[91] Some Paolian leaders (like Zhang Liansheng) and veteran cadres (like Zhu Pingfan) were kept in detention.[92] But it seemed clear that this phase of the Cultural Revolution would soon end.

It was becoming clear to military officers that their withdrawal from civilian administration was imminent. To prepare for this outcome, they began to re-cruit former Liansi leaders into the party and pave the way for putting them into leading positions in the civilian power structure. When the labor union, the poor and lower-middle peasants association, the women's federation, and the Communist Youth League organizations were restored, Liansi leaders were appointed to important posts in them. The Liansi leader, Li Zongzhou, became deputy director of the county trade union.[93] These appointments would change a person's occupational status from worker to cadre. As these individuals were recruited into the party, they would be prepared for higher appointments in the party and government structures of the county.

In October 1973, however, the situation in the county became unsettled, and open resistance emerged. A large number of wall posters appeared in the

89. Qi He notebooks.

90. *Zhonggong Feng xian difangshi dashiji,* pp. 248–249; Zhonggong Feng xian weiyuanhui, "Guanyu chengguan zhen deng ershiyi ge jiceng dangwei gaixuan de pifu" (Reply regarding the revised selection of members of the party committees of the county seat and 20 other basic level committees), May 25, 1973.

91. Qi He notebooks.

92. Zhang Liansheng notebooks; Zhu Pingfan, *Wangshi,* p. 32; Gao Dalin, *Yu xiu yuan wanji,* pp. 109–111.

93. Zhonggong Feng xian weiyuanhui, "Guanyu Ji Xingchang, Chao Daiqin deng liu tongzhi renzhi de tongzhi" (Notice regarding the appointment of Ji Xingchang, Chao Daiqin, and four other comrades), October 6, 1973; *Jiangsu sheng Feng xian zhi,* pp. 531–542; and Zhang Liansheng notebooks.

county seat that accused the PAD of carrying out the "bourgeois reactionary line," "suppressing the revolutionary masses," "replacing law with power," and most tellingly, for being complicit in the disgraced Lin Biao's "reactionary line." Internal public security bureau reports expressed alarm that some of these wall posters were put up by released victims of the May 16 elements campaign, and many of those who had been released from the study classes after having confessed were now openly telling people that their confessions were extracted through torture. Some were even tracking down their former investigators and threatening them. In the county's May 7 Cadre School, some cadres who had been investigated were now openly criticizing Xu Shiyou, the head of the Jiangsu Province Revolutionary Committee, in mass meetings.[94]

The tectonic plates of national politics were about to shift once again, and change was in the air. The county's leaders and case group investigators seemed to be increasingly demoralized. On October 11, 1973, despite having been affirmed as the "chief boss of the May 16 elements in Feng County," Zhang Liansheng's case group investigator told him that he had permission for a few days' home visit.[95] Zhang would not return.

94. Feng xian gongan jiguan junguanhui, "Qingkuang jianbao, dishiliuqi, shiyue fen di, she qingkuang" (Situation report, no. 16, Enemy activities and social situation in October), October 30, 1973. These situation reports, previously issued monthly, were being issued more frequently, reflecting dramatic local developments that troubled the authorities.

95. Zhang Liansheng notebooks; and Zhang Liansheng interview.

7

Backlash

ZHANG WAS EXPECTED to return to the study class when his leave expired on October 14. Instead, he fled the county to present a petition in Beijing. After darkness fell on October 13, he walked across the provincial border to Dangshan County, Anhui, and jumped onto a freight train headed west for the city of Zhengzhou, in Henan Province. Hiding in the home of a relative for two weeks, he wrote a long and detailed petition about Paolian's persecution by the local PAD. On October 28 he climbed aboard a northbound freight train, arriving in Beijing on November 2, 1973, and presented his petition at a reception station in central Beijing that afternoon.

The Petition Campaign

Zhang's petition was nearly 50,000 characters in length and laid out Paolian's complaints about its persecution at the hands of the PAD, explaining in detail the sequence of events over the previous several years. The document was separated into subsections titled, "Why I must report the situation to the Center and Chairman Mao"; "What a handful of people did during Feng County's Criticizing and Cleansing movement"; "How we should understand the line struggle in Feng County's Cultural Revolution"; "What I did during the Great Proletarian Cultural Revolution"; "My viewpoints on Feng County's situation"; and finally "Several explanations and requests." Zhang concluded his petition with the following words: "I earnestly request that the higher leadership responsibly carry out Chairman Mao's revolutionary line and reinvestigate certain events in the history of Feng County's Cultural Revolution. . . . If we fail to thoroughly clarify these events, if we tolerate the prevailing incorrect viewpoints, Feng County's revolution and production will suffer an irrevocable damage."[1]

As Zhang waited in the reception station for his turn to hand in his petition, he was surprised to meet another petitioner from Feng County. He learned that there were a number of other petitioners from Feng County and elsewhere in the Xuhai region who were in Beijing, staying in a cheap hostel. He went there immediately, and met with five other petitioners from Feng County and four from Xuzhou. Some in the latter group were members of Xuzhou's Kick faction who had been persecuted after the "Wang Xiaoyu line" was reversed. Zhang was not familiar with any of these people, and he had little sympathy with the Kick faction, because they had for a period supported the Liansi cause. But he knew that the Xuzhou Kick faction had been the victims of the May 16 elements investigations, so it made sense to create an alliance with them to present petitions together as a single group in Beijing.[2]

Over the next few days, Zhang wrote two letters to Paolian leaders, giving his views on what had happened in the county and how they might seek redress for their persecution. He asked them to mobilize victims in the recent campaign to join in a petition campaign. He also coordinated with the other petitioners from Feng County, several of whom were from rural communes, to collect information about the crackdowns and the violations of central policy in the recent campaigns, and about abuse of power, corruption, and sex scandals.

On November 15, in the name of the Xuzhou Prefecture Petitioners Group (*Xuzhou diqu shangfang tuan*), Zhang and the others submitted their petition and supporting materials at the reception station. The office staff informed them that the central leaders were already aware of the Xuzhou problems and promised to hand over the materials to the top leaders. They advised the group to return home and wait for a response.

On November 16, the petitioners left Beijing by train and arrived the next day in the Shandong capital of Ji'nan, where they checked into the railway bureau guesthouse. Shortly after arriving, they held a meeting to plan their next steps. One of the main topics of discussion was a statement issued publicly by former rebels in Xuzhou ten days earlier, a political manifesto that sought to take advantage of the recent purge and denunciation of Lin Biao to

---

1. Zhang Liansheng, "Gei Mao Zedong zhuxi ji Zhou Enlai zongli, Wang Hongwen fu zhuxi de xin," October 28, 1973.

2. Zhang Liansheng notebooks; and Zhang Liansheng interview.

protest their recent mistreatment. The manifesto called for the current "Criticize Lin Biao Campaign" to "thoroughly expose the crimes" of Lin Biao's followers inside the leadership of the Ji'nan Military Region. It charged that the May 16 elements investigations had violated the "correct line" of the Ninth Party Congress, that the use of torture and forced confessions constituted dictatorship over the proletariat, and that the campaign was an error of political line that essentially disavowed Chairman Mao's Cultural Revolution. It demanded that all of the verdicts reached in the "Cleansing of the Class Ranks," the "One Strike, Three Anti" and the "Investigation of May 16 Elements" campaigns should be reversed, the victims compensated, and the perpetrators punished. It also demanded the reinvestigation of all alleged suicides by targets of these campaigns to determine whether they were actually cases of murder. The document went on to demand that all newly admitted party members be investigated to determine whether they were appointed based on factional affiliation. Finally, the manifesto demanded that the leadership of all revolutionary committees be reshuffled to overcome these injustices.

Zhang Liansheng's excitement upon reading this manifesto is easy to understand—it expressed clearly and powerfully all of Paolian's grievances and indicated that rebel groups had suffered all over the Xuhai region, and likely beyond, in the same way that Zhang experienced in Feng County. Inspired, Zhang applied these demands in an essay titled "An Open Letter to the Revolutionary Cadres, Party Members, and Revolutionary Masses of Feng County" on November 18, and had it printed and circulated the same day.[3]

The next day, the petitioners arrived in Xuzhou by train. When they contacted the city's party committee, the office staff claimed that it had received nothing from the central authorities about their case and refused to meet. The next day the petitioners were able to meet with two officials who dealt with them on behalf of the city authorities. The officials said they had received nothing from Beijing or the provincial party committee, so they had no idea how to deal with the problems raised in the petition. They suggested that the petitioners disband their group, return to their work units, and participate in the Criticize Lin Biao campaign there.

This aggravated the petitioners, and the meeting broke up in discord. So later that day, the petitioners went instead to the offices of the Xuzhou Prefecture

---

3. Zhang Liansheng notebooks.

party committee, where they met with the prefecture's two top officials.[4] Those officials told the petitioners that they had no idea how to deal with the problems that they raised but promised to handle them properly whether or not they received instructions from Beijing. They said that the party committees at various levels always acted in accord with Mao Zedong Thought, so the petitioners should go back to their work units to present their complaints. The prefecture leaders then abruptly ended the meeting.[5]

Undeterred, over the next two months Zhang and the other petitioners stayed in Xuzhou to continue their campaign. Other aggrieved individuals came from Feng County to join their cause. They developed ties with other groups of petitioners from Xuzhou and the surrounding counties, and presented these new petitions to the authorities. They communicated with Paolian leaders and members back in Feng County to collect further information and compile more evidence of abuse. They traveled back to the county to encourage local people to put up wall posters and organize protest demonstrations. And they repeatedly tried to contact the prefecture's leaders to complain about events in the county in recent years.

The prefecture's leaders refused any further meetings. When the petitioners put up wall posters that aired their complaints, soldiers and office staff immediately pulled them down. Later, the leaders agreed to meetings but did not show up. Eventually, the petitioners gave up.

Getting nowhere in Xuzhou, Zhang and the petitioners decided to present their petition in the provincial capital of Nanjing. They arrived in Nanjing on December 10 and visited the provincial reception center over the next several days. A junior official met with them and welcomed their petition as the right of all citizens, but he tried to minimize their complaints as relatively minor issues that could be handled effectively by party organs at lower levels. After a long and inconclusive discussion, the official promised to report the meeting to the supervisors.[6]

After several days, another group of petitioners from Xuzhou arrived in Nanjing. They drafted a petition and agreed to form a united delegation of

---

4. They were Chai Rongsheng (commander of military subdistrict, chairman of the Prefecture revolutionary committee and secretary of the prefecture party committee) and Guan Yaoting (veteran civilian cadre, vice-chairman of the prefecture revolutionary committee and deputy party secretary).

5. Zhang Liansheng notebooks.

6. Ibid.

petitioners from all the cities and counties in the Xuzhou area. The expanded group resolved to put up wall posters all around the streets of Nanjing if the authorities refused its petition. Several days later, it met with the same junior official in the reception center, who gave them the same response as before. Getting nowhere in Nanjing, the Feng County petitioners returned to Xuzhou in December along with several others from Xuzhou City. Refused an audience at the prefecture party headquarters, they aired their complaints at the public security bureau before returning to Feng County by bus.

As these events were taking place, shifts in Jiangsu's political situation created more favorable circumstances for the petitioners' cause, while threatening to weaken Shao Wen's position back in the county. In mid-December 1973, Beijing transferred Xu Shiyou, head of Jiangsu's revolutionary committee and party committee, and commander of the Nanjing Military Region, to the Guangzhou Military Region. General Xu had been in charge of military control in the province prior to the formation of its revolutionary committee in 1968, and he had pushed the recent persecution campaigns to restore political order, an effort in which the local PAD played a central role. Xu's transfer was part of an effort by Beijing to weaken military control over civilian administration throughout China in the wake of the Lin Biao incident. The authority of veteran cadres in Jiangsu's provincial leadership was strengthened by Xu's departure. These veteran cadres were more sympathetic to the petitioners' campaign. They were not implicated in the recent persecution campaigns, and they themselves had suffered criticism and demotion earlier in the Cultural Revolution. More importantly, the petitioners' campaign would help them regain authority and push military figures out of civilian administration.

Tensions in Feng County

Back in Feng County, the authorities were cracking down. Some production brigades in Malou Commune seized and tortured Paolian members, accusing them of secret communications and holding "black meetings." More than twenty people in the commune were beaten, and more than one hundred farmers fled from their production brigades to escape persecution. Three farmers in Huashan Commune were arrested for putting up wall posters.[7]

At a conference held on November 26, Shao Wen gave a speech to the county's cadres about "how to consolidate the general situation." It indicated

7. Ibid.

clearly that he was on the defensive and that he was preparing to counterattack. He stated that "Recently certain class enemies have tried to make trouble for us," and "Taking advantage of certain shortcomings in our work, they are spreading rumors." Shao argued that the recent campaigns in the county were correctly conducted and that nobody could deny their positive achievements. The verdicts were reached correctly, and "If some people persist in making trouble, we should punish them by law."[8] Two days later the county's public security bureau issued an internal document charging that "former mass organization leaders" and people who were criticized in the class-cleansing campaigns were "spreading rumors," "instigating factionalism," and "submitting illegal petitions." The document ordered grassroots leaders to intensify social control.[9]

On December 26, Zhang Liansheng and the other petitioners went to the county party committee offices where an official told them that Shao was too busy to meet. They returned the next day and were told that they could only present their complaints as individuals and that the county's leaders would decide when and where the meetings would be held. Frustrated, the group put up wall posters around the county headquarters demanding a resolution to the problem of the "Lin Biao line" in the county. Staff from the offices came out and covered up the posters. Several days later, Zhang and the others went to the county headquarters once again and were told that they would only meet with them individually. The delegation left in frustration.[10]

On December 30, Zhang went to the county power plant to meet with former Paolian leaders. As he left the meeting, a Liansi leader and around a dozen supporters seized him, wrapped him in heavy quilts, and drove him on a tractor to Danlou Commune, where Zhang's home village was located. They held him there for three days, trying to convince him to stop his petitioning, but Zhang refused and demanded to be released. On January 3, 1974, several county leaders arrived and also tried to convince him to desist, and he again refused.

During his days in captivity, the public media reported the news about Xu Shiyou's transfer as part of a reshuffling of military commanders in China. This

8. Shao Limin notebooks.

9. Feng xian gongan jiguan junguanhui, "Qingkuang jianbao, dishiqiqi, shiyiyue fen di, she qingkuang" (Situation report, no. 17, Enemy's activities and social situation in November), November 28, 1973.

10. Zhang Liansheng notebooks.

made clear that military authority over civilian administration was being cur-
tailed across China. After Zhang's kidnapping, other local petitioners became
alarmed, and they contacted petitioners in Xuzhou and nearby counties, and
made phone calls to provincial and central reception centers, reporting that
Zhang Liansheng, member of the standing committee of the county revolutionary committee, had been kidnapped by the county authorities and that it
was not known whether he was dead or alive. These moves frightened the
county's leaders, who released Zhang on January 3.[11]

Over the next several weeks, Zhang and his comrades continued to mobilize petitioners. They contacted Paolian members but also cast a wider net,
linking up with former Kick faction members in Xuzhou and other victims in
nearby counties. On February 5, Zhang went to Beijing alone to present another petition to the central reception station. While in Beijing, he met with
seven other petitioners from Feng County, including one of the university
students who returned to their hometown in Feng County to support Paolian's
rebellion back in 1967. This petitioner, Wang Dunmian, was a student at Beijing Petroleum Institute at the time and was later assigned a job in Shandong
Province. During the May 16 elements investigations, he was arrested and
brought back to Feng County, where he was interrogated and tortured.[12]
Accompanied by Wang, Zhang visited Peking University, Tsinghua University,
the Chinese Academy of Sciences, and other organizations and gathered information about the "Criticize Lin Biao and Confucius"[13] campaign, which
was just then getting underway. He also obtained transcripts of recent speeches
by central leaders about the campaign. Staff at the reception station still had
no response to his earlier petition, so in mid-February Zhang returned home
by train.[14]

During January and February 1974, the county's leaders took steps to stem
the tide of dissent. They dispatched propaganda teams into the countryside, organized a crackdown by public security forces, and increased patrols by volunteer

11. Ibid.; and Zhang Liansheng interview.

12. Interview no. 8.

13. Mao launched the "Criticize Lin Biao and Confucius" campaign in early January 1974. It
was an attempt to reaffirm the aims of the Cultural Revolution while undermining the authority
of military forces who had exercised a harsh dictatorship over many regions. The campaign
served to reawaken factional conflict across China and had a particularly dramatic effect in
Jiangsu. See Walder, *China under Mao*, pp. 295–302; and Dong and Walder, "Nanjing's 'Second
Cultural Revolution' of 1974." *China Quarterly* 212 (December 2012): 893–918.

14. Zhang Liansheng notebooks; Zhang Liansheng interview.

security workers.[15] They intensified political propaganda and celebrated the alleged success of the recent investigation campaigns, while emphasizing the care with which final verdicts were reached.[16] They highlighted the significance of the Criticize Lin Biao and Confucius campaign and insisted that it would be carried out under tight control by the party committee. They would not tolerate efforts to undermine or disrupt it.[17]

The political environment in Jiangsu Province and elsewhere in China would soon shift in ways that would have a major impact on Feng County politics. As the Criticize Lin Biao and Confucius campaign developed into April 1974, it went beyond Beijing's original intentions and turned into a nationwide movement of petitioners who had suffered in the campaigns of recent years. In Jiangsu Province, the dissident campaign became a major force in the capital city of Nanjing, as petitioners used the campaign as an opportunity to denounce the military officials who had conducted the persecution campaigns. What made these protests effective was the fact that the veteran civilian cadres who had recently been placed at the head of the province after the transfer of General Xu Shiyou lent their support to the public upwelling of complaints against military officials. These civilian leaders, headed by Peng Chong and Xu Jiatun, both originally members of the provincial party committee secretariat in 1966, used the dissident campaign as a way to further weaken the remaining military officers in the province and to strengthen their return to authority after a long hiatus.[18]

These national and provincial trends altered the political situation in the county. First, the remaining officers from the 202nd Division of the PLA left Feng County in April, leaving Shao Wen, head of the PAD, as the only remaining military official in the county leadership.[19] Second, the prefecture's party committee head, Chai Rongsheng (military subdistrict commander), was replaced by a veteran civilian cadre, Hu Hong, who had lost his post as head of another prefecture at the outset of the Cultural Revolution and had no prior history in Xuzhou's conflicts. Third, Yin Shibin, a veteran cadre who also had lost his post in the Cultural Revolution, was transferred in from another

---

15. Feng xian geweihui zhengfazu, "Guanyu dui shehui da qingcha de qingkuang baogao" (Report on the status of the social cleansing investigations), January 17, 1974.

16. Shao Limin notebooks.

17. Ibid.

18. Dong and Walder, "Nanjing's 'Second Cultural Revolution' of 1974."

19. *Feng xian zuzhishi ziliao,* p. 145.

county to become Feng County's deputy party secretary. A few months later, two other veteran cadres from elsewhere were appointed as deputy party secretaries.[20] Fourth, several Paolian leaders and junior cadres who originally had been appointed to positions on the county revolutionary committee but were suspended during the recent persecution campaigns were returned to their posts. Zhang Liansheng was one of them. Fifth, former Paolian leaders contacted purged veteran cadres in the county to make common cause with them in their opposition to Shao Wen.[21]

Revival of the Liansi-Paolian Conflicts

Under these circumstances, a new political struggle emerged in Feng County. One force consisted of Paolian members persecuted during the recent suppression campaigns, along with veteran cadres; the other force consisted of officers and functionaries in the PAD network in the county, along with Liansi activists. These struggles were not limited to bureaucratic infighting and furious arguments in meetings of the revolutionary committee. They also resulted in the revival of violent clashes in work units and rural communes.

The animosities broke into the open in revolutionary committee meetings to discuss how to carry out the Criticize Lin Biao and Confucius campaign. Zhang Liansheng and other former Paolian leaders participated in the first of these conferences in February. The county's leaders insisted that the campaign was an abstract ideological campaign, while Zhang and his colleagues argued that it should be focused on criticizing the Lin Biao line in the army and the mistakes committed by the party's leaders in carrying out the May 16 elements investigations. When Paolian sympathizers made their speeches, they were interrupted, shouted down, and even dragged out of the conference. Paolian leaders were forbidden from reading party documents pertaining to the campaign. During small group meetings, Paolian leaders repeatedly insisted that Shao Wen attend to hear their complaints, but they were refused. In protest, Paolian members withdrew from the conference. The meetings concluded after Shao made a brief appearance and closed the proceedings with a short speech.[22]

20. Ibid.
21. Zhang Liansheng notebooks.
22. Ibid.

Stymied in officially sanctioned meetings, Paolian leaders decided to organize themselves to carry out the Criticize Lin and Confucius campaign independently in various work units and villages. They contacted other victims in neighboring counties and planned a mass rally to be held on March 3. They put up wall posters to publicize the event in the county seat and selected speakers, including several veteran cadres who joined with them in their effort. They went to the county headquarters to invite the county's leaders to attend the rally, but the county leaders charged that the meeting was illegal and refused.

The rally was held at the county's sports field, with more than two thousand people in attendance. It went off without incident, and the organizers planned for another rally one week later. They decided to mobilize cadres and ordinary citizens, compiled evidence for more pointed criticisms of wrongdoing in the county, and set up a publicity group to spread their findings. The second rally was held, once again at the county sports field.[23]

The county's leaders and former members of Liansi felt threatened by this campaign, because it was clearly aimed at them. Their supporters began to fight back. Wall posters appeared that insisted upon party committee leadership of the Criticize Lin Biao and Confucius campaign. At the Feng County Middle School and cotton mill, Liansi leaders blocked the exits to prevent Paolian members from attending the rallies. Some rural communes forbade farmers to travel to the county seat on the days of the rallies, using commune broadcasting networks to warn against attendance. Other commune leaders destroyed dissident handbills. Some Paolian activists were driven out of factories by force when they arrived to spread the news.

The most serious incident took place in the county seat on March 11. A furious argument about how the Criticize Lin campaign should be conducted broke out between Liansi and Paolian activists in the county's transport team. That same evening, a meeting of Paolian activists was attacked by around one hundred armed Liansi members from the Beidianzi production brigade, who broke in and assaulted the participants. Most escaped, but three Paolian leaders were captured and beaten as they were dragged around the county seat, finally being dumped at the town's north gate.[24]

Paolian supporters publicized the incident to discredit the county's leaders. They organized a delegation to visit the hospitalized victims, and they had the

23. Ibid.
24. Ibid.

most heavily wounded one transported by ambulance to Xuzhou on March 15 to dramatize their report to prefecture officials about the violence being meted out to them in the county. They issued demands for an investigation of the incident, an interview with prefecture leaders, and payment for medical care. They learned the next day that the prefecture was sending a team to Feng County to investigate. To win support from the investigation team and the public, and to put pressure on the county leaders, Paolian held a third mass rally to criticize Lin Biao and Confucius in the county on March 17. The county leaders still refused to meet with the group or acknowledge their complaints.

Next, Paolian planned another mass meeting for March 21, this time around the theme of "Welcoming the Feng County Petitioners Group's Return." It then created a formal organization in the name of the petitioners' group and set up offices in the first floor of the county guesthouse. That afternoon, two junior county leaders came to the guesthouse and told the petitioners that the county authorities welcomed their return to the county, but they should not occupy rooms at the guesthouse and instead return to their jobs and concentrate on production. The junior leaders promised to relay their request for a meeting with the county's senior leaders.

Despite these half-hearted attempts to placate the petitioners, the county's leaders did nothing to restrain their supporters in Liansi. When complaints were lodged with the county seat's party secretary about the violent attacks of March 11, he told the aggrieved parties that they should not have provoked an argument. Liansi members continued to pull down petitioners' wall posters. Liansi activists from Malou Commune beat up Zhang Liansheng at the entrance to the county guesthouse, but when he went to the county headquarters to complain, Shao Wen refused to meet. On March 24, farmers from several communes assembled at the county guesthouse to seize the petitioners inside and expel the group. One Paolian leader was beaten up, and several were kidnapped. Shao expressed little concern when he was informed of the event. Similar incidents occurred across the county in March, and supporters of the power structure were openly making speeches and putting up wall posters that attacked Paolian and defended the party committee. In one Songlou Commune production brigade, the party secretary announced that the brigade militia should get together for dinner and drinks each evening, and then go on patrol in the village. If they found someone "holding a black meeting" or "conducting underground investigations," they should teach them a lesson and would not be held responsible even if they beat someone to death.[25]

At end of March, the new prefecture leaders ordered the Feng County party committee to address the complaints of the petitioners. Under direct orders, the county's leaders agreed to talk with Paolian leaders in April 1974 but continued to resist their claims. Paolian considered the local problems to be a "fundamental one of political line," demanding that the county leaders acknowledge their errors and finally handle the petitioners' appeals regarding job assignments, delayed wage payments, and reimbursement for travel costs. The county leaders, in contrast, argued that the petitioners' activities "disrupted the Criticize Lin and Confucius campaign," "disrupted industry and agriculture," and "rekindled factional animosities" across the county. For them, the top priority was to strengthen party leadership.[26]

For Zhang Liansheng, the only positive result of the early April discussions was that the county authorities agreed to provide him with an official letter in support of his medical treatment in Xuzhou and Nanjing, along with a cash subsidy for his expenses. They may have calculated that having Zhang leave the county would relieve the pressure on them by depriving the petitioners of one of their most active organizers. Whatever their intentions, Zhang did need medical attention and funds. He suffered from chronic bronchitis and psychosomatic symptoms due to his torture in detention during the May 16 elements investigations. He could not afford medical treatment on his own. Originally from a rural household, his status changed from student back to farmer after he completed high school back in 1966. After receiving grain rations from his production team, he had almost no cash income. Commune medical insurance and other benefits were very modest. After Zhang was selected as a member of the county revolutionary committee in 1969, he was eligible for small daily cash subsidy as a part-time rural cadre, but without the other benefits provided to full-time staff on the state payroll. The subsidy amounted to around twenty yuan per month, after deductions for Sundays. Half the subsidy had to be paid to his production brigade in compensation for missed labor days and to pay for his basic grain rations. The subsidy was suspended, however, when Zhang fled his case investigation study class to engage in the petition campaign. Medical costs were completely beyond his means.[27]

25. Ibid.
26. Shao Limin notebooks.
27. Zhang Liansheng interview.

Upheaval in Nanjing

On April 9, Zhang traveled to Xuzhou for medical treatment, where he en-
countered large numbers of petitioners from around the prefecture. They told
him that Nanjing was filled with petition delegations from across the province
and that the new provincial leaders, the veteran civilian cadres Peng Chong
and Xu Jiatun, were cooperating with the petitioners and former rebel leaders
to push back against the remaining military officers in the provincial government. Several thousand Nanjing residents who had been expelled from the
city under military rule had poured back into Nanjing and were engaged in a
wall poster campaign and daily street protests.[28] Excited by this news, and
reasoning that better medical care was available in Nanjing, Zhang and several
other petitioners from Feng County went to Nanjing on April 18.

Over the next few days, the petitioners moved around the city to familiarize
themselves with the burgeoning petitioners' campaign in the city and the civilian leaders' sympathetic response. They sent a telegram back to the county to
invite key Paolian leaders to come to Nanjing and join the activities of the
Xuzhou Prefecture petition delegation. On April 23, the group staged a demonstration at the offices of *New China Daily* (*Xinhua ribao*), the party newspaper that had earlier published an article that praised Xuzhou as an "advanced
model" for its conduct of the cleansing campaigns. The chief editor acknowledged the error and promised that the paper would not publish anything else
about the region without the permission of the petitioners' delegation. The
next day, more Paolian leaders arrived in Nanjing to join their activities, and
they went back to the newspaper's offices to investigate the sources for two
positive articles about Feng County that were published back in October and
November 1973.[29]

On April 28, the provincial leaders Wu Dasheng and Peng Chong, and the
Xuzhou prefecture leaders Hu Hong and Guan Yaoting met with the Xuzhou
region petitioners at the Jiangsu Hotel. Zhang Liansheng and other Feng
County petitioners attended. After discussing the situation in the prefecture,
the province and prefecture leaders agreed that they would summon the party
leaders of the eight counties to join in their negotiations in Nanjing and that
petitioners from each county should send two representatives to participate
in the negotiations over their grievances.

28. As described in Dong and Walder, "Nanjing's 'Second Cultural Revolution' of 1974."
29. Zhang Liansheng notebooks.

At end of April, several thousand former Nanjing residents, who had been expelled from the city during the recent persecution campaigns, blocked the rail lines at the main Nanjing station. Beijing sent urgent telephone instructions to the Jiangsu leadership demanding that the protests be resolved and rail transportation be restored. A few days later, they issued a central document that reiterated the telephone instructions. Wu Dasheng, a PLA subordinate of Xu Shiyou and still the top provincial leader at this point in time, was criticized by name.[30]

The meetings of the province and prefecture leaders with the petitioners from Xuzhou's counties took place shortly after this dramatic event. They met three times from May 4 to May 8, along with top party officials from the province, prefecture, and counties, including Shao Wen and Dong Hongzhi, and more than sixty petitioners from the eight counties and Xuzhou.

The petitioners charged that the former military leaders of Xuzhou violated the Ninth Party Congress decisions, set up power structures based on factionalism, labeled more than 5,000 people in the prefecture as counterrevolutionaries and more than 100,000 people as May 16 elements. When their turn came, the Feng County petitioners reported that more than five hundred people in the county had been charged as May 16 elements, and more than two hundred had died under interrogation. They focused particularly on one case in Shahe Commune, where a large group of people were framed as members of an "underground anticommunist regiment," during which twelve people were tortured to death. They criticized the local leaders' unwillingness to handle their complaints about this case. Under pressure from the new provincial and prefectural civilian leaders, Shao Wen had no choice but to make a self-criticism. He did so, but he argued that this case was handled under direct orders from the previous prefecture authorities.

Petitioners from other places made similar complaints. In the course of these meetings, the provincial and prefectural leaders—including in one meeting Jiangsu's top party official, Peng Chong—expressed support for the petitioners' demands. Local PAD officials admitted that most of the complaints were based in fact. They promised to respond to the complaints and properly handle problems left over from the previous period.[31]

---

30. Ibid., and Dong and Walder, "Nanjing's 'Second Cultural Revolution' of 1974."

31. Zhang Liansheng notebooks; and Xuzhou diqu fu ning shangfang tuan, "Jiefa pipan Xuzhou diqu wenti huiyi jiyao zhiyi," "Jiefa pipan Xuzhou diqu wenti huiyi jiyao zhier," and "Jiefa

In addition to these conferences with the entire Xuzhou delegation, the Feng County petitioners met several times individually with provincial and prefectural leaders, and in each case these leaders responded positively to their complaints. At a May 4 meeting at the provincial guesthouse, Hu Hong responded to reports of beatings in Feng County by saying that the perpetrators would be punished, especially if they were PAD officers. At a May 6 meeting with Hu and Shao Wen, the two leaders announced measures to stop the beatings and other efforts to appease petitioners in Feng County. At a May 7 meeting, Shao and Dong Hongzhi stated that they agreed with these measures, but they hesitated to publicize them in the county unless they were ordered to do so by the prefecture. And on May 9, in a meeting with Hu, Zhang Liansheng and his comrades demanded that Shao and Dong be sent to the provincial party school, where the Feng County petitioner delegation was stationed, to hear the masses' criticisms, and that the recently appointed deputy party secretary of the county, Yin Shibin, come to Nanjing to participate in their discussions. Hu dissuaded them, arguing that Shao seemed to have changed his attitude and that the petitioners should not insist on further measures after their specific complaints have been addressed.

Yin Shibin did come to Nanjing shortly afterward, but Shao refused to let him meet with the petitioners, who expressed their discontent in a complaint to Hu Hong. On May 10, Hu met with the petitioners and repeated what he had said earlier. On May 11, Hu met with the county's leaders and the petitioners, asking them to return to Feng County and to try to stabilize the situation. He sent Shao and three petitioners back to the county in one car. During the trip home, Zhang told Shao that "currently the key problem is for you to change your stance." Shao replied, "You have the same problem."[32]

After returning to the county, the Paolian leaders felt that Shao was dragging his feet in halting the countermovement against the petitioners' activities. They met with Shao several times in mid-May, demanding that he call a cadre conference and a mass rally. Shao argued that Liansi leaders would be provoked by such measures and that if a mass rally was held, chaos might result. It is possible that he felt that the decisions reached in Nanjing should be implemented gradually to prevent a backlash, but Paolian interpreted his stance as an unwillingness to carry out agreements. Shao did convene a cadre conference

pipan Xuzhou diqu wenti huiyi jiyao zhisan" (Minutes of the exposure and criticism meeting about the Xuzhou Prefecture problem, nos. 1–3), May 14, 1974.

32. Zhang Liansheng notebooks.

to hear a broadcast from Nanjing regarding criticisms of the recent investigation campaigns, but he did not organize a mass rally. A number of commune leaders who attended the conference minimized the significance of the criticisms. They argued that the criticism of the provincial leaders had little relevance to Feng County, and in any case, they had at worst gone too far in implementing a correct policy; they had not implemented an incorrect policy. They continued to insist that the petitioners were troublemakers who should be resisted firmly, and if they persisted, they should fight back.

Frustrated by what they perceived as stonewalling by the county power structure, Paolian leaders sent another delegation to Nanjing, including Zhang, to report the situation to the provincial leaders. More than forty new local petitioners accompanied them. Over the next two weeks, they met several times with prefecture leaders in Nanjing and Xuzhou to report on local officials' refusal to accept the agreements reached in Nanjing. They asked that the prefecture suspend Shao from his post, that the province summon him to Nanjing, and that new civilian cadres be sent to Feng County to implement the new policies. They requested that the original revolutionary committees at all levels (that is, before the purges of Paolian members carried out by Shao) be restored. They also requested that all cadres suspended from their posts be assembled in a conference to reveal the injustices done to them.

While Paolian's leaders were presenting their new petition in Nanjing, Liansi leaders were continuing their resistance back in the county. Paolian leaders in Shizhai and Malou Communes were beaten up by Liansi members. Liansi and their cadre supporters staged their own rallies and defended the military officers Wu Dasheng and Shao Wen from the criticisms lodged against them. They openly denounced recent *New China Daily* editorials as "poisonous weeds" and denounced policy shifts in Nanjing as "tricks" by a handful of provincial leaders who were trying to "pit the masses against one another." This amounted to a budding countermovement by the beneficiaries of military rule in the county against recent policy shifts by civilian provincial leaders. Paolian's leaders reported these developments to the provincial authorities.

Despite these provocations, prefecture leaders continued to counsel reconciliation. They clearly wanted to muffle local conflicts and play a longer game and were unwilling to sack Shao and make decisive moves against budding resistance by Liansi and the PAD hierarchy in the county. They counseled moderation in meetings with Paolian petitioners and stated a desire to work out problems in meetings held in Xuzhou, repeating that "change will not come overnight." In Nanjing, the Xuzhou petitioners were informed in a meeting that the province's leaders were preoccupied with sorting out the demands of the many thousands of petitioners who had been expelled from the city, and they could no longer devote attention to their demands. It was time for them to return home.

On May 31, the Feng County petitioners met with Hu Hong at the provincial guesthouse in Nanjing. He told them that it was now the busiest season for agriculture, and the political problems raised in the petitions should be set aside for the time being. The abuses could only be addressed gradually, step by step. Problems at the provincial level should be rectified first, followed by the prefecture, and then ending with the counties. The process would take time and the petitioners should not demand an immediate resolution. The next day the petitioners met with Hu once again, and he told them that they should continue to document their charges carefully. Whether Shao would be suspended from his post and replaced, and whether he turned out to be a follower of the "Lin Biao line," depended on further investigation. Ultimately the party center would rule on these issues. "You asked me to express my opinion," Hu said, "but it is not appropriate for me to express my personal opinions before the prefecture's standing committee of the party makes a decision." The Feng County petitioners decided to return home, leaving four petitioners in Nanjing to report on further developments in the provincial capital. On June 3, they boarded trains for home.[33]

Stalemate in the County

The shift in Jiangsu's political tides, which favored the petitioners' cause and ultimately the Paolian faction, had the seemingly paradoxical effect of sharpening local conflicts and reviving the factional animosities between Liansi and Paolian. From early June through October 1974, the conflicts became sharper, and the two sides organized.

During June, rural communes organized armed patrols to "dissuade" petitioners by frightening them into silence and inactivity. They declared that petition delegations violated central document no. 12, which forbade the restoration of mass organizations, and were therefore illegal.[34] One commune leader

33. Zhang Liansheng notebooks; Zhang Liansheng interviews.
34. Zhonggong zhongyang, "Guanyu zai pi Lin pi Kong yundong zhong jige wenti de dafu" (Responses to certain questions that have arisen in the Criticize Lin Biao and Confucius campaign), Zhongfa [74], no. 12, April 10, 1974.

gave a speech in which he declared that recent attacks on military officials in the province and prefecture were in violation of central policy and would ultimately need to be resolved by Beijing. In the meantime, he said, the petitioners should be resisted. Liansi's Li Zongzhou and Shao Limin convened a meeting in the county guesthouse where they advocated learning from Suzhou's example, where the local militia cracked down hard on petitioners and stabilized order. Liansi-inspired wall posters appeared in the county that argued that the restoration of former civilian cadres to leading positions was a step backward and undermined the campaign to criticize Lin Biao and Confucius.[35]

Paolian activists intensified their contacts with grassroots members and also with veteran cadres who had sided with them in the past and who were still awaiting new posts. They tread carefully, because the central document had explicitly repudiated petitioner delegations and fighting teams during the Lin Biao and Confucius campaign. Some advocated disbanding their petitioners' delegation, but they decided to wait for further developments.[36]

In July, Paolian organized two rallies, but both were disrupted by Liansi. More wall posters attacked Paolian-affiliated veteran cadres. At a July 13 meeting convened by the county authorities of former participants of the May 7 Cadre School study classes, Liansi members broke in and beat up Paolian members, including Zhang Liansheng. County officials at the scene did nothing to stop them. In late July, Shao Wen spoke at a meeting of county cadres and denounced petitioners who left work to petition. "These were instances of class struggle," he argued, "and violations of discipline." He called for mobilizing the masses to criticize and expose them.[37] Another leader presented statistics to show that the petitioners were harming the economy.[38]

These trends continued in August and into the early fall. Shao and his supporters were encouraged by mid-August instructions issued from Beijing to the Xuzhou Prefecture authorities. The directives focused on disruptive events that continued in the cities of Xuzhou and Lianyungang. It ordered the pre-

35. Zhang Liansheng notebooks.

36. Ibid.

37. Zhonggong Feng xian weiyuanhui, "Shao Wen tongzhi zai xian nongcun sanji ganbu huiyi shang de jianghua, jianjue guanche luoshi zhongyang 21 hao wenjian, duoqu pi Lin pi Kong he quan nian nongye shengchan xin shengli" (Comrade Shao Wen's speech at the county's three-level rural cadre conference, resolutely carry out central document no. 21, strive for new victories in the Criticize Lin Biao and Confucius Campaign and annual agricultural production), July 29, 1974.

38. Shao Limin notebooks.

fectural authorities to disband mass organizations that were formed in the name of "revolutionary workers" and a "Criticize Lin Biao and Confucius Liaison Station" because they violated central policy. It ordered an end to all mobilization across work organizations and occupational lines, and people who had left work for petitioning were to return as soon as possible. Publication of newssheets was deemed illegal and should be stopped; instigators of these activities behind the scenes should be exposed and punished. All the cross-occupation and cross-region factional communications should be forbidden. All property that these groups seized should be returned, and all buildings that they occupied should be surrendered.[39] This central directive was a response to disorders that were far more severe than anything in Feng County at the time, but the county authorities took advantage of them to press their case against Paolian and the veteran cadres who sided with them. The county suspended wage payments and grain rations to the petitioners and ignored their subsequent complaints.

39. Zhonggong Jiangsu sheng weiyuanhui, "Zhonggong Jiangsu shengwei dianhua zhishi" (Telephone instructions from Jiangsu provincial party committee), August 14, 1974.

8

The Final Struggle

THE LOCAL STANDOFF was broken in the last three months of 1974. At a central party work conference in mid-October, Wang Hongwen and Zhang Chunqiao, ranking central leaders associated with the radical group that had supported Mao in launching the Cultural Revolution, harshly criticized the crackdown against May 16 elements in Jiangsu Province. This was part of their drive to push military officers out of revolutionary committees in the wake of Lin Biao's purge. It was also due to their perception that the crackdowns were part of a military effort to persecute genuine rebel groups who had spearheaded the mass movements that they had sponsored back in 1967.

The veteran cadres who now headed Jiangsu immediately relayed these instructions to party committees across the province, because it helped them push out lingering army control over civilian administration. The remaining military officers in Jiangsu's leadership, headed by Wu Dasheng, lost their posts in mid-November, and the veteran civilian cadre Peng Chong was appointed first party secretary of the province and head of its revolutionary committee.[1] On December 30, the Jiangsu party committee and the Jiangsu Military District jointly ordered all military personnel working in civilian governments to return to their military units.[2]

These changes reverberated downward through the prefecture and into the county. Xuzhou Military Subdistrict commander Chai Rongsheng, head of the local PADs, had already been transferred out of the prefecture the previous

1. Dong and Walder, "Nanjing's 'Second Cultural Revolution' of 1974."

2. Jiangsu sheng dang'an ju, ed., *Jiangsu sheng dashiji (1949–1985)* (Jiangsu Province chronology [1949–1985]) (Nanjing: Jiangsu renmin chubanshe, 1988), p. 329.

February. Hu Hong and the other veteran cadres consolidated their dominance over his successor in the military subdistrict.[3]

In December 1974, Shao Wen was transferred far away from Feng County. His new post would be political commissar of the PAD in Haimen County, Nantong Prefecture, in the far southeastern corner of Jiangsu Province. The veteran civilian cadre, Yin Shibin, was promoted to succeed him as top county leader. Two other veteran cadres, Xu Zhendong and Lu Shaoshi, who were transferred in shortly after Yin, respectively, from positions in Xuzhou and Donghai County, became the number two and number three leaders in the county.[4]

One would think that Shao Wen's removal and the appointment of an entirely new leading group would bring a dramatic shift in local politics, but these outsiders presided over political structures that had been filled with PAD and Liansi loyalists during Shao's reign.[5] These political structures were the only way for them to exercise their authority, so it was not possible for them to decisively reverse past policies without causing disruptions in the county's party committee and revolutionary committee. They had to tread carefully.

Prior to Shao's removal, not much had been done about Paolian's grievances against Liansi and the PAD officers riddled throughout the county power structures. And not much changed in the first months afterward. Perhaps sensing that they were sitting atop a political powder keg, or perhaps being unfamiliar with the specifics of the county's recent political history, the new county leaders seemed indifferent to Paolian's pleas and the demands of the petitioners. This seeming indifference frustrated Paolian's leaders, who expected

3. In February 1974, Hu Hong replaced Chai Rongsheng as chairman of the Xuzhou Prefecture revolutionary committee and as the prefecture's party secretary, and in October Chai became deputy commander of the Jiangsu Military District. *Xuzhou shi zuzhishi ziliao*, pp. 291–292 and 486–487.

4. *Feng xian zuzhishi ziliao*, p. 145; *Xuzhou shi zuzhishi ziliao*, p. 301; and Zhang Liansheng interview.

5. Zhang Liansheng notebooks; Li Zhi, "Di shiyici luxian douzheng zhong jingyan jiaoxun xiaojie" (A preliminary summary of lessons learned from experience during the eleventh line struggle), February 1978; Feng xian nongji chang; "Guanyu Zhang Haiqing de jiaodai jiefa zonghe cailiao" (On Zhang Haiqing's comprehensive confession and exposure materials), December 24, 1976; Zhonggong Feng xian weiyuanhui, "Guanyu He Quanfu deng shiba wei tongzhi zhiwu renmian tongzhi" (Notice on the appointment and removal of He Quanfu and 17 other comrades), October 3, 1974, Zhonggong Fengxian weiyuanhui, "Guanyu Song Chuanhe deng tongzhi zhiwu renmian wenti de tongzhi" (Notice on the appointment and removal of Song Chuanhe and other comrades), February 15, 1974.

to be actively supported in their cause in the same way that Shao had earlier promoted Liansi's. This is the primary reason why, after these leaders were later attacked by Liansi at the end of 1975 and early 1976, Paolian did not actively defend them.[6]

The "Overall Rectification" of 1975

The local political situation shifted decisively in the middle of 1975. This was due to yet another reversal in the ever-fluctuating politics of 1970s China. In early 1975, Deng Xiaoping, one of the primary targets of the Cultural Revolution along with Liu Shaoqi, who had died in detention in 1969, was restored to a leading position in Beijing. Mao Zedong had soured on the political disorders inadvertently stimulated by the Criticism of Lin Biao and Confucius campaign. He charged Deng with re-establishing stability and political unity, and with reviving a lagging economy. Deng set about energetically to enact a program of "overall rectification" (*quanmian zhengdun*).

On March 5, the central authorities issued a document that called for the strengthening of the railway system.[7] It had major implications for the political situation in Xuzhou, and by extension Feng County, because one of the most deeply disrupted sectors of the railway system was at the major terminus in Xuzhou, which was repeatedly disrupted by continued factional conflict between the Kick faction and local authorities. The minister of railways and Jiangsu's provincial authorities jointly formed a work team to go to Xuzhou and sort out its chronic factional conflicts. Xuzhou was one of the most deeply disrupted cities in China at the time, its factional warfare having been rekindled the previous year in ways that continued to disrupt railway traffic across eastern China. Xuzhou would be a model "test point" of Deng Xiaoping's overall rectification, and the work team adopted strong measures to get to the bottom of local conflicts and root them out once and for all.

The work team announced that it would systematically address the complaints of the Kick faction's cadres and workers who were persecuted as alleged May 16 elements and, at the same time, moved decisively to restore order in the railway system. It also moved against the most disruptive leaders in each

---

6. Zhang Liansheng interview.

7. Zhonggong zhongyang, "Guanyu jiaqiang tielu gongzuo de jueding" (Decision on strengthening railway work), Zhongfa [75], no. 9, March 5, 1975.

faction. A notoriously militant Kick faction leader was arrested, along with a Support faction militant. The Kick leader was charged and sentenced for organizing public demonstrations and disrupting production. The Support leader suffered the same fate for "running an underground factory" and "sabotaging the socialist economy." The work team went into the workplaces that had the most severe factional conflicts and completely reorganized their leading bodies, removing those who pushed factional agendas and replacing them with more moderate figures. Their leading bodies had earlier been filled with Support faction activists, and the work team replaced them with veteran cadres who had lost their posts during the Cultural Revolution. These measures, taken over a two-month period, seemed to have their intended effects, and the disruptions of the railway system ended. On June 2, 1975, the central authorities issued another central document that praised the efforts of the Xuzhou work team and offered it as a model for curtailing stubborn factional conflict elsewhere in China. The key point in the document was the imperative to remove leaders at all levels who acted according to factional allegiances and thereby sabotaged social order and economic activity.[8]

This document marked a starting point for breaking the logjam of factional animosities embedded in local power structures across China. On June 4, the central authorities issued a similar set of orders for these measures to be carried out in the steel industry.[9] On July 17, they issued an order that faction members who recently had been rushed into party membership and leadership positions should be re-examined for suitability and removed from leading bodies if found to be unqualified.[10] On the same day, they also issued a document calling for a national focus on fulfilling industrial production plans in the coming year and distributed a speech by Deng Xiaoping in which he called for

8. Zhonggong zhongyang, "Pizhuan 'zhonggong Jiangsu shengwei guanyu Xuzhou diqu guanche zhixing zhongyang 9 hao wenjian de qingkuang xiang zhonggong zhongyang, guowuyuan de baogao'" (Relaying with instructions "Report to the Central Committee and State Council by the Jiangsu provincial party committee on the thorough implementation of central document no. 9 in Xuzhou Prefecture"), Zhongfa [75], no. 12, June 2, 1975.

9. Zhonggong zhongyang, "Guanyu nuli wancheng quannian gangtie shengchan jihua de pishi" (Instructions on striving to complete the annual production plan for iron and steel), Zhongfa [75], no. 13, June 4, 1975.

10. Zhonggong zhongyang, "Zhuanfa Zhejiang shengwei 'Guanyu zhengque chuli tuji fazhan de dangyuan he tiba de ganbu de qingshi baogao'" (Circulating Zhejiang provincial party committee's "On the correct handling of those who were rushed into party membership and promoted as cadres"), Zhongfa [75], no. 16, July 17, 1975.

further rectification of the military leadership at all levels to eliminate the negative influence of the errors they had made in "support the left" interventions.[11] Through the very end of 1975, Deng Xiaoping's "overall rectification" was the guideline for all party work nationwide, and Deng became associated with a vigorous effort to stem factional conflict, suppress disruptive activists, and restoring order and economic progress.

These moves did not have much impact on the stalemate in Feng County until the middle of the year. Little progress was made in addressing the petitioners' grievances, and Liansi members and their civilian cadre allies remained firmly entrenched in positions of power throughout the county. With the conclusion of the rectification carried out by the Xuzhou work team, however, the situation began to change, and the provincial authorities began to focus on the political problems in counties, which in many ways mirrored those in Xuzhou.

In early May, the provincial authorities convened a Xuhai Region Theoretical Study Class (*Xuhai diqu lilun xuexi ban*) in Nanjing. This was yet another edition of the "study class" used repeatedly over the years to reconcile political strife. A total of 163 participants were ordered to the class, including standing committee members of both party committees and revolutionary committees at the prefecture and county levels, and a large number of commune party secretaries and heads of prefecture and county government departments. Most of the members of revolutionary committees who were assigned to the class were former leaders of mass factions.[12]

The study class participants from Feng County included the county's deputy party secretary Xu Zhendong, two members of the county's party standing committee who were Liansi supporters, and seven individuals who were affiliated with Liansi or Paolian. Five of these were former Liansi leaders who now held positions as heads of communes or government departments. Two were affiliated with Paolian and had lost their initial positions under the original revolutionary committee. One of the Paolian participants was Zhang Liansheng. One of the Liansi participants was Shao Limin, a former

---

11. Zhonggong zhongyang, "Zhuanfa guowuyuan 'Guanyu jinnian shangban nian gongye shengchan qingkuang de baogao'" (Relaying the State Council's "Report on the production situation during the first half of this year"), Zhongfa [75], no. 17, July 17, 1975; Zhonggong zhongyang, "Pizhuan Deng Xiaoping zai zhongyang junwei kuoda huiyi shang de jianghua" (Relaying Deng Xiaoping's speech at the enlarged Central Military Commission conference), July 15, 1975.

12. Zhang Liansheng notebooks.

county hardware factory worker who was now deputy head of the county industrial bureau.[13]

The study class did not go well for Liansi members, because they had been
a core part of the power structures that carried out the cleansing campaigns.
Under the sponsorship of Shao Wen, they had been rushed into party membership and leadership positions as a result of their factional activities. They
were forced to confess their actions during the coercive investigations of alleged May 16 elements and in a series of violent events across the county. They
confessed to extracting confessions under torture, to factional bias, and to violations of central policy. They confessed to attacking and intimidating petitioners. They confessed to kidnapping Zhang and other Paolian leaders. They
confessed to blindly following Shao in his mistaken line. They confessed that
they were motivated by a desire for personal advantage. They pledged to drop
their factional viewpoints and reform their thoughts. At the same time, the
leaders of the study group gave thinly veiled warnings to Paolian members that
they should not take these changes as an opportunity to continue to pursue
their grievances more actively. Both factions, they stressed, must stop their
factional activity and drop their factional viewpoints. This was party policy,
and both sides must respect the party's authority.[14]

Zhang attended most of the rallies and small group discussions during the
study class, but he was not required to make a self-criticism or write a summary of what he had learned. This reflected the trust and sympathy that he
enjoyed with the current prefecture and county leaders. One side benefit for
him was that he was permitted to frequently consult doctors in the provincial
medical hospital for treatment during his three-month stay in Nanjing.[15]

Finally, on the morning of July 29, 1975, Peng Chong and other provincial
leaders gave speeches at the final session of the study class. They reminded the
participants that they should drop factionalism, maintain party discipline, fully
investigate and correct all false charges, and reconcile former conflicts. The
participants boarded trains back to Xuzhou that night.[16]

In August, after the conclusion of the study class in Nanjing, the "overall
rectification" was extended into Feng County. The main objectives were to
reorganize leadership at all levels to reduce factionalism, redress false charges

13. Shao Limin notebooks; and Zhang Liansheng notebooks.
14. Zhang Liansheng notebooks.
15. Zhang Liansheng interview.
16. Ibid.

in the recent campaigns and compensate the victims, and promote industrial and agricultural production. The county leaders established a four-hundred-person "theoretical study work team" (*lilun xuexi gongzuo dui*). It included large numbers of Paolian leaders who had been members of the revolutionary committee when it was first formed but who were subsequently purged, and many Paolian leaders and local cadres who had been subjected to the investigation campaigns. The purpose of the work team was to rehabilitate these individuals and prepare them for assignment to new leadership positions.[17]

In September, the county's party standing committee was reshuffled yet again. Two new civilian cadres from outside were transferred in as members of the standing committee, along with a model "educated youth" from Nanjing who had been sent down to Feng County back in 1968. Simultaneously, four civilian cadres were appointed to the standing committee of the county revolutionary committee. The four members of the party standing committee who had been appointed by the military were now outnumbered by the six recent appointees.[18] At the first meeting of the new party committee in early September, resolving the problem of persistent factionalism at lower levels was designated as the primary task for the coming months.[19]

On September 10, the county authorities, at long last, publicly redressed the cases of the close to seven hundred victims of the May 16 elements investigations. Cadres purged during the campaign were assigned to new jobs. Those who had been assigned to bad jobs as punishment were given new ones. The leadership of various units under the county government was also assessed to replace unqualified appointees with those who were more capable.[20] The staff offices under the revolutionary committee were abolished and the former government bureaus were restored. In the course of these changes, a number of prominent leaders of the Liansi faction (including Li Zongzhou, Li Peng, Bai Hexiu, and Shao Limin) lost their posts, while veteran cadres were restored to positions in the new administrative deparments.[21] In October, the

17. Zhang Liansheng notebooks; and Zhang Liansheng interview.

18. *Zhonggong Feng xian zuzhishi ziliao*, pp. 145 and 249; and Zhang Liansheng interview.

19. Zhonggong Feng xian weiyuanhui, "Diwei fuze tongzhi zai Zhonggong Feng xian xianwei changwei huiyi shang de zhishi" (The prefecture leaders' directives at the county party standing committee meeting), September 4, 1975.

20. *Zhonggong Feng xian difangshi dashiji*, p. 257.

21. *Feng xian zuzhishi ziliao*, pp. 147, 149–152, and 251–255; and Zhonggong Feng xian weiyuanhui, "Guanyu Qin Yuxuan deng san tongzhi zhiwu renmian de tongzhi" (Notice on the appointment and removal of Qin Yuxuan and two other comrades), November 27, 1975.

county authorities set up a "Learn from Dazhai in Agriculture Office," which sent work teams into communes in an effort to effect similar rectifications in the leadership of communes and production brigades. Zhang Liansheng and other participants in the theoretical study work team became members of the new work team.[22]

In the course of these actions, the county authorities issued a series of orders. One of them redressed the grievances of the victims of the May 16 elements investigations.[23] Another voided the sentences of Paolian members framed in the false gang rape case.[24] Yet another ordered financial compensation to those who were assigned to labor reform, fired, or imprisoned in 1971 and 1972.[25] Addressing the problem of entrenched PAD and Liansi power in the rural communes, they ordered all commune PAD personnel who were earlier appointed as commune party secretaries or vice-secretaries to be removed from their posts.[26]

Through these decisive moves, with the full support of provincial and prefectural leaders, the veteran cadres who now led the county consolidated their political control. But the "overall rectification" carried out under Deng Xiaoping's energetic leadership throughout 1975 left aggrieved parties in its wake. People at all levels who had lost their positions or had been transferred to lesser ones were unhappy with the latest shift in political winds, in particular Liansi members and officials in the PADs rural networks.

Liansi Fights Back

Mao Zedong's support for Deng Xiaoping's "overall rectification" was short-lived. He became convinced that Deng was essentially reversing what he still considered to be the "positive accomplishments" of the Cultural Revolution. The systematic elimination of former rebels from leadership positions and

---

22. Zhang Liansheng interview.

23. *Jiangsu sheng Feng xian zhi*, p. 30; and *Zhonggong Feng xian difangshi dashiji*, p. 257

24. "Jiangsu sheng Xuzhou diqu zhongji renmin fayuan xingshi panjue shu," September 24, 1975.

25. Zhonggong Feng xian weiyuanhui, "Guanyu jiejue qingcha yundong zhong liangshi gongying wenti de tongzhi" (Notice on how to resolve the problems regarding victims' grain rations during the investigation campaign), October 15, 1975.

26. Zhonggong Feng xian weiyuanhui, "Guanyu gongshe wuzhuangbu ganbu renzhi wenti de tongzhi" (Notice regarding the question of offices held by commune People's Armed Department cadres), December 18, 1975.

their replacement by veteran cadres who had been overthrown earlier in the Cultural Revolution appeared to repudiate the entire episode. Mao was ultimately persuaded that Deng had gone too far, and as he came under fire near the end of 1975, the rectification campaigns stalled. Instead, a new campaign was initiated during December 1975 to push back against "rightist" tendencies that restored too much of the status quo ante. The campaign intensified with the issuance of the first central document of 1976, which took away Deng's control over the rectification process and launched a national criticism campaign against "rightist restorationism." This culminated in the official expulsion of Deng Xiaoping from all of his party and government posts in April, as a consequence of the massive demonstrations in Tiananmen Square on April 4 and 5.[27] There followed a campaign to "Criticize Deng" for his "rightist counterattack to reverse verdicts."[28]

Taking advantage of the latest in this series of reversals emanating from Beijing, Liansi's leaders and Liansi-affiliated cadres who had been pushed aside as a result of Deng's rectification policies sprung into action in February 1976. The new shift in central policy was a godsend, tailor-made to pave the way for their vindication, and permitting *them* to reverse the verdicts that were issued against them in 1975. They targeted the veteran cadres who had taken power the previous year, after the departure of Shao Wen, and also those who were subsequently put into leadership positions at all levels by them as they rectified the county's power structures.

Trouble began on February 22, 1976, when the county authorities held a conference of the revolutionary committee and relayed the central documents that signaled the latest shift in the party's political line. At these sessions, a series of former Liansi leaders, including Bai Hexiu, Li Zongzhou, Shao Limin, and Cheng Yinzhen, criticized the county's leaders. They claimed that after Yin Shibin and the other civilian cadres took power, they violated Mao's instructions to promote unity and economic progress, and that the overall rectification had caused more serious problems than the investigations of May 16

27. See MacFarquhar and Schoenhals, *Mao's Last Revolution*, pp. 413–434; Teiwes and Sun, *The End of the Maoist Era*, pp. 462–496; Ezra F. Vogel, *Deng Xiaoping and the Transformation of China*, pp. 145–172; and Dong Guoqiang and Andrew G. Walder, "Foreshocks: Local Origins of Nanjing's Qingming Demonstrations of 1976," *China Quarterly* 220 (December 2014): 1092–1110.

28. The full name of the campaign was "Criticize Deng's Right-wing Counter-attacking Wind of Reversing Verdicts" (*pi Deng fanji youqing fan'an feng*).

elements. These, they charged, were fundamental errors of political line. The May 16 elements investigations were simply a matter of going too far in pursuit of a correct line, but the overall rectification was a mistake of orientation and political line. The new leaders' only aim, they argued, was simply to restore former cadres to their original positions. They charged that the cadres now leading the county had never really rectified the errors that led originally to their being overthrown, and they rose to power "through the back door" during the overall rectification. There was little that Yin Shibin could say in response, since he had been placed in a vulnerable position by this latest shift in Beijing's political line. He did not dispute the accusations and said that he welcomed criticism.[29]

Aggrieved Liansi members who had been pushed aside in 1975 mobilized to protest their mistreatment. More than a dozen of them led followers to occupy a county guesthouse in February, which became their headquarters.[30] Shao Limin, Li Zongzhou, and one former cadre rebel leader convened meetings of Liansi leaders and activists, and drew up lists of cadres to target. They put up wall posters that attacked these officials for alleged crimes, reviving language of a decade before. In March, they disrupted mass rallies organized by the county authorities, and they sent teams to Xuzhou that invaded and disrupted leadership conferences there. They also traveled to neighboring Pei County to put up wall posters attacking Xu Zhendong, who recently was transferred to the county as the top leader. In April, they disrupted a conference for commune leaders and heads of county agencies, during which Liansi's leaders publicly denounced Yin Shibin, Lu Shaoshi, and other county leaders and read out a speech by the Shanghai radical leader Ma Tianshui, an associate of the Politburo radical Zhang Chunqiao.[31]

The county's leaders were on the defensive, unable to move against the newly mobilized Liansi forces. In August, Shao Limin and other Liansi leaders broke into a county conference and expelled Yin Shibin from the meeting by force. Taking over the meeting, they reported on how they had debated with officials in Xuzhou, and on their discussions with dissidents there about strategies for overthrowing prefecture leaders. They sent people to document the errors of the county's leaders as part of their denunciation campaign. Liansi

29. Zhang Liansheng notebooks.

30. Li Zhi, "Di shiyici luxian douzheng zhong jingyan jiaoxun xiaojie," February 1978; "Guanyu Zhang Haiqing de jiaodai jiefa zonghe cailiao," December 24, 1976.

31. "Guanyu Zhang Haiqing de jiaodai jiefa zonghe cailiao, "December 24, 1976.

leader Shao Limin took over the county's agricultural machinery factory, where he worked, from the county-appointed manager. Shizhai commune organized a mass rally of some ten thousand participants to denounce the county's leaders. The party heads of seventeen out of the twenty-one communes denounced their superiors in the county leadership, and furious arguments broke out in meetings of the county party committee.[32]

Throughout this period, Feng County's leaders were in a difficult position. They could not move against the Liansi activists and their cadre followers. They dutifully relayed central documents mandating the criticism of Deng Xiaoping and his "overall rectification." In April, they held a mass rally to announce the appointment of Hua Guofeng as prime minister and the demotion of Deng Xiaoping. That same day, they issued a document revoking their previous removal of commune PAD personnel from party leadership positions. The work teams organized to rectify commune and brigade leaderships ceased activity in May.[33]

Former Paolian leaders were unhappy about the Liansi rebellion against the county's leaders, because these were challenges to policies that had addressed their grievances, reversed the charges against them, provided compensation, and assigned them jobs. But they did not mobilize to resist the revival of Liansi or defend the county's leaders. Veteran cadres, not Paolian leaders, had been elevated into leadership positions as Liansi followers were removed. They had little motivation to jump to the defense of these cadres, who had done nothing to address their concerns in the first months after their appointment and did not act until prompted to do so during the overall rectification that began in May 1975. That rectification, moreover, had addressed their primary grievances, and it was clear that to oppose Liansi would put them in a position of defying a new trend in Beijing's ever-shifting political line.[34]

---

32. Ibid.; and Shi Yuemei interview.

33. Zhonggong Feng xian weiyuanhui, "Tongzhi" (Notice [on the Tiananmen incident]), April 7, 1976; Zhonggong Feng xian weiyuanhui, "Zai shengwei zhaokai dianhua huiyi shang Peng Chong tongzhi de jianghua" (Comrade Peng Chong's speech on the provincial telephone Conference [about Hua Guofeng's appointment and Deng Xiaoping's purge]), April 8, 1976; Zhonggong Feng xian weiyuanhui, "Tongzhi" (Notice [On the Tiananmen Incident and Criticism of Deng Xiaoping]), April 14, 1976. Zhonggong Feng xian weiyuanhui, "Tongzhi" (Notice [on commune PAD cadres' position and public administration]), April 8, 1976.; Zhang Liansheng notebooks; and Zhang Liansheng interview.

34. Zhang Liansheng notebooks.

Liansi's oppositional activism continued after Mao's death and right up to the arrest of the Gang of Four in October 1976. Liansi members took their protests to the prefecture capital in Xuzhou during the summer, and they set their ambitions even higher in the early fall. In early October, Liansi leaders Shao Limin, Cheng Yinzhen, and Li Peng traveled to Suzhou to establish contacts with factions that were mobilizing to unseat the provincial leaders Peng Chong and Xu Jiatun, who had pushed the overall rectification policies in Jiangsu. While they were in Nanjing, preparing to participate in demonstrations to demand the overthrow of these provincial leaders, they learned that four radical members of the central party leadership had been arrested. Panicked, they agreed not to divulge any information about their oppositional activities in Suzhou and Nanjing, and they quietly returned to Feng County.[35] The final twist in Cultural Revolution politics was about to take place.

Final Reckoning

Mao Zedong died on September 9, 1976. Less than one month later, on October 6, four ranking members of the party leadership, Wang Hongwen, Zhang Chunqiao, and Yao Wenyuan, and Mao's wife, Jiang Qing—were arrested in a coordinated sweep of their supporters by security forces.[36] This was done at the behest of the party's new leader, Hua Guofeng, who was officially appointed to the posts of party chairman and chairman of the Central Military Commission, ending any speculation that one of the Maoist radicals would obtain them.[37] Central and regional leaders were briefed on the events immediately, including Peng Chong and Xu Jiatun, who were summoned to Beijing and assured that their positions were secure.[38] There

---

35. "Guanyu Zhang Haiqing de jiaodai jiefa zonghe cailiao," December 24, 1976.

36. "Zhonggong zhongyang tongzhi" (Notice issued by the CCP Central Committee), October 7, 1976. See also MacFarquhar and Schoenhals, *Mao's Last Revolution*, pp. 433–449; and Teiwes and Sun, *The End of the Maoist Era*, pp. 569–594.

37. Zhonggong zhongyang "Guanyu Hua Guofeng tongzhi ren Zhongguo gongchandang zhongyang weiyuanhui zhuxi, Zhongguo gongchandang zhongyang junshi weiyuanhui zhuxi de jueyi" (On the decision to appoint Comrade Hua Guofeng to the posts of chairman of the CCP Central Committee and the Central Military Commission), Zhongfa [76], no. 15, October 7, 1976.

38. "Zhonggong zhongyang tongzhi," October 7, 1976; "Zhonggong zhengzhiju lingdao tongzhi shiyue qiri wan zhi bari lingchen zai si shengshi san junqu fuze tongzhi huishang de jianghua (genju jilu zhengli)" (Speeches by leading comrades of the Politburo at a meeting with

PHOTOGRAPH 5. Memorial meeting for Mao Zedong, September 18, 1976. In the first row are Liansi leaders Li Peng (*fourth from left*) and Li Zongzhou (*fifth from left*)

followed a political campaign to denounce the policies associated with this "Gang of Four," who were blamed for the disorder and persecutions of the Cultural Revolution.

On October 23, the Feng County party committee convened a mass rally of 16,000 citizens to celebrate the arrest of the Gang of Four. In late November, it convened a conference of cadres at the county, commune, and brigade level to study central documents regarding the crimes of these figures and called for all local cadres and citizens to prepare for a new campaign to expose and criticize the Gang of Four. In late December, it convened an expanded session of the county party committee to relay orders from the provincial leadership that

responsible comrades from four provinces and cities and three military regions on the evening of October 7 and early morning hours of October 8 (compiled from minutes), October 7–8, 1976; "Zhongyang zhengzhiju tongzhi jiejian Peng Chong, Xu Jiatun tongzhi shi de tanhua jilu" (Minutes of the talks between Politburo comrades and Comrades Peng Chong and Xu Jiatun), October 7, 1976.

called for the mobilization of a criticism campaign against the Gang of Four's agents in Feng County.[39]

This movement hit Liansi and its supporters among local cadres very hard, because they had been the ones who had mobilized most recently in a rebellion against party authorities. During the subsequent campaign to eliminate the lingering influence of Gang of Four radicalism in the county, seventy-eight Liansi leaders and cadres were put in isolation, investigated, and subjected to public denunciation.[40] Through April 1977, more than 20,000 criticism meetings, 17,000 articles, and 130,000 wall posters denounced Liansi leaders and activists in the county. The chief targets were the senior cadre Teng Zetian, who refused a transfer to a new post in Xuzhou during the overall rectification and joined the protests against the county' new leaders; He Quanfu, a cadre in the county seat who lost his position in 1975 and then became active in the Criticize Deng campaign in 1976; and a number of dissident cadres and Liansi leaders.[41]

These individuals were accused of a series of political crimes: they had targeted county and prefecture authorities during 1974 and 1975; they rushed their followers into the party and into leading posts; they abused their offices and engaged in corruption. They were placed in study classes and removed from their posts; if they refused to recant, they were placed in a more coercive form of isolation.[42] In June, the county's trade union denounced several Liansi leaders for turning their organization into a tool for factional activities and

39. Zhonggong Jiangsu shengwei, "Xu Jiatun tongzhi zai di shi xianwei shuji huiyi jieshu shi de jianghua" (Comrade Xu Jiatun's speech at the conclusion of the conference of prefecture, city, and county party secretaries), December 9, 1976.

40. Xu Jiashun interview.

41. Zhonggong Feng xian weiyuanhui, "Yin Shibin tongzhi zai ge gongshe dangwei fuze ren huiyi jieshu shi guanyu chuanda guanche zhongyang gongzuo huiyi jingshen de jianghua" (Comrade Yin Shibin's speech at the conclusion of the conference of party leaders of various communes regarding the spread and implementation of the spirit of the central work conference), April 29, 1977.

42. Zhonggong Feng xian weiyuanhui, "Jianjue luoshi Hua zhuxi zhuagang zhiguo de zhanlüe juece, cong daluan zouxiang dazhi" (Resolutely implement Chairman Hua's strategic decision to grasp key issues regarding state administration and move from chaos to order), May 12, 1977; Zhonggong Feng xian weiyuanhui, "Zai Hua zhuxi zhuagang zhiguo zhanlüe juece zhiyinxia liji xingdong qilai jianjue dahao sixia zhe yi zhang—Yin Shibin tongzhi zai quan xian guangbo dahui shang de jianghua" (Take actions instantly under the direction of Chairman Hua's strategic decision to grasp key issues regarding state administration, resolutely win the battle of agricultural production in the summer season—Comrade Yin Shibin's Speech at the

conspiring with factions in Xuzhou and Suzhou.[43] Liansi's leaders and their cadre supporters were denounced for the extensive economic damage that their mobilization had wrought—Shao Limin's agricultural machinery factory had not fulfilled its annual production plan for several years and could not even afford to pay salaries. The cotton mill, long under the control of Li Zongzhou, had completed only 25 percent of its annual plan for cotton cloth in 1976. The pharmaceutical factory, under leadership of Bai Hexiu in recent years, also was in a mess.[44]

In November, Xuzhou broadcast a public trial of "counterrevolutionaries" in the prefecture. Four individuals from Feng County were among the accused—Teng Zetian, He Quanfu, Bai Hexiu, and Shao Limin.[45] Shortly afterward, the Feng County Court announced prison sentences for Teng, He, Bai, and three other Liansi activists that ranged from two to ten years for involvement in actions that resulted in fatalities and, more importantly, for involvement in actions against the county authorities in 1976.[46]

During 1978 and 1979, the prefecture and county worked continuously on the rectification of leadership at all levels and the return of veteran cadres to responsible posts. New veteran cadres were promoted or transferred in from elsewhere to remake the county party committee and revolutionary committee, and similar changes took place in administrative posts under the county government.[47] The leaders of the county's factories were replaced—forty-nine new cadres were promoted to leading positions, while thirteen former leaders were demoted.[48] In December 1978, the county authorities systematically reviewed old cases for 998 local state cadres who had been dismissed and inves-

all-county broadcast meeting), May 22, 1977; *Feng xian zuzhishi ziliao*, p. 155; and Shi Yuemei interview.

43. Feng xian zong gonghui, "Guanyu zhengjian jiceng gonghui zuzhi de baogao" (Report on the adjustment of basic-level labor union organizations), June 22, 1977.

44. Feng xian niukui zengying bangongshi, "Guanyu niukui zengying gongzuo de baogao" (Report regarding the work of reversing deficits and increasing surpluses), November 3, 1977.

45. *Zhonggong Xuzhou lishi dashiji*, p. 443.

46. Xu Jiashun interview.

47. *Feng xian zuzhishi ziliao*, pp. 157–168 and 266–287.

48. Zhonggong Feng xian weiyuanhui, "Gaoju Mao Zhuxi de weida qizhi, yanzhe dang de shiyi da luxian, wei gao sudu fazhan wo xian gongye er fendou—Zhang Benshu tongzhi zai Feng xian gongye xue Daqing xianjin daibiao huiyi shang de jianghua" (Raise high the great banner of Chairman Mao's Thought, follow the line of the 11th Party Congress, strive to rapidly develop our county's industry—Comrade Zhang Benshu's Speech at the Feng County conference of learning from Daqing in industry advanced representatives), March 17, 1978.

tigated in the decade after 1966.[49] In February 1979, they issued a document that reversed all wrongful verdicts, rehabilitated the victims, and destroyed the case files compiled against them.[50] In June, the re-examination of the cases of state cadres came to an end: only in 105 cases were the original verdicts upheld; 276 cases were found to be complete fabrications. Memorial services and monetary compensation was provided for the families of the twenty cadres who died under investigation.[51] A separate review of cases against 4,528 lower-ranking cadres over the past two decades who worked in grassroots organizations led to the reversal of the original charges in roughly half of the cases, and 1,143 were restored to their former jobs.[52] Beginning in 1980, the central authorities emphasized that party cadres should be better educated, more professionally competent, and younger. Many veteran cadres who had become involved in factional activities were replaced by younger cadres over the next decade.[53]

Remarkably, Paolian escaped almost entirely during the systematic campaign against agents of the Gang of Four. If anything, they had followed the call of Mao and his associates to rebel against party leaders even more enthusiastically than the activists in Liansi, and they had been just as active in factional activity as their opponents. They had rebelled against the county authorities for years, and they had armed themselves and had fought battles that resulted in a number of fatalities. They were saved largely by the timing of their most active period of rebellion, and in many ways by their suppression during the anti–May 16 elements campaign, which was, after all, intended to target the most militant rebel leaders. As victims of this campaign, Paolian had benefited from the campaign against alleged military abuses in the wake of Lin Biao's fall, and they aligned themselves with veteran cadres during the overall rectification directed by Deng Xiaoping. These veteran cadres did not allocate them positions of authority in 1975 but instead replaced Liansi activists with other veteran cadres. Fortunately for Paolian, it had refrained from mobilizing

49. Zhonggong Feng xian weiyuanhui, "Lu Shaoshi tongzhi zai xianwei sanji ganbu huiyi shang de jianghua" (Comrade Lu Shaoshi's speech at the three-level cadre conference of the county party committee), December 1, 1978.

50. Zhonggong Feng xian weiyuanhui, "Guanyu chexiao wenhua da geming chuqi dui yibufen tongzhi chezhi baguan, kaichu dangji deng chuli jueding" (Decision on reversing the Cultural Revolution decisions to fire and remove from office and expel from the party certain comrades), February 15, 1979; *Zhonggong Feng xian difangshi dashiji*, p. 277.

51. *Zhonggong Feng xian difangshi dashiji*, p. 280.

52. *Feng xian zuzhishi ziliao*, pp. 155–156.

53. Ibid., pp. 157–158.

against Liansi during 1976, preferring instead to lie low. This largely coinciden-tal sequence of events meant that it was Liansi who bore the brunt of the campaign against radical followers of the Gang of Four. Liansi's campaign to rebound from losses they suffered in Deng Xiaoping's rectification reached its zenith shortly before the arrest of the Beijing officials associated with the launching of the Cultural Revolution. In so doing, they became the designated enemies of the new regime. If Shao Wen had not been transferred out of the county two years before, the fate of the two factions would likely have been reversed.

It is ironic that Paolian's members had for so long been disappointed that officials at higher levels were uninterested in investigating their claims in their rivalry with Liansi over the years. They had hoped that the military officers in the Xuhai Study Class in Beijing would investigate their claims against Liansi by looking carefully at the history of conflict in the county, which they felt would certify them as the county's genuine rebel force and their opponents as "conservative" tools of the PAD and the old political order. Later, when the tide began to turn in their favor, they were again disappointed that officials in Xuzhou and Nanjing refused to explore the specifics of local conflicts and simply counseled them to set aside factional animosities. And they were disap-pointed with the new veteran cadres who replaced Shao Wen at end of 1974, who also seemed uninterested in delving into the complex history of factional conflict in the county.

In the end, Paolian was fortunate that the post-Mao leaders in the prefec-ture and county were still unwilling to look carefully at its history of factional conflict. If they had done so, it would have been hard to avoid the conclusion that Paolian was every bit as disruptive a force and was in every sense also followers of the Gang of Four. But it was saved by timing; it had been largely a spent force by 1975. In 1977, the authorities, once again, were unwilling to delve into factional histories, and it was politically expedient for them to go after the Liansi activists who had resisted the rebuilding of political order in the county. This was the last of the odd and confusing twists of Feng County politics during the Cultural Revolution.

Shao Wen, Paolian's enemy and primary tormentor during the Cultural Revolution, had been transferred out of Feng County at the end of 1974, to a lesser position in distant Nantong Prefecture. In December 1979, the new lead-ers of Feng County submitted a report to Xuzhou Prefecture, accusing Shao of financial irregularities and corruption during his reign over the county. They asked their superiors to send the case file to the Jiangsu Province Military

District for further investigation and punishment.[54] The prefecture authorities circulated the report within the prefecture hierarchy, but no punishment followed.[55] Shao remained as the political commissar of the Haimen County PAD until he retired in 1981.[56]

In the mid-1980s there was a national campaign to investigate and punish "three types of people" (sanzhong ren): those who had risen to positions of authority after engaging in rebellion as followers of the "Jiang Qing–Lin Biao clique"; those who had stubbornly persisted in factional activities; and those who were implicated in "beating, smashing, and looting" during the Cultural Revolution. This was the final major campaign to rid leading bodies across China of individuals who had risen into positions as a result of their earlier factional activity—whichever side they had been on.[57] The campaign had a relatively limited impact on Feng County. Its muted impact may be due to the fact that most of the cadres who were involved in the factional conflicts had already been replaced by younger ones or had been transferred elsewhere. Most of the former Liansi leaders who had been rushed into party membership and promoted into leading posts had already been purged during the overall rectification of 1975 and the continuing purges after 1976. The new county leaders put in place during the early 1980s did not view former Liansi leaders and affiliated cadres as a threat. Focused on reviving the economy of a

54. Zhonggong Feng xian weiyuanhui, Xuzhou diwei gongzuo zu, "Guanyu Feng xian yanzhong weifan caijing jilü wenti de diaocha baogao" (Investigation report on the problem of serious violations of financial discipline in Feng County), December 12, 1978.

55. Zhonggong Xuzhou diwei, "Guanyu Feng xian yanzhong weifan caijing jilü wenti de tongbao" (Circular on the problem of serious violations of financial discipline in Feng County), March 20, 1979.

56. Zhonggong Jiangsu sheng Nantong shiwei zuzhibu, Zhonggong Jiangsu sheng Nantong shiwei dangshi gongzuo weiyuanhui, Jiangsu sheng Nantong shi dang'an guan, Zhongguo gongchandang Jiangsu sheng Nantong shi zuzhishi ziliao (Materials on the organizational history of the Chinese Communist Party in Nantong City, Jiangsu), Beijing: Zhonggong dangshi chubanshe, 1991, pp. 348 and 355.

57. Zhonggong zhongyang, "Guanyu qingli lingdao banzi zhong 'sanzhong ren' wenti de tongzhi" (Notice on the problem of cleansing the "Three Types" from leading groups), Zhongfa [82], no. 55, December 30, 1982; Zhongyang zhengdang gongzuo zhidao weiyuanhui bangongshi, "Guanyu zuohao qingli 'sanzhong ren' diaocha heshi gongzuo jige wenti de tongzhi" (Notice on several problems in verifying the investigation work of "Three Types"), April 26, 1984; Zhonggong zhongyang, "Guanyu qingli 'sanzhong ren' ruogan wenti de buchong tongzhi" (Supplementary notice on various problems in the investigation of "Three Types"), Zhongfa [84], no. 17, July 31, 1984.

still-impoverished county, they seemed unwilling to pursue old political vendettas.

Only twenty-four cadres and former faction leaders were put under investigation during this final rectification campaign, which ran from 1984 to 1987. Only three of them were found to be a "Three Types" activist. One was Gao Xiamin, a former Shahe Commune party leader who was responsible for the notorious false case of the "Shahe Underground Anti-Communist Regiment." He previously was suspended from his duties and investigated for the false case in the "overall rectification" of 1975, then was saved by the Criticize Deng movement of 1976 and reappointed as the top party leader of Huashan Commune. In 1979, he was demoted to deputy director of a county bureau. In this new campaign, he lost his leadership position and was expelled from the party. He eventually retired as an ordinary office worker in a county bureau. The second one was former Liansi combat team leader Zhang Guichun. Originally a demobilized soldier and worker in the coal-mine construction company, he was recruited into the party and appointed deputy party secretary of the county department store in the early 1970s. In the "overall rectification" of 1975, he was removed from that post and reassigned a humble job. He was designated as a "beating, smashing, and looting element" and expelled from the party. The third was former Paolian combat team leader Hou Li. Originally a clerk in the county department store, he survived the May 16 elements investigations and was appointed section chief of the store after the Cultural Revolution. He was also designated as a "beating, smashing and looting element", an accusation intended to show impartiality toward the two factions. Since he never joined the party, he was only removed from the post of section chief. The remaining twenty-one suspects were released with minor sanctions—an inner-party warning or demotion from leading positions.[58]

Zhang Liansheng escaped censure as a prominent rebel leader in the early post-Mao years. After the charges against him were reversed in 1975, the county authorities appointed him to the work team for the overall rectification. During

---

58. Zhonggong Feng xian weiyuanhui, "Zhonggong Feng xian weiyuanhui hecha 'sanzhong ren' gongzuo zongjie" (Feng County party committee summary of work in verifying the investigations of "Three Types of People"), June 18, 1987; Zhonggong Xuzhou diwei, "Guanyu dui Zhang Guichun dingxing chuli yijian de pifu" (Response on the opinion regarding the verdict and sentencing of Zhang Guichun), February 25, 1987; and Zhonggong Xuzhou diwei, "Guanyu dui Hou Li dingxing he chuli yijian de pifu" (Response on the opinion regarding the verdict and sentencing of Hou Li), January 17, 1987.

PHOTOGRAPH 6. Zhang Liansheng as a medical student, Nanjing, 1979

the campaign waged by Liansi against the county's leaders during the Criticize Deng campaign of 1976, he stayed at home and avoided political activity. After the arrest of the Gang of Four, he worked for several months in 1977 as a deputy work group head in a production brigade in Shizhai Commune, and while working in that position he took the newly re-established college entrance examinations, which had been canceled shortly before he would have sat for them in 1966.

At the age of twenty-eight, more than a decade after his senior year at Feng County Middle School, Zhang began his university education at Nanjing

Medical College. During his four years there, the leadership qualities he had honed as a rebel organizer of Paolian were well in evidence. He was selected leader of his class (*banji*) and was admitted to the party. After graduation in 1982, he was assigned a job in the health care department of the Xuzhou Coal Mining Bureau. It was only at this point that his history as a rebel leader came back to haunt him. In the mid-1980s, during the campaign to investigate "Three Types of People," he was penalized in his work unit because of his past history. His party branch gave him a severe warning but he was not expelled. Instead, he was put under a form of probation. Zhang felt that his superiors used the campaign as an excuse to penalize him because he was often at odds with them. As a result of this sanction, his career suffered, and he was never subsequently promoted. Zhang's last petition of protest complained about this perceived injustice in a letter that he sent to China's party chairman Hu Jintao seven years before his retirement in 2007.[59] Zhang's years as a leader of Paolian, which began when he was a high school senior in a small rural town, improbably brought him into contact with some of China's most powerful national leaders. In many ways, those years were the most exciting and meaningful of his life.

59. Zhang Liansheng interview; and Zhang Liansheng, "Gei Hu Jintao de shensu xin" (Petition to Hu Jintao), November 22, 2000.

9

Troubled Decade

WHAT WERE FENG County's factional conflicts really all about? Why did these factions form, and why did they prove so hard to reconcile? These are questions that the authors have struggled with in a series of publications about other settings. In the case of this rural county, the lines of conflict and the logic of factional alliances are in many ways clearer than in large cities that had scores or even hundreds of rebel groups. This is a much simpler setting, the local rebel movement was small, and by the standards of large cities, not particularly "radical" in the way that this term is usually understood.

Let us start with the most obvious interpretation—that the Liansi faction represented a "conservative" political orientation based on the vested interests that its leaders had in the existing political system. The primary evidence for this interpretation is that local officials connected with the People's Armed Department, headed by one of the top handful of party officials in the county (Shao Wen), provided steadfast support for Liansi and, in fact, helped to organize it. A major resource that lent great strength to the Liansi faction in its fight with Paolian was the PAD networks that stretched down into rural communes and villages. This, in turn, allowed the PAD to mobilize farmers on behalf of Liansi through the rural militia. This fragment of the local power structure was essentially intact after the collapse of the old Party Committee and county government. In this interpretation, as defenders of the status quo, the surviving repressive apparatus of the old power structure fought against more radical elements with strong grievances against the existing system.

Certain inconvenient facts complicate such an interpretation. The first and perhaps most important is that Shao Wen, his subordinates in the PAD, and his allies in Liansi in fact overthrew the old powerholders as completely as any rebel group might have done. Gao Ying, the county's party secretary, was removed from office and was tormented by both factions in the county, with

Shao's apparent approval. Only two out of the nine members of the standing committee of the county's communist party committee in 1966 played any role in the revolutionary committee that was formed in late 1969. Out of the twenty-six members of the old Feng County party committee, only three were granted positions on the revolutionary committee. Although several other veteran cadres who had connections with Liansi and the PAD were added to the county leadership in 1970 and 1971, the rest only gradually were assigned new leadership posts some years later, after Shao had been transferred elsewhere.[1]

It is therefore hard to argue that Shao acted to protect incumbent power-holders or to keep the status quo intact. When he was in charge of the county, he pushed to appoint as many Liansi activists as he could to leadership posts and prepared them quickly for entry into the Communist Party—which indicates that Liansi leaders were outside the party establishment. Why did Shao act as he did, essentially substituting the PAD for the old civilian party establishment? The short and obvious answer is that the January 28, 1967, orders from Beijing that called for China's military to "support the left" essentially made officers associated with the PAD the only members of the former party leadership who were immune from overthrow, and in the absence of a rebel power seizure, they in fact became the instrument for the overthrow of local authorities.

The PAD was the grassroots extension of the regional PLA subdistrict, and it was the frontline force for "support the left" work. In the many localities in China where a rebel group had seized power, with excluded rebel groups hotly contesting the power seizure, PAD commanders had to decide which of the contending rebel groups to support.[2] Shao did not have to do this, because there was no rebel power seizure. As the member of the county's former party standing committee who simultaneously was the political commissar of the PAD, he was the only member of the standing committee to continue to hold real power. The only other member of the county's former party standing committee that he chose for continued service was Dong Hongzhi, former head of the discipline inspection committee. Of the twenty-six total members of the old county party committee, only one other official survived to serve on the standing committee of the revolutionary committee—Zhu Guangren, former head of the county finance department. If we conceive of the PAD as a con-

1. *Feng xian zuzhishi ziliao,* pp. 113, 145–148, and 249–255.
2. See Walder, *Agents of Disorder,* pp. 108–126.

servative force, it is hard to square this with its remarkably thorough purge of the old power structure, and its continued resistance to restoring the old cadres to their posts well into the 1970s. Only after Shao, Dong, and other cadres selected for service by the PAD were transferred out of Feng County in 1974 could veteran county officials be returned to their posts.

If Shao was not motivated to preserve the old power structure, then what were his motivations and those of his followers? It is important to recall that one of the largest and most aggrieved groups of rebels who joined Paolian in late 1966 were teachers and staff in the county's schools who were herded into coercive "training class" in the summer of 1966, where they were subjected to harrowing and often violent loyalty investigations. Hundreds were attacked for political disloyalty and were given verdicts that would have ruined their future careers. Another group consisted of students who had clashed with the work team sent into the county's middle schools. Both of these moves were based on decisions taken by the county's Cultural Revolution committee, which carried out what it understood to be the aims of the campaign in the summer and early fall of 1966. Gao Ying, the county's party secretary, was the chair of the committee, but Shao was his top-ranking deputy and was in charge of the coercive training classes in collaboration with the public security bureau. This is an important reason why Shao had a defensive and hostile attitude toward Paolian—if Gao implemented the "bourgeois reactionary line," then Shao could have been denounced as his instrument.

This same self-protective motivation applied to the rebel faction in the public security bureau that aligned itself firmly with Shao Wen and became a firm supporter of Liansi. The bureau was targeted by those who had suffered in the county-run loyalty investigations. As rebel attacks on the county authorities escalated in early 1967, a number of officers in the bureau formed a rebel group and overthrew the director of their bureau, who was a member of the county party committee. Their rebellion against their own leader was partly intended to inoculate them against rising accusations from rebel activists by blaming the recent abuses on their superior, permitting them to pose as rebels. As it turns out, the rebel group was composed of Feng County natives who were already at odds with the head of their bureau, who was from outside Feng County. When they refused Paolian's request to halt attacks by their rivals, Paolian turned against them, setting the two sides on a collision course.

Even if there are difficult questions about an interpretation that portrays the PAD-Liansi alliance as a conservative force motivated to preserve the former power structure, can we not portray Paolian as a more "radical" political force? This is certainly the way that Paolian portrayed itself, and it never hesitated to accuse the PAD and Liansi of conservative motivations at odds with the goals of the Cultural Revolution. The first complication to such an interpretation is the fact that Paolian never moved to seize power over the county government or had any intention to do so. It was urged to do so by the militant university students who came back to their native Feng County to support the rebel campaign. The students saw Paolian as the most likely vehicle for this move. But Zhang Liansheng and other leaders of Paolian refused—they knew that they had no ability to manage an entire county, and Gao Ying had already agreed to all of their demands. Another complication is that Paolian was not alone in targeting Gao Ying for mass criticism—other rebels who later aligned with Liansi were equally motivated to do so, and in fact the two sides fought over who would hold Gao Ying in custody and organize struggle sessions against him.

The political divisions among the county's rebels originated in reaction to local events and emerged only in the heat of mass activities. Disagreements began to appear during denunciation rallies over the questions of whether Gao Ying had the right to wear a PLA uniform, whether he should stand or sit during the sessions, and whether he should be expelled from the party. Because the returned university students were so much more aggressive and outspoken, and because they supported Paolian and tried to push it into a more militant stance, rebels who were unaffiliated with Paolian began to push back against the interfering "outsiders." They moved against the outsiders, eventually driving them out of the county, and these animosities were directed also at Paolian.

In other cases, splits emerged that were tangential to the broader political themes of the Cultural Revolution. At Feng County Middle School, divisions appeared immediately between faculty, staff, and students from the two middle schools that had been merged several years before. In the county government, most strikingly in the public security bureau, splits emerged between natives of the county and leaders who had been transferred from outside. At the cotton mill, the county's largest enterprise, splits emerged primarily over the legitimacy of demands for better pay and working conditions, which were a particular concern of the many temporary and contract workers. The smaller faction, affiliated with Paolian and composed exclusively of permanent employees, insisted that these demands were a deviation from the political goals of the movement. The larger faction, which disagreed, included large numbers of temporary workers and aligned with Liansi. However, the mill's two factions adopted the same critical stance toward the managers of their mill and the county authorities.

If the early differences between Paolian and the rebels who eventually formed Liansi were not particularly clear cut, what about the groups that joined Paolian? We have already seen that the PAD and public security rebels were a key force behind Liansi. The eventual membership profile of Paolian provided the PAD and Liansi with ammunition for their charge that Paolian was in fact a conservative organization, tied to the former powerholders. The first element to this charge was the fact that a number of the purged members of the former party committee—the highest-ranking being deputy party secretary Zhu Pingfan—pledged their support to Paolian. Why? Their motivation closely paralleled those of Shao Wen and the public security bureau rebels. These leading cadres had been purged by Shao's PAD-led power seizure, and pledging support to Paolian would benefit them if the rebel group prevailed. Second, among the most important early components of Paolian were two alliances of cadres composed primarily of office staff who had returned from conducting the Socialist Education Campaign in neighboring counties. The campaign that they had been sent to conduct was denounced as a prime example of the "bourgeois reactionary line," and these younger cadres were motivated to denounce their former superiors for forcing them to carry out this mistaken line. They joined Paolian in large numbers and were welcomed because they had been absent from the county and had been uninvolved in the conflicts prior to early 1967. Third, the former head of the county's public security bureau, who had been overthrown by the department's rebels who were subsequently so hostile to Paolian, pledged his support to the Paolian alliance and was welcomed by them. In light of the way that large segments of the former power structure flocked to Paolian, Shao Wen and Liansi argued that Paolian was attempting to restore to power capitalist roaders who had been purged from office as revisionists. In other words, Paolian harbored the real conservatives. In their view, this was not true of Liansi, which supported a militarized power structure that had pushed aside almost the entire former county elite.

Liansi's struggles during 1975 and 1976 in many ways vindicate its self-presentation as Feng County's true rebels. Its members were the victims of the "overall rectification" pushed by Deng Xiaoping in 1975, and from their point of view Deng was one of the most important officials stripped of power for revisionism earlier in the Cultural Revolution. In their view, which aligned with that of the Politburo radicals who were later purged as the Gang of Four,

Deng's campaign was intended to take revenge against rebels who had earlier overthrown the "capitalist roaders" in China's power structure. When the tide turned against Deng and his campaign to restore veteran cadres to power, Liansi moved against the veteran cadres who replaced Shao Wen and other military officers in Feng County. These veteran officials were transferred from other localities, where they had been overthrown by rebels earlier in the Cultural Revolution. Liansi therefore saw itself, with some justification, as a radical force that fought to prevent the restoration of the old order. Paolian, by contrast, sat out this final phase of the conflict.

Finally, there is the complicating matter of PLA support. In most other regions of China, rebels divided over the question of military control. Rebel factions who resisted military control conceived of themselves as true rebels who demonstrated their militant spirit and "rebel to the end," while denouncing factions that supported military control as conservatives. These labels, and the reasoning behind them, were in fact accepted by many early analysts of this period, just as they were embraced by anti-army rebels. In Feng County, however, the factions did not line up as for and against military control—the struggle was over which branch of China's military would implement it. The PLA officers from the 68th Army were the protectors and virtual allies of Paolian, and they persisted in supporting Paolian against the PAD-Liansi alliance until they were no longer able to do so.

There is also the matter of how this all ended. Paolian had long fought to defend its claim to be the county's true revolutionary force, insisting that the PAD and Liansi were the coercive apparatus of the old power structure who were stubbornly clinging onto their positions. But in the end, it did not matter. The rebels who were punished as agents of the radical Gang of Four were members of Liansi, not Paolian, and only Liansi's leaders were sentenced to prison terms after the death of Mao. Paolian was fortunate in the end that its longstanding claim to be the true rebels in the county was denied, ignored, and eventually forgotten.

If the political orientations that drove the county's conflicts throughout this decade defy easy characterization, does that mean that Feng County's ten-year history of conflict was highly atypical? In what ways did the county's history depart from broader patterns that have been documented elsewhere? The first and most obvious distinctive feature of the Feng County experience is that its local rebel movement was small, weak, and late in developing. This was broadly true of most rural counties, especially so for poor and agrarian ones. In many rural counties, especially those with smaller student populations, there was almost no local rebel activity until December 1966, after the students returned from their approved autumn trips to Beijing and elsewhere. In this respect, Feng County was by no means unusual.[3] What was unusual was that no rebel group attempted to seize power from the county authorities. Local rebels limited themselves to denouncing party secretary Gao Ying for carrying out the "bourgeois reactionary line." Just under 20 percent of China's counties never experienced a rebel power seizure, and Feng County was among them.[4] In most rural counties, given the modest scale of the student and worker rebellion, it was in fact rebel groups *within* party and government agencies that seized power from their own superiors.[5] This did occur within the Feng County's public security bureau, but it did not translate into a broader movement by rebel cadres.

The People's Armed Department under Shao Wen took over the administration of the county in early March 1967. This was typically the first action by military units in a locality. By February, military units had done this in 37 percent of all counties, but by the end of March, this proportion reached 79 percent—so this act and its timing in the county fit closely with the national pattern.[6] What was unusual is what happened next. Shao began to make aggressive moves to suppress Paolian, but regular PLA troops that arrived shortly afterward strongly dissented from the PAD's moves against Paolian. This was the primary source of Feng County's long history of active factional antagonism. The move had the effect of creating antagonisms between the PLA and PAD, and it stimulated the formation of Liansi and its essential alliance with the PAD.

But Feng County was not highly unusual in this respect. This sequence of events also occurred in Xuzhou City, and it was apparently common across Xuzhou Prefecture.[7] Accounts of Shandong Province, where Wang Xiaoyu also sent in PLA units to supervise and in many cases reverse the decisions of local PAD officers, revealed similar effects in many Shandong localities.[8] The

3. Walder, *Agents of Disorder,* pp. 72–78.

4. Calculated from the dataset used in Walder, *Agents of Disorder.*

5. See ibid., pp. 82–100; Andrew G. Walder, "Rebellion of the Cadres: The 1967 Implosion of the Chinese Party-State," *China Journal* 75 (January 2016), 102–120; and Walder and Lu, "The Dynamics of Collapse in an Authoritarian Regime."

6. Calculated from the dataset in Walder, *Agents of Disorder.*

7. See Dong and Walder, "Forces of Disorder."

8. See Bu Weihua, *Zalan jiu shijie,* pp. 525–528. This was another reason why Wang Xiaoyu was purged; as in Xuzhou, his decisions inadvertently undermined established revolutionary committees and perpetuated factional conflicts in ways that proved very difficult to resolve.

problem of different military units working at cross-purposes was also wide-spread in Shaanxi Province, where factional warfare was particularly perni-cious and difficult to stamp out.[9] And when the Xuhai Study Class brought civilian rebels and military officers to Beijing to resolve their factional differ-ences, there were many other regions that sent delegations for their own study classes at the same time. This suggests that the involvement of military units in civilian factionalism was a relatively common problem across China. We can only speculate about how deeply these differences were reflected at the county level to the same extent as Feng County.

The splits between military actors and their support for opposite sides was a major reason why the factional battles in Feng County proved impossible to resolve. The extent to which this was unusual is indicated by the remarkably late formation of the county's revolutionary committee. By the time that Feng County finally formed its revolutionary committee in September 1969, only 1.6 percent of China's 2,066 counties had yet to do so.[10] This was a very late formal resolution to the county's factional conflicts, though as we have seen, it was only a temporary respite.

The severe persecution campaigns that were so prevalent across China after the formation of revolutionary committees were therefore late in coming to Feng County, but they were harsh and focused on Paolian, which had lost its PLA supporters and was under the heel of Shao, his PAD, and their Liansi allies. These persecution campaigns were widespread across China, and they generated many more deaths and other victims than the factional fighting that preceded it. This was also the case in Feng County.[11] Although there is little systematic evidence that these campaigns focused overwhelmingly on the los-ing side in the factional conflicts, we can reasonably speculate that this was the case in many regions.

As harrowing as the experience of Paolian was during the investigation of "May 16 elements," and as stubbornly persistent and violent the battles were between the two factions over several years, it does not appear that Feng

9. Shinichi Tanigawa, *The Dynamics of the Chinese Cultural Revolution in the Countryside: Shaanxi, 1966–1971*, PhD diss., Stanford University, 2007; and Tanigawa, "The Policy of the Military 'Supporting the Left.'"

10. Calculated with the dataset used in Walder, *Agents of Disorder*.

11. Walder, *Agents of Disorder*, p. 180. This was equally true across rural China. See Andrew G. Walder and Yang Su, "The Cultural Revolution in the Countryside: Scope, Timing, and Human Impact," *China Quarterly* 173 (March 2003): 82–107.

County was among the most bloody. Our best estimate for the county's death toll during this entire period, based on the evidence at our disposal, is that there were roughly 250 deaths in the county attributable to either factional warfare or subsequent persecution campaigns.[12] Feng County was far from the notorious case of Dao County, Hunan, where more than four thousand were killed in a several-month period, or some forty-two other counties where more than one thousand died between 1966 and 1971.[13] The battles described in Feng County were almost all small in scale, and rarely involved military-grade weaponry. Fighters from the county did not stream into a nearby city for large-scale battles of the kind that were common in many localities in 1968. The violent rivalry between the Kick and Support factions in Xuzhou had little resonance with the Paolian-Liansi split in the county. Despite the intensity of factional animosities, it was not unusually violent by the standards of the period.

The period from 1970 to 1973, in the course of these prolonged persecution campaigns, gives us a clear sense that the social order of the county was beginning to unravel. The "One Strike, Three Anti" campaign in particular uncovered widespread misallocation of funds and illegal seizure of property. There was considerable evidence that rebels who occupied new positions of power were engaged in widespread self-dealing and corruption. And the campaigns were creating serious morale problems in large segments of the population, even among those who were charged with carrying out the seemingly endless investigations of political deviance. Since these campaigns were very broadly implemented across China, we can consider Feng County as a window into some of the grassroots consequences of sustained levels of conflict and oppression.

One of the most dramatic aspects of the 1970s in Feng County is the 1974 mobilization by petitioners to protest their persecution in the suppression campaigns. This, to be sure, followed directly from the county's unusually prolonged factional strife, but protests of this kind broke out across broad regions

---

12. This includes 83 reported deaths in factional fighting, 129 suicides, and 35 deaths under interrogation mentioned at various points in the earlier chapters.

13. Tan Hecheng, *The Killing Wind*, detailed the evidence for Dao County. The other numbers are based on the dataset employed in Walder, *Agents of Disorder*. Of the 42 counties with more than 1,000 reported deaths, 31 were in Guangxi Province, where mass killings were widespread. The cases of Guangxi and Guangdong are analyzed in depth by Yang Su, *Collective Killings in China during the Cultural Revolution* (New York: Cambridge University Press, 2011).

of China that year, a period that at the time was labeled the "Second Cultural Revolution." The links between these protests and the earlier factional divisions, and their connection to the suppression campaigns carried out under military auspices, have been well documented in Guangzhou, Nanjing, Hangzhou, Guilin, and other cities.[14] Feng County's activists became directly involved in this nationwide wave of protest, and our account details the ways in which activists from rural counties could become involved.

The fallout from these persecution campaigns, and the revival of open factional conflict in 1974, did not prevent a modest revival of the county's impoverished economy during the mid-1970s, a trend reflected across rural China. The county's grain harvests, which had barely recovered to 1955 levels by the onset of the Cultural Revolution, dropped again over the next three years, and in 1969 they were still 13 percent lower than 1966. Grain production revived steadily thereafter, and by 1976 output was 38 percent higher than 1966. The county's modest industrial base began to grow once again in 1970, when four small state enterprises were opened, bringing the total to fourteen; by 1976 the number had increased to twenty-six. Commune and brigade enterprises (known later as township and village enterprises) also expanded. In 1970 their total output was only 11 percent higher than in 1965, but by 1976 it was four times higher. These and many other improvements during the mid-1970s, however, paled in comparison to the advances recorded shortly after the end of the Cultural Revolution. The 1985 grain harvest was *more than double that of 1976.* The 1980 output of township and village enterprise was already *21 times* larger than in 1975.[15] These and other indicators suggest that the imposition of a repressive but still conflict-ridden political order after 1969 permitted economic recovery from the disruptions of the previous three years. But the county's economic advance was still hampered in ways that became evident only in retrospect. The advances recorded during the mid-1970s are more accurately

14. See, e.g., Dong and Walder, "Nanjing's 'Second Cultural Revolution' of 1974"; Anita Chan, Stanley Rosen, and Jonathan Unger, eds. *On Socialist Democracy and the Chinese Legal System: The Li Yizhe Debates* (Armonk, NY: ME Sharpe, 1985); Forster, *Rebellion and Factionalism in a Chinese Province,* pp. 120–172; Stanley Rosen, "Guangzhou's Democracy Movement in Cultural Revolution Perspective," *China Quarterly,* no. 101 (March 1985), pp. 1–31; and Song Guoqing, "The Floating Fate of a Rebel Leader in Guangxi, 1966–1984," in *Victims, Perpetrators, and the Role of Law in Maoist China,* ed. Daniel Leese and Puck Engman (Berlin and Boston: Walter de Gruyter, 2018), pp. 174–199.

15. *Jiangsu sheng Feng xian zhi,* pp. 236–237, 271, 299.

viewed as a delayed and fitful recovery from setbacks dating back to the Great Leap Forward of 1958–1960.

From these observations, we offer the following conclusions. The political battles in Feng County, as in many localities in China, did not clearly pit the defenders of the status quo against those with grievances against it. It did represent the splintering and destruction of the old power structure. In Feng County, as in many rural counties, this left the People's Armed Department as the arbiter of winners and losers among contending rebel factions. What was different in Feng County was that a separate branch of the military intervened to restrain the hand of the PAD and dispute its judgments, and it stayed involved in the county for several years thereafter. The deep-seated and long-lasting factional conflicts that resulted were distinctive, and in many ways unusual, but they were a variation on a common theme across China, where the decisions of military units became the axis around which factional conflicts revolved. Where Feng County fits in the broad spectrum of county-level politics during the Cultural Revolution is still far from clear, but its history shows how even poor and remote regions could be drawn into national political struggles, with devastating consequences.

What, then, were these struggles really about? Once factions had clearly formed, and after violent encounters between them spread, the driving force of the escalating conflicts was the realization that defeat would mean victimization at the hands of your enemies. This was as true for PLA and PAD officers—who would suffer reprimands, demotions, or worse—as much as for members of civilian factions. The struggle in Feng County was pushed forward by the absence of a neutral authority that could credibly enforce a ceasefire and ensure the evenhanded treatment of the two sides. This problem existed not simply at the county level, but in twenty communes and more than four hundred villages. Agreements reached on several occasions at the county level proved unenforceable, in part because both factions were little more than loose alliances of relatively independent rebel groups and in part because there were no credibly neutral mechanisms in *local* communities to enforce a truce. Each agreement reached between the leaders of Paolian and Liansi over the years was sabotaged by renewed fighting by subordinate groups in the communes. Paolian affiliates could not trust a settlement that was enforced by Shao Wen and a PAD that had close ties with Liansi. Liansi could not trust a settlement that was enforced by PLA units that had all along supported Paolian. This turned the "great alliances" forced upon factions in coercive study classes into a largely symbolic charade. It provided cover for higher authorities to withdraw their involvement by declaring victory and washing their hands of local problems that they had inadvertently created.

Paolian's treatment at the hands of Shao Wen after the final withdrawal of the supportive PLA unit—not only the harrowing persecution campaigns marked by torture and suicide, but the loss of jobs and the denial of back pay and benefits for leaders and followers alike—illustrates clearly the outcome that each side was fighting to avoid. It would be superficial to understand this as simply a struggle for power, with each side fighting to obtain advantages. In a more fundamental sense, it was a struggle for survival. This was not a struggle that any of the participants could have anticipated when they took their first steps toward political activism at the outset of the Cultural Revolution.

CHRONOLOGY

1966

January 16–18: Feng County People's Congress meets and appoints a new county People's Government, with Qian Xiufu as county magistrate.

May 18–20: Feng County CCP Congress meets and appoints a new county party committee headed by Gao Ying, who becomes the first-ranking party secretary.

May 25: County authorities issue a "Notice on Unfolding the Study of the Cultural Revolution," in response to the CCP Central Committee's May 16 Circular, which launches the Cultural Revolution.

Mid-June: Activist students and teachers at Feng County Middle School and other middle schools put up the first group of Cultural Revolution wall posters on their campuses, in imitation of the famous wall posters at Peking University.

Early July: County authorities send work teams to the county's three middle schools, and they label several activist students as "obstacles" to the healthy development of the campaign and orchestrate mass criticism against them.

July 20: County authorities establish a "Leading Small Group" to coordinate the Cultural Revolution in the county, along with a special office to guide the campaign. The chairman of the group is the county's party leader Gao Ying. Shao Wen, a member of the CCP standing committee of the county, and political commissar of the People's Armed Department (PAD), is deputy head.

July 22: County authorities establish a "summer training class" for teachers and staff of local secondary schools, with Shao Wen in charge. The "training" involves loyalty investigation and thought reform, conducted via denunciation, coercive interrogation, and physical abuse over the next two months.

Mid-August: County authorities recall work teams from the middle schools, after Mao Zedong denounces the practice several weeks before, but the demands by students and teachers that the work teams be criticized are denied.

September to November: Students and teachers travel to Beijing and elsewhere to "exchange revolutionary experience."

December: The first Red Guard organizations appear at Feng County Middle School. The county authorities finally permit the former heads of work teams to be criticized at the schools but refuse the demand to expel them from the CCP, causing friction with activist students.

1967

Mid-January: Close to one hundred university students, natives of Feng County, return to push forward county's rebel movement against local authorities. Rebel organizations appear in workplaces across the county, and rivalries between them appear.

January 21: Rebels in the prefectural capital of Xuzhou seize power from the city's party and government authorities. Five days later, a similar power seizure occurs in the provincial capital of Nanjing.

January 26: Rebel organizations in Feng County jointly convene a mass rally to criticize the county's leaders. The rebel alliance known as Paolian is established, but it does not attempt to seize power.

February 4. Rebels in Xuzhou seize power over Xuzhou Prefecture, the government jurisdiction immediately above that of Feng County.

February 9: A violent clash occurs between Paolian and rival mass organizations as they fight over the custody of the county's top party official, Gao Ying.

Mid-February: The PLA 68th Army, the Xuzhou Military Subdistrict, and other PLA units in the region are ordered to intervene in Xuzhou City and Xuzhou Prefecture. The PLA 68th Army, under the Ji'nan Military Region, is placed in charge of military control. As a result, Wang Xiaoyu, a civilian cadre recently appointed as head of the Shandong Province Revolutionary Committee, with authority over the Ji'nan Military Region, plays a major role in the Xuzhou region over the next two years.

March 6: In the absence of any moves by rebel organizations to seize power, the county PAD takes over power in the county, setting aside the civilian party and government. It sets up a production management office to handle routine administration. Shao Wen becomes the head. The county's deputy party secretary, Teng Zetian, and a few other civilian officials are retained.

March 9: PLA Unit 6174, part of the 68th Army, sends a "support the left" work team to Feng County. The head of this military work team is Zheng Guoxin, Unit 6174's political commissar.

April 4: The Feng County military control committee is established, headed by Zheng Guoxin. The county's PAD leaders became his deputies. Discord between the PLA officers and the PAD personnel soon follow.

April 12: The military control committee establishes the Feng County Proletarian Revolutionary Great Alliance Preparatory Committee. To avoid factional disputes, Paolian and certain rival mass organizations are excluded.

May 25: With the support of the local PAD, a rival mass organization opposed to Paolian, known as Liansi, is established. The preparatory committee is undermined when mass organizations withdraw from it to join Liansi.

June 23: The preparatory committee merges with Paolian to form the Feng County Proletarian Revolutionary Alliance Committee, dominated by Paolian. All sides consider the alliance committee an expanded version of Paolian.

July 4: Wang Xiaoyu, on behalf of Beijing authorities, arrives in Xuzhou to handle disputes between Xuzhou's Kick and Support factions. He blames the Xuzhou PLA for the problem and forces it to back down from its opposition to the Kick faction. This causes discord among local military commanders and worsens factional struggles in Xuzhou.

July 15: As part of Wang Xiaoyu's intervention, the PLA Unit 6174 work team temporarily withdraws from Feng County. As a result, the county's military control committee falls into hands of the PAD officers, who favor the Liansi faction. The struggles between Paolian and Liansi, and between PLA and PAD officers, intensifies over the next two months. Local civilian cadres begin to choose sides in the worsening factional disputes.

September: Large-scale factional combat breaks out in the county. Liansi is defeated and withdraws from the county seat, accompanied by PAD personnel and civilian cadres who had aligned with the faction. Troops from PLA Unit 6174 return to the county. Paolian takes over the county seat and nearby communes, while Liansi retreats to rural communes and nearby counties.

Early November: Paolian sets up a new production management office to replace the one set up by the PAD back in March. Some of the former county leaders, led by former deputy party secretary Zhu Pingfan, are appointed as its nominal heads.

December 27: Liansi organizes an armed brigade to carry out guerrilla warfare in rural communes; Paolian takes over the PAD arsenal and distributes weapons to its affiliates in the county seat and rural communes. Factional combat and raids to seize control of resources spread over the following months, leading to widespread casualties and property damage.

1968

March 2: A PLA Unit 6174 Mao Zedong Thought propaganda team, headed by commander Xia Jidao, replaces the previous military work team; the military control committee is revived with Xia Jidao as its new leader, replacing Zheng Guoxin, who withdraws from the county.

March 5: Paolian and Liansi sign an agreement to halt violent clashes, surrender weapons, and have their members to return to work.

March 13: Xuzhou military authorities convene a "study class" (*xuexi ban*) for military officers and factional leaders across Xuzhou Prefecture's eight counties. Led by officers from the PLA 68th Army and the Xuzhou Military Subdistrict, the meetings fail to resolve the conflicts in Feng County.

Mid-June: Paolian and Liansi are instructed to select delegates to attend a Xuhai Study Class in Beijing. PLA officers and PAD personnel who are deeply involved in local factional struggles are also summoned to the class.

September 27: Delegates from Paolian and Liansi reach an agreement in Beijing, repeating the main points of the failed March 5 agreement. The new agreement is ignored by the two factions back in Feng County, and violent clashes continue.

December 29: Liansi militants return to the county seat and take it over by armed force. Paolian members flee to rural communes and other counties.

1969

January 31: Beijing authorities force Paolian and Liansi delegates in the Xuhai Study Class to sign another agreement that repeats the main points of the March 5 and September 27 accords, but factional fighting escalates back in Feng County.

April 1–24: The CCP's Ninth National Congress is held in Beijing. The congress announces a "decisive victory" for the Cultural Revolution, and calls for the restoration of the nation's party organizations. Wang Xiaoyu is disgraced and blamed for the ongoing problems in Xuzhou and other political errors.

April 12: During a telephone conference between Beijing delegates and local faction leaders in Feng County, Liansi activists violently invade the meeting site, kidnapping and torturing some of the Paolian representatives.

April 25: Paolian and Liansi delegations at the Xuhai class reach an agreement that renounces their connections with their factional headquarters back in the county.

May 26: Zhou Enlai and other central leaders meet with all members of the Xuhai class. Wang Xiaoyu makes a self-criticism before the participants.

June 10: The Feng County delegates at the Xuhai class reach a tentative agreement about the composition of the county revolutionary committee but disagree about who will fill which roles, especially the selection of Shao Wen to head the new government.

July 30: Central leaders meet with the entire Xuhai class and announce the composition of the Xuzhou City revolutionary committee, and the Xuhai class is disbanded. Feng County's problems, still unresolved, are passed back to the new Xuzhou authorities to resolve.

August 1: Revolutionary committees for Xuzhou City and Xuzhou Prefecture are established, headed respectively by the 68th Army's commander Zhang Zhixiu and the Xuzhou Military Subdistrict commander Chai Rongsheng.

August to early September: Xuhai Study Class delegates, upon their return from Beijing, are sent to a new study class run by the Xuzhou military authorities in the eastern suburbs of Xuzhou, in an effort to reconcile the two factions and form an alliance.

September 20: The Feng County Revolutionary Committee is established, along with a party core leading small group, both headed by the PAD leader, Shao Wen. Revolutionary committees in the county seat, rural communes, and various workplaces are filled with Liansi members and supporters of the PAD. Members of Paolian continue resistance in workplaces and communes.

November 6: Beijing transfers control over the Xuzhou municipal and prefecture revolutionary committees from the Ji'nan Military Region to the Jiangsu provincial revolutionary committee.

1970

February 11: A new PLA propaganda team, headed by the 68th Army's 202nd Division's deputy commander Wei Xianlai is sent into Feng County to ensure more evenhanded treatment of the two factions by Shao Wen and the local PAD. The county's new revolutionary committee is put under the authority of the PLA propaganda team and its provisional party committee.

March 1: The PLA propaganda team initiates the "Cleansing of the Class Ranks" and the "One Strike, Three Anti" campaigns. During the next two months, many leaders from both Paolian and Liansi are detained in study classes for self-criticism and confession.

Late May: Wei Xianlai and several subordinates from the PLA depart from Feng County, and Shao Wen once again assumes power.

July: The "Investigation of May 16 Elements" campaign is launched, to be run simultaneously with the ongoing "Class Cleansing" and "One Strike, Three Anti" campaigns. The three campaigns are merged into a single "Criticizing and Cleansing" campaign. The campaign is turned against Paolian leaders and their supporters among former civilian cadres.

September to December: Several new study classes are held, with Paolian leaders and affiliated cadres as the main targets for criticism and investigation.

1971

February: The Second Class-Cleansing Office is set up to take charge of the investigation of alleged "May 16 elements." The suppression of former Paolian members is intensified, and many are detained in isolation for investigation and coercive interrogation.

May 25–28: The Sixth CCP County Congress appoints a new county party committee, with Shao Wen as its head. In succeeding months, subcounty party organizations are restored and are filled with PAD officers, civilian cadres loyal to Liansi, and commune PAD personnel.

July to December: The May 16 elements investigation intensifies. Paolian leaders and affiliated cadres who were included as members of the revolutionary committees in 1969 are suspended from their posts and detained for interrogation and investigation.

September: China's second-ranking leader and Mao Zedong's designated heir and successor dies in disgrace in what is known as the "Lin Biao Incident." This begins the removal of military officers from regional leadership positions as members of a suspected conspiracy by officers loyal to Lin Biao.

1972

January 10: Mao Zedong signals a shift in policy: the removal of military officers from civilian administration and the rebuilding of civilian party organizations. But military leaders in many regions resist these changes.

January to March: Feng County's May 16 elements investigations reach a climax; many suspects are forced to make false confessions.

May to August: The May 16 elements investigations finalize the verdicts, and investigators are asked to ensure that the case files were strong enough to withstand overturning in the future.

August 21: The central authorities announce the gradual withdrawal of military officers from civilian administration.

August to December: County authorities narrow the focus of the investigation campaigns and begin to release suspects. Only two dozen or so key suspects remain in detention.

1973

January to October: The May 16 elements investigations are discontinued, but the county's leaders continue to insist on their correctness. Many victims of the investigation campaigns begin to present petitions of complaint in Xuzhou, Beijing, and elsewhere.

August 24–28: The CCP's Tenth National Congress is convened in Beijing. It confirms the correctness of the Cultural Revolution but blames its excesses on the Lin Biao Clique. This demoralizes military officers who had been in charge of local investigation campaigns and encourages former rebels who had been persecuted in them.

October: Remaining targets of the persecution campaigns are released from custody in Feng County. They join in petition campaigns in Beijing and elsewhere. The county authorities take measures to stop the petitioners. Anticipating their withdrawal from county administration, they speed the recruitment of former Liansi leaders into party and leadership posts.

Mid December: Xu Shiyou is transferred out of Jiangsu Province, and military control of the province begins a sharp decline.

1974

January: Beijing initiates a "Criticize Lin Biao and Confucius" campaign. The victims of the Cultural Revolution in Jiangsu, including veteran cadres and former rebels, take advantage of this new movement to defy military authorities.

February: The Xuzhou Prefecture party committee and revolutionary committee are reorganized, and veteran civilian cadre Hu Hong replaces the Xuzhou Military Subdistrict commander Chai Rongshen as the top leader.

March: Former Paolian leaders convene three mass rallies to criticize Lin Biao and Confucius in the name of the Feng County petition delegation.

April: Officers from PLA's 202nd Division are recalled to their military units and leave Feng County. A veteran civilian cadre from outside Feng County, Yin Shibin, is transferred in as deputy secretary of the county party committee and deputy director of the county revolutionary committee. The county's power structure begins to shift.

July: Two more veteran civilian cadres are transferred in as deputy party secretaries and deputy heads of the revolutionary committee. Former veteran cadres in the county return to administrative posts. Shao Wen and his supporters speed up their effort to recruit their loyalists into the party and to appoint them to leading positions.

November: Jiangsu's top remaining military leader, Wu Dasheng, is replaced by veteran cadre Peng Chong. The new provincial leadership decrees that all remaining military personnel must withdraw from civilian administration.

December: Shao Wen and other PAD officers are transferred out of Feng county. Yin Shibin and two other veteran cadres take over.

1975

January to February: The new county party committee meets with resistance from workplace and rural commune leaders formerly aligned with the PAD officers and Liansi. Paolian members continue to suffer from discrimination.

March to June: Deng Xiaoping sends a joint work team into Xuzhou to carry out an "overall rectification." It adopts harsh measures to extinguish continuing factional rivalries and restore the operation of the railway system and other enterprises.

May to July: The Jiangsu Province party committee convenes a Xuhai region theoretical study class. Some four dozen cadres and two faction leaders from Feng County are summoned to participate. Former Liansi leaders and cadres loyal to them are severely criticized for resisting the new county authorities and are forced to make thorough confessions.

August 16: The new county authorities set up a "Work Team for Theoretical Studies," composed of many veteran cadres and Paolian leaders who had suffered suppression by the PAD.

September 1: The work team for theoretical studies is renamed the "Work Team for Learning from Dazhai in Agriculture" and is sent to four rural communes to reduce the influence of former PAD and Liansi loyalists.

September 10: The county authorities announce the withdrawal of all charges against the victims of the May 16 elements investigations.

October to early 1976: Many former Liansi leaders and loyalists lose their positions.

1976

February: Deng Xiaoping loses favor and is removed from leading posts; Beijing initiates the "Criticize Deng and Counterattack against the Right-wing Resurgence" campaign. Former Liansi leaders and affiliated cadres take advantage of the campaign to defy the county authorities.

April 5: Central leaders order a crackdown on massive demonstrations on Tiananmen Square; the campaign to criticize Deng and the right-wing resurgence intensifies.

April to September: Former Liansi leaders and affiliated cadres launch an offensive to undermine the new prefecture and county leaders.

September 9: Mao Zedong dies; political struggles within the central leadership end with the arrest and denunciation of the Gang of Four and other radical leaders on October 6.

Early October: Former Liansi leaders travel to Suzhou and Nanjing to contact other dissidents and coordinate their offensive against provincial leaders. They cease their efforts and return to Feng County in mid-October after learning of the arrest of the Gang of Four.

October 23: The county authorities convene mass rallies to celebrate the arrest of the Gang of Four. A mass campaign to expose and criticize the Gang of Four and their followers in the county ensues, with Liansi and its supporters as the primary targets.

1977

January to April: The campaign to expose and criticize the Gang of Four and its clients continues; Teng Zetian, He Quanfu, and a few others became the main targets.

May: Two party standing committee members formerly aligned with Liansi and the PAD are removed from their positions and isolated for further investigation.

November: Teng Zetian, He Quanfu, and four former Liansi leaders are sentenced to prison for factional activities.

1984

March 6: The county authorities set up a leading small group and a special office for cleansing the "Three Types of People" (factional activists during the Cultural Revolution).

1987

June 18: The county party committee hands over a document to the prefecture, reporting that one veteran cadre and two former rebel leaders have been punished as "Three Types" activists. This is the final reckoning of the factional struggles initiated in Feng County two decades before.

GLOSSARY OF NAMES

Leaders of Mass Organizations

Bai Hexiu (白鹤修). Junior cadre in the county grain management bureau in 1966; party member; important leader of Liansi; member of county revolutionary committee in 1969; party leader of the county pharmaceutical factory in the early 1970s; removed from his post in the "overall rectification" of 1975; imprisoned as an agent of the Gang of Four in 1977.

Cheng Yinzhen (程银真). Student in his senior year at Feng County Middle School in 1966; Communist Youth League member; important leader in the Liansi faction; member of county revolutionary committee in 1969; later assigned a job in a local potassium mine. After the Cultural Revolution, became a teacher in the Huashan Commune Middle School.

Dong Ligui (董立贵). Office staff in the county personnel bureau in 1966; selected as deputy director of the preparatory committee in summer of 1967; aligned with Paolian but not actively involved. Retired as a section chief in the county's party school after the Cultural Revolution.

Hou Li (侯立). Demobilized soldier and clerk in the county department store in 1966; non-party member; major leader of Paolian. Selected as a member of the county revolutionary committee in 1969; suffered during the May 16 elements investigation; appointed section head in the county department store after the Cultural Revolution. Removed from his post in 1987 after being designated as a "Three Types" activist.

Li Peng (李鹏). Office staff in Feng County Party Committee's rural work department in 1966; party member and major leader of Liansi; member of county revolutionary committee's standing committee in 1969; appointed head of county broadcasting station soon afterward; demoted to a position as a commune production aide after the Cultural Revolution.

Li Zhi (李直). Office staff in the county party propaganda department in 1966; party member aligned with Liansi; promoted to middle-level leading posts after the Great Alliance; became deputy director of the Pei County broadcasting and television bureau after the Cultural Revolution and remained in that post until retirement.

Li Zongzhou (李宗周). Demobilized soldier and machinery repairman at the county textile mill in 1966; non-party member and major leader of Liansi; member of county revolutionary committee's standing committee in 1969; joined the party and promoted to middle-level leading posts in the early 1970s; dismissed from the posts during the "overall rectification" of 1975; expelled from the party after the Cultural Revolution and transferred to the county distillery as ordinary worker.

Shan Shutang (单树堂). Demobilized soldier and bus driver in the Xuzhou Prefecture transportation company in 1966; non-party member and major leader of Paolian; member of the county revolutionary committee's standing committee in 1969; suffered during the May 16 elements investigations; assigned to a job in Xuzhou City in 1974.

Shao Limin (邵理民). Worker in the county hardware factory in 1966; party member and one of the top leaders of Liansi; member of the county revolutionary committee in 1969; member of the county party committee and deputy director of the county industry bureau in the early 1970s; dismissed from all posts during the "overall rectification" of 1975 and deeply involved in factional resistance afterward; given severe disciplinary warning after being investigated for factional activities after the Cultural Revolution.

Shi Hongde (史洪德). Instructor in the county rural cadre school in 1966; party member; became director of the preparatory committee in the summer of 1967; aligned with Paolian; member of the county revolutionary committee in 1969; suffered during the May 16 elements investigations; appointed party secretary of the county cotton textile mill after the Cultural Revolution.

Wang Dunmian (王敦勉). Native of Feng County and a student at Beijing Petroleum Institute in 1966; assigned to a job in the petroleum industry in Shandong in 1968; hauled back to Feng County for the May 16 elements investigations in early 1970s; released from custody in 1973 and assigned a temporary job in the county chemical fertilizer plant; appointed head of a small work unit after the Cultural Revolution.

Zhang Guichun (张桂春). Demobilized soldier and worker in the county coal mine construction company in 1966; major Liansi leader; member of the county revolutionary committee in 1969; joined the party and appointed deputy party secretary of the county department store in the early 1970s; dismissed from his post in the "overall rectification" of 1975; investigated as an agent of the Gang of Four after the Cultural Revolution and expelled from the party as a "Three Types" factional activist in 1987.

Zhang Liansheng (张连生). High school senior student at Feng County Middle School in 1966; Communist Youth League member and one of the top leaders of Paolian; member of the county revolutionary committee's standing committee in 1969; detained during the May 16 elements investigations in 1971 and not released until 1973; actively involved in petitioners' campaign about the abuses of military control in 1974; joined in the county's "Work Team for Learning from Dazhai in Agriculture" in 1975; restored to responsible positions in 1977. Entered Nanjing Medical College in 1978 and joined the party; worked at the Xuzhou bureau of coal mines from 1982; received a disciplinary warning during the "Three Types" investigation in the mid-1980s but was not expelled from the party.

Zhang Ludao (张鲁道). Office staff in the county party propaganda department in 1966; party member and lesser leader of Paolian; survived the May 16 elements investigations in the early 1970s; promoted to the posts of deputy director of the county education bureau and head of county party school after the Cultural Revolution.

Civilian Cadres

Cai Zhenhong (蔡振洪). Deputy county magistrate in charge of security and legal affairs in 1966; aligned with Liansi and the county PAD; member of the county revolutionary committee and the county party committee in the early 1970s; became deputy chairman of the Xinyi County People's Congress after the Cultural Revolution.

Dong Hongzhi (董洪芝). Head of the county party discipline committee in 1966; aligned with Liansi and the county PAD; member of the county revolutionary committee's standing committee in 1969; member of the county party committee's standing committee in 1971; appointed director of the Xuzhou Prefecture meat processing plant in 1975.

Gao Xiamin (高侠民). Junior cadre in a rural commune in 1966; aligned with Liansi and the county PAD; appointed director of Shahe Commune Revolutionary Committee in 1969 and party secretary of the commune in 1971; fabricated the false case against the alleged "Shahe Anti-Communist Regiment," for which he was suspended from all posts during the "overall rectification" of 1975. Reappointed as the top leader of Jinling Commune in early 1976 during the Criticize Deng Xiaoping campaign and stayed in that post until the late 1970s; investigated in the mid-1980s and expelled from the party after being designated a "Three Type" activist in 1987.

Gao Ying (高膺). First secretary of the county party committee in 1966; criticized and suspended from his post in the first months of 1967; became deputy director of Xuzhou Prefecture grain management bureau in 1972; eventually retired after the Cultural Revolution as head of the Xuzhou Prefecture finance and trade office.

Guan Yaoting (关耀庭). Deputy secretary of the Xuzhou Prefecture Party Committee in 1966; aligned with Xuzhou Military Subdistrict authorities early in the Cultural Revolution; became deputy director of the prefecture's revolutionary committee and deputy party secretary of the prefecture party committee in 1971; removed from his posts during the "overall rectification" of 1975.

He Quanfu (何泉福). Deputy party secretary of the Feng County town before the Cultural Revolution; aligned with Liansi; became party secretary of Shazhuang Commune in 1971; promoted to head the county revolutionary committee's general office in 1974; lost his post in early 1976 as part of the "overall rectification"; became deeply involved in factional activity during the Criticize Deng campaign; sentenced to prison after the Cultural Revolution as an agent of the Gang of Four.

Hu Hong (胡宏). Party secretary of Yangzhou Prefecture, Jiangsu, in 1966; suspended from all posts early in 1967; appointed deputy secretary of Yancheng Prefecture Party Committee and deputy director of the Yancheng Prefecture Revolutionary Committee in 1972; became secretary of the Xuzhou Prefecture Party Committee and director of the Xuzhou Prefecture Revolutionary Committee in 1974; promoted to posts of deputy director of Jiangsu Province Revolutionary Committee in 1975 and first party secretary of Fujian Province in 1982.

Lu Shaoshi (鲁少时). Party secretary of Donghai County in 1966; criticized and suspended from posts early in 1967; appointed deputy secretary of the Feng County Party Committee in 1974 and party secretary in 1978; became director of the Xuzhou Prefecture propaganda department in 1982.

Peng Chong (彭冲). Member of the Jiangsu Province Party Committee secretariat in 1966; removed from all posts early in 1967; became deputy director of the Jiangsu Province Revolutionary Committee in 1968 and deputy secretary of the Jiangsu Province Party Committee in 1969; coordinated a campaign against military leaders in 1974, after which he became party secretary of Jiangsu Province later that year; eventually retired as deputy chairman of the National People's Congress.

Qian Xiufu (钱秀夫). Deputy party secretary and county magistrate in 1966; criticized and suspended from his posts early 1967; became deputy director of the county revolutionary

committee and deputy secretary of the county party committee during the "overall rectification" of 1975; retired from these posts soon after the Cultural Revolution.

Sun Shudian (孙树典). Director of the county public security bureau in 1966; removed from his
post by rebels in his bureau early in 1967, aligned with Paolian; suffered in the investigation
campaigns after 1969; became director of Tongshan County Public Security Bureau in 1975;
promoted to deputy chief procurator of Xuzhou City after the Cultural Revolution and
eventually retired from that post.

Teng Zetian (滕泽田). Deputy secretary of the county party committee in 1966; aligned with
Liansi and the county PAD; became leader of the production command group under the
county revolutionary committee in 1969; became actively involved in factional activity in
opposition to the county's leaders during the "Criticize Deng" campaign; sentenced to six
years in prison as an agent of the Gang of Four after the Cultural Revolution.

Wang Xiaoyu (王效禹). Deputy mayor of Qingdao City, Shandong, in 1966; initiated rebel
power seizures in Qingdao and Ji'nan with prior permission from Beijing; appointed head
of the Shandong Province Revolutionary Committee and first party secretary and political
commissar of the the Ji'nan Military Region in early 1967; intervened in Xuzhou on the
orders of Beijing on behalf of the Kick faction; criticized and purged at the end of the Ninth
CCP Party Congress in 1969.

Xu Jiatun (许家屯). Member of the Jiangsu Province Party Committee secretariat in 1966;
criticized and removed from office in early 1967; reappointed to provincial party leadership
posts in the early 1970s; helped to coordinate the campaign against military leaders in 1974;
succeeded Peng Chong as head of the Jiangsu Province Party Committee at the end of 1976.
Elevated to the Central Committee in the 1980s; as head of the Hong Kong branch of the
New China News Agency in 1989, he denounced the June 4 military crackdown and went
into exile in the United States until his death in 2016 at age 100.

Xu Zhendong (徐振东). Deputy chief of staff of the Xuzhou Prefecture Party Committee in
1966; lost his post in early 1967; appointed deputy secretary of the Feng County Party Committee in 1974; became secretary of the Pei County Party Committee in 1975; retired as
deputy director of the Xuzhou Prefecture administration office after the Cultural
Revolution.

Yin Shibin (尹士彬). Party secretary of Xinyi County in 1966; criticized and purged in early
1967; appointed deputy secretary of the Feng County Party Committee in March 1974 and
promoted to secretary in December; became deputy director of the Xuzhou Prefecture
administration office in 1978.

Zhu Guangren (朱广忍). Head of the county finance department in 1966; along with Shao Wen
and Dong Hongzhi, one of three members of the 1966 county party committee to hold a
responsible post in the 1969 revolutionary committee. He had no factional affiliation prior
to his selection to the revolutionary committee, and therefore was acceptable to both sides,
especially to Paolian, which sought a counterweight to Liansi's Dong Hongzhi. Later persecuted during the "cleansing" campaigns along with other Paolian leaders.

Zhu Pingfan (朱平凡). Deputy party secretary of the county party committee in 1966; aligned
with Paolian in the summer of 1967; suffered criticism and investigation after the great alliance in 1969; became deputy director of the Donghai County revolutionary committee and
deputy party secretary of its party committee in 1975; retired as chairman of the Donghai
County People's Congress after the Cultural Revolution.

Military Officers

Chai Rongsheng (柴荣生). Commander of the Xuzhou Military Subdistrict in 1966; aligned with Xuzhou's Support faction; appointed director of the prefecture revolutionary committee in 1969 and secretary of prefecture party committee in 1971; promoted to deputy commander of the Jiangsu Province Military District in 1974.

Guo Fengcai (郭凤才). Chief of staff of PLA Unit 6174 in 1966; member of the "support the left" work team in Feng County in 1967; withdrew from the county in 1970.

Li Bude (李布德). Political commissar of the PLA 68th Army in 1966, aligned with Xuzhou's Kick faction; transferred to the Shanxi Province Military District as political commissar in 1969.

Li Gengxin (李庚新). Acting political commissar of the PLA 68th Army's engineering corps in 1966; in charge of "support the left" work in Feng and Pei Counties beginning early 1967; intervened repeatedly in Feng County politics.

Liu Zongbin (刘宗斌). Commander of Feng County PAD in 1966; firmly aligned with Liansi; transferred to Donghai County as commander of its PAD in 1969; later became head of the Donghai County Revolutionary Committee and county party secretary but lost his post in 1975.

Ma Chi (马驰). Deputy commander of the Feng County PAD in 1966; firmly aligned with Liansi; transferred to the same position in Tongshan County's PAD in 1970.

Shao Wen (邵文). Political commissar of the Feng County PAD and member of the county party standing committee in 1966; appointed deputy director of the county cultural revolution small group in the summer of 1966; active in "support the left" work and firmly aligned with Liansi; became head of the county revolutionary committee in 1969 and secretary of the county party committee in 1971; transferred to Haimen County PAD, Nantong Prefecture, in 1974 and retired there in 1981.

Wang Ruzhen (王如珍). Deputy commander of the Xuzhou Military Subdistrict in 1966; joined in "support the left" work in Xuzhou Prefecture during 1967; appointed deputy director of the prefecture revolutionary committee in 1969 and deputy secretary of the prefecture party committee in 1971; withdrew from civilian leadership posts in 1975.

Wei Xianlai (卫先来). Deputy commander of the PLA 68th Army's 202nd Division in 1966; appointed head of the PLA Unit 6063 Mao Zedong Thought propaganda team sent to Feng County in early 1970; left the county several months afterward.

Wu Dasheng (吴大胜). Deputy director of the Nanjing Military Region's logistics department in 1966; aligned with Nanjing's pro-army rebel faction; appointed deputy director of the Jiangsu Province Revolutionary Committee in 1968 and deputy secretary of the Jiangsu Province Party Committee in 1969; became the top provincial leader at the end of 1973; removed at the end of 1974 and retired from the military after the Cultural Revolution.

Wu Huaicai (吴怀才). Deputy commander the PLA 68th Army in 1966; aligned with Xuzhou's Support faction; appointed deputy director of the Xuzhou municipal revolutionary committee in 1969; became commander of the 68th Army the same year; became the top leader in Xuzhou in 1971; withdrew from party and government posts in 1974.

Xia Jidao (夏计道). Commander of PLA Unit 6174 in 1966; became head of its PLA Mao Zedong Thought propaganda team in Feng County in March 1968; appointed deputy director of the county revolutionary committee in 1969; suspended from leading posts in the early 1970s and forced to retire soon afterward.

Xu Fang (徐方). Deputy commander of the PLA 68th Army's engineering corps in 1966; joined in Feng County "support the left" work in early 1967; supported Paolian and was criticized by Liansi and the county's PAD officers; was in Feng County for only a few months and was afterward uninvolved in the county's politics.

Xu Shiyou (许世友). Commander of the Nanjing Military Region in 1966; aligned with Nanjing's pro-army rebel faction; appointed head of the Jiangsu Province Revolutionary Committee in 1968 and secretary of the Jiangsu Province Party Committee in 1969; transferred as commander of the Guangzhou Military Region in 1973.

Zhang Zhixiu (张钰秀). Commander of the PLA 68th Army in 1966; aligned with Xuzhou's Support faction; became head of the Xuzhou municipal revolutionary committee in 1969; promoted to posts of deputy commander of the Ji'nan Military Region and vice-chairman of the Shandong Province Revolutionary Committee shortly afterward.

Zheng Guoxin (郑国信). Political commissar of PLA Unit 6174 in 1966; head of its "support the left" work team in Feng County from 1967 to early 1968; aligned with Paolian and deeply involved in local factional conflicts; suspended from leading posts in the early 1970s and forced to retire.

BIBLIOGRAPHY

Secondary Sources

Bu Weihua. *Zalan jiu shijie: Wenhua da geming de dongluan yu haojie* (Smashing the old world: The catastrophic turmoil of the Cultural Revolution). Hong Kong: Zhongwen daxue chubanshe, 2008.

Chan, Anita. "Dispelling Misconceptions about the Red Guard Movement—The Necessity to Re-examine Cultural Revolution Factionalism and Periodization." *Journal of Contemporary China* 1, 1 (September 1992): 61–85.

Chan, Anita, Richard Madsen, and Jonathan Unger. *Chen Village: The Recent History of a Peasant Community in Mao's China.* Berkeley: University of California Press, 1984.

Chan, Anita, Stanley Rosen, and Jonathan Unger, eds. *On Socialist Democracy and the Chinese Legal System: The Li Yizhe Debates.* Armonk, NY: ME Sharpe, 1985.

Cultural Revolution Database. *The Chinese Cultural Revolution Database,* edited by Song Yongyi. Hong Kong: Universities Service Centre for China Studies, Chinese University of Hong Kong, 2002. CD-ROM, online at http://ccrd.usc.cuhk.edu.hk.

Dong Guoqiang and Andrew G. Walder. "Forces of Disorder: The Army in Xuzhou's Factional Warfare, 1967–1969." *Modern China* 44, 2 (March 2018): 139–169.

———. "Foreshocks: Local Origins of Nanjing's Qingming Demonstrations of 1976." *China Quarterly* 220 (December 2014): 1092–1110.

———. "From Truce to Dictatorship: Creating a Revolutionary Committee in Jiangsu." *China Journal* 68 (July 2012): 1–32.

———. "Local Politics in the Chinese Cultural Revolution: Nanjing under Military Control." *Journal of Asian Studies* 70, 2 (May 2011): 425–447.

———. "Nanjing's Failed 'January Revolution' of 1967: The Inner Politics of a Provincial Power Seizure." *China Quarterly* 203 (September 2010): 675–692.

———. "Nanjing's 'Second Cultural Revolution' of 1974." *China Quarterly* 212 (December 2012): 893–918.

Elvin, Mark. *The Retreat of the Elephants: An Environmental History of China.* New Haven, CT: Yale University Press, 2004.

Forster, Keith. *Rebellion and Factionalism in a Chinese Province: Zhejiang, 1966–1976.* Armonk, NY: ME Sharpe, 1990.

———. "Spontaneous and Institutional Rebellion in the Cultural Revolution: The Extraordinary Case of Weng Senhe." *Australian Journal of Chinese Affairs* 27 (January 1992): 39–75.

Friedman, Edward, Paul G. Pickowicz, and Mark Selden. *Revolution, Resistance, and Reform in Village China.* New Haven, CT: Yale University Press, 2005.

Hinton, William. *Shenfan: The Continuing Revolution in a Chinese Village.* New York: Random House, 1983.

Jiangsu sheng dang'an ju, ed. *Jiangsu sheng dashiji (1949–1985)* (Jiangsu Province chronology [1949–1985]). Nanjing: Jiangsu renmin chubanshe, 1988.

McFarquhar, Roderick. *The Origins of the Cultural Revolution.* Vol. 3, *The Coming of the Cataclysm 1961–1966.* New York: Columbia University Press, 1997.

MacFarquhar, Roderick, and Michael Schoenhals. *Mao's Last Revolution.* Cambridge, MA.: Harvard University Press, 2006.

Nelsen, Harvey W. *The Chinese Military System: An Organizational Study of the Chinese People's Liberation Army.* 2nd ed. Boulder, CO: Westview Press, 1981.

———. "Military Forces in the Cultural Revolution." *China Quarterly* 51 (July–September 1972): 444–474.

Oi, Jean C. *State and Peasant in Contemporary China: The Political Economy of Village Government.* Berkeley: University of California Press, 1989.

Perry, Elizabeth J. *Rebels and Revolutionaries in North China, 1845–1945.* Stanford, CA: Stanford University Press, 1980.

Rosen, Stanley. "Guangzhou's Democracy Movement in Cultural Revolution Perspective." *China Quarterly* 101 (March 1985): 1–31.

Schoenhals, Michael. "'Why Don't We Arm the Left?' Mao's Culpability for the Cultural Revolution's 'Great Chaos' of 1967." *China Quarterly* 182 (June 2005): 277–300.

Song Guoqing. "The Floating Fate of a Rebel Leader in Guangxi, 1966–1984." Pp. 174–199 in *Victims, Perpetrators, and the Role of Law in Maoist China,* ed. Daniel Leese and Puck Engman. Berlin and Boston: Walter de Gruyter, 2018.

Su, Yang. *Collective Killings in China during the Cultural Revolution.* New York: Cambridge University Press, 2011.

Tan Hecheng. *The Killing Wind: A Chinese County's Descent into Madness during the Cultural Revolution.* New York: Oxford University Press, 2017.

Tanigawa, Shinichi. *The Dynamics of the Chinese Cultural Revolution in the Countryside: Shaanxi, 1966–1971.* PhD diss., Department of Sociology, Stanford University, 2007.

———. "The Policy of the Military 'Supporting the Left' and the Spread of Factional Warfare in China's Countryside: Shaanxi, 1967–1968." *Modern China* 44, 1 (January 2018): 35–67.

Teiwes, Frederick C., and Warren Sun. *The End of the Maoist Era: Chinese Politics During the Twilight of the Cultural Revolution, 1972–1976.* Armonk, NY: ME Sharpe, 2007.

Unger, Jonathan. "Cultural Revolution Conflict in the Villages," *China Quarterly* 153 (March 1998): 82–106.

Vogel, Ezra F. *Deng Xiaoping and the Transformation of China.* Cambridge, MA: Harvard University Press, 2011.

Walder, Andrew G. *Agents of Disorder: Inside China's Cultural Revolution.* Cambridge, MA: Harvard University Press, 2019.

———. *China under Mao: A Revolution Derailed.* Cambridge, MA: Harvard University Press, 2015.

———. *Fractured Rebellion: The Beijing Red Guard Movement.* Cambridge, MA: Harvard University Press, 2009.

———. "Rebellion of the Cadres: The 1967 Implosion of the Chinese Party State." *China Journal* 75 (January 2016): 102–120.

Walder, Andrew G., and Qinglian Lu. "The Dynamics of Collapse in an Authoritarian Regime: China in 1967." *American Journal of Sociology* 122, 4 (January 2017): 1144–1182.

Walder, Andrew G., and Yang Su. "The Cultural Revolution in the Countryside: Scope, Timing, and Human Impact." *China Quarterly* 173 (March 2003): 82–107.

Wang, Shaoguang, *The Failure of Charisma: The Cultural Revolution in Wuhan*. Oxford: Oxford University Press, 1995.

Wang Wensheng, ed. *Feng xian jian zhi* (Brief annals of Feng County). Feng xian: Feng xian yinshua chang, 1986.

Xie Duanyao, ed., *Zhonggong Xuzhou lishi dashiji* (Chronology of the Chinese Communist Party in Xuzhou). Beijing: Zhonggong dangshi chubanshe, 1999.

Yu Ruimao, ed., *Jiangsu sheng Feng xian zhi* (Annals of Feng County, Jiangsu). Beijing: Zhongguo shehui kexue chubanshe, 1994.

Zhonggong Feng xian xianwei dangshi gongzuo weiyuanhui, ed., *Zhonggong Feng xian difangshi dashiji (1928.1–2002.6)* (History of the Chinese Communist Party in Feng County). Internal publication. Xuzhou, 2002.

Zhonggong Feng xian xianwei zuzhibu, Zhonggong Feng xian dangshi gongzuo weiyuanhui, Feng xian dang'an ju, *Zhongguo gongchandang Jiangsu sheng Feng xian zuzhishi ziliao* (Materials on the organizational history of the Chinese Communist Party in Feng County, Jiangsu). Beijing: Zhonggong dangshi ziliao chubanshe, 1989.

Zhonggong Jiangsu sheng Nantong shiwei zuzhibu, Zhonggong Jiangsu sheng Nantong shiwei dangshi gongzuo weiyuanhui, Jiangsu sheng Nantong shi dang'an guan, *Zhongguo gongchandang Jiangsu sheng Nantong shi zuzhishi ziliao* (Materials on the organizational history of the Chinese Communist Party in Nantong City, Jiangsu), Beijing: Zhonggong dangshi chubanshe, 1991.

Zhonggong Xuzhou shiwei zuzhibu, zhonggong Xuzhou shiwei dangshi gongzuo weiyuanhui, Xuzhou shi dang'an ju, *Zhongguo gongchandang Jiangsu sheng Xuzhou shi zuzhishi ziliao* (Materials on the organizational history of the Chinese Communist Party in Xuzhou City, Jiangsu). Beijing: Zhonggong dangshi chubanshe, 1991.

Primary Sources

Personal Diaries and Notebooks

Anonymous. Work notebooks, 1970–1972 (staff of the Feng County Revolutionary Committee "Second Office").

Guo Chaogang (郭朝刚). PLA "Support the Left" notebooks, 1967–1969 (platoon-level officer, member of PLA Unit 6174 propaganda team in Feng County from 1968 to 1970).

Qi He (齐河). Work notebooks, 1971–1973 (staff of the Feng County Revolutionary Committee "Second Office").

Shao Limin. Work notebooks, 1968–1975 (worker in Feng County hardware factory; major leader of Liansi).

Zhang Liansheng. Work notebooks, 1967–1976 (student at Feng County Middle School in 1966; major leader of Paolian).

Zhang Ludao. Meeting notebooks from the Xuhai Study Class, 1968–1969 (office staff of the Feng County propaganda department in 1966; minor leader of Paolian).

Interviews

Interview no. 1. Student in Huankou Middle School in 1966; leader of the Paolian faction in Huankou Commune; became a farmer in his village. July 5, 2018.

Interview no. 2. Worker at the County Textile Mill in 1966; leader of the Mill's Paolian faction; became a work unit party leader after the Cultural Revolution. July 4, 2018.

Interview no. 3. Teacher at Feng County Middle School in 1966; member of the school's Paolian faction; middle school teacher in Xuzhou after the Cultural Revolution. July 3, 2018.

Interview no. 4. Primary school teacher in the county seat in 1966; Paolian activist; county seat's cultural and education advisor after the Cultural Revolution. July 11, 2018.

Interview no. 5. Pharmacist in the county medicine company; Liansi activist in the county health system; appointed to middle-level leading posts after the great alliance; removed during the "overall rectification" of 1975. July 10, 2018.

Interview no. 6. Cook at Liangzhai Middle School in 1966; uninvolved in factions; worked at the same school after the Cultural Revolution until his retirement. January 8, 2019.

Interview no. 7. Student in Feng County Middle School in 1966; Liansi leader in the school; became a teacher after graduation until retirement. July 5, 2018.

Interview no. 8. Native of Feng County and second-year university student in 1966; actively involved in Feng County's factional struggles in 1967; suffered the repression campaigns in early 1970s. July 4, 2018; January 8, 2019.

Hou Xianli (侯先礼). Part-time primary school teacher in Zhaozhuang Commune in 1966; leader of the commune's Liansi faction; full-time teacher in the early 1970s. January 7, 2019.

Huang Xiuhua (黄秀华). Student in Liangzhai Middle School in 1966; leader of the Paolian faction in Liangzhai Commune. July 8, 2018.

Li Zhi (李直). Staff of the county propaganda department in 1966; aligned with Liansi; promoted to middle-level leading posts after the great alliance. July 5, 2018.

Li Zongzhou (李宗周). Machinery repairman at the county textile mill in 1966; major leader of Liansi; promoted to middle-level leading posts after the great alliance; removed during the overall rectification of 1975. June 18, 2013, and July 4, 2018.

Qi Zhongmin (齐忠民). Zhaozhuang Commune farmer; military dependent; leader of commune's Paolian faction; returned to his village after the great alliance. January 7, 2019.

Shi Yuemei (史月梅). Branch party secretary of Huangdikou Brigade, Shizhai Commune, in 1966; aligned with Liansi; appointed vice-secretary of Feng County party committee in 1971; removed in 1977; retired from the county tax bureau as ordinary employee. January 6, 2019.

Xu Jiashun (徐家顺). Brigade cadre in Huashan Commune in 1966; Liansi leader in the commune; member of the commune revolutionary committee; sentenced to prison in late 1970s because of factional activities in the Cultural Revolution. July 11, 2018.

Zhang Liansheng (张连生). Feng County Middle School student in 1966; major leader of the county's Paolian faction over the next decade. June 17–20, 2013; October 24–26, 2014; December 3, 2014; November 20–21, 2016; February 8–10, 2017; July 2–4, 2018.

Confession Materials, Petitions, and Memoirs

Dong Ligui. "Huiyi chouweihui" (Reminiscence about the preparatory committee). April 28, 2016.

Feng xian nongji chang. "Guanyu Zhang Haiqing de jiaodai jiefa zonghe cailiao" (On Zhang Haiqing's comprehensive confession and exposure materials). December 24, 1976.

Gao Dalin. *Yu xiu yuan wanji* (An old man's memoirs written in the Yuxiu garden). Self-published, 2016.

Li Zhi. "Di shiyici luxian douzheng zhong jingyan jiaoxun xiaojie" (A preliminary summary of lessons learned from experience during the eleventh line struggle). February 1978.

Xu Zuolun. "Xu Zuolun shensu xin" (Xu Zuolun's petition). November 20, 1977.

———. "Xu Zuolun shensu xin" (Xu Zuolun's petition). June 19, 1978.

Xuzhou diqu fu ning shangfang tuan. "Jiefa pipan Xuzhou diqu wenti huiyi jiyao zhiyi" (Minutes of the exposure and criticism meeting about the Xuzhou Prefecture problem, no. 1). Pamphlet. May 14, 1974.

Xuzhou diqu fu ning shangfang tuan. "Jiefa pipan Xuzhou diqu wenti huiyi jiyao zhier" (Minutes of the exposure and criticism meeting about the Xuzhou Prefecture problem, no. 2). Pamphlet. May 14, 1974.

Xuzhou diqu fu ning shangfang tuan. "Jiefa pipan Xuzhou diqu wenti huiyi jiyao zhisan" (Minutes of the exposure and criticism meeting about the Xuzhou Prefecture problem, no. 3). Pamphlet. May 14, 1974.

Zhang Liansheng. "Gei Mao Zedong zhuxi ji Zhou Enlai zongli, Wang Hongwen fu zhuxi de xin" (Letter to Chairman Mao Zedong, Premier Zhou Enlai, and Vice-Chairman Wang Hongwen). October 28, 1973.

———. "Gei Hu Jintao de shensu xin" (Petition to Hu Jintao). November 22, 2000.

Zhu Pingfan, *Wangshi* (Past events). Self-published. October 10, 2013.

Unpublished Compilations

Feng xian jiaoyu ju. *Feng xian jiaoyu dashiji (1903–2016)* (Feng County education chronology [1903–2016]). Unpublished book draft. March 2016.

Feng xian shizhi bangongshi, Feng xian dangshi di er juan di si bian, ed. *"Wenhua da geming" shinian dongluan (1966.5–1976.10)* (The "Cultural Revolution" decade of turmoil [May 1966–October 1976]). Unpublished book draft. August 2016.

Xuzhou shi shizhi bangongshi bian. *Zhonggong Xuzhou difang shi (1949–1978) (Zhengqiu yijian gao)* (History of the Chinese Communist Party in Xuzhou [1949–1978] [Draft for comments]). Internal document. Xuzhou. May 2008.

Materials Issued by the Paolian Faction (in Chronological Order)

Feng xian shachang paolian pai "er.san shijian diaocha zu." "Er yue san ri zhuan'an diaocha baogao" (Investigation report on the "February 3 incident"). June 3, 1967.

Feng xian yinshua chang hongyin zaofan tuan. "Renwu bu shi zenyang yakua women zuzhide" (How the People's Armed Department crushed our organization). June 19, 1967.

Feng xian paoda silingbu lianhe zongbu he Feng zhong honglian. "Feng bai hongweidui shi zenyang kuade" (How the Red Guard Brigade of the Feng County department store collapsed). June 1967.

Feng xian paoda silingbu lianhe zongbu. "Zhongguo renmin jiefangjun 6174 budui zaici jinzhu Fengcheng, Fengcheng geming xingshi dahao chengnei kaishi huifu xin zhixu" (People's

Liberation Army Unit 6174 redeployed to Feng County Seat, order is being restored). *"Paoda silingbu" haowai*, September 14, 1967.

"Paolian zhanshi shizuo geming lianhe de cujin pai" (Paolian fighters resolve to promote the revolutionary great alliance). *Paoda silingbu*, no. 35, March 15, 1968, p. 2.

Jiangsu sheng Feng xian paoda silingbu lianhe zongbu. "Mao Zhuxi huishou wo qianjin—Feng xian liangtiao luxian douzheng dashiji (er gao)" (Chairman Mao waves us forward—Chronology of the two-line struggle in Feng County [second draft]). June 5, 1968.

Jiangsu sheng Feng xian paoda silingbu lianhe zongbu. "Guanyu Feng xian wuzhuang bu de wenti (di er pi cailiao)" (On the problem of Feng County's People's Armed Department [second batch of materials]). June 1968.

Xuhai ban Feng xian "paolian" daibiao tuan. "Feng xian paoda silingbu lianhe zongbu qingkuang jianjie" (Brief introduction to the situation of the Feng County Bombard the Headquarters Allied General Headquarters). July 1968.

"Chedi dadao Gao Ying de hei ganjiang Liu Zongbin" (Thoroughly overthrow Gao Ying's reliable tool, Liu Zongbin). *Paoda silingbu*, no. 55, August 15, 1968.

"Chedi qingsuan Gao Ying de hei ganjiang Liu Zongbin sanbu 'duo zhongxin lun' de liudu" (Thoroughly liquidate the lingering poison of Gao Ying's reliable tool Liu Zongbin's dissemination of "many centers"). *Fenglei ji*, no. 142, August 21, 1968.

Hongweibing Feng xian zhihuibu. "Guanyu Feng xian muqian xingshi de shengming" (Declaration on the current situation in Feng County). Handbill. August 25, 1968.

"'Qisan,' 'qiersi' bugao xuanpanle Gao, Qian, Teng, Cai, Liu yihuo de sixing" (The "July 3" and "July 24" proclamations pronounce a death sentence on the Gang of Gao, Qian, Teng, Cai, and Liu). *Fenglei ji*, no. 146, September 1, 1968.

Xuhai ban Feng xian paolian daibiao tuan. "Zhi Feng xian paolian zongbu xin" (Letter to the Feng County Paolian headquarters). September 1968.

Xuhai ban Feng xian paolian daibiao tuan. "Zhi zhongyang ban de Mao Zedong sixiang xuexi ban bangongshi he zhongyang shouzhang de xin" (Letter to the office of the Center-sponsored Mao Zedong Thought study class and to central party leaders). September 2, 1968.

Xuhai ban Feng xian paolian daibiao tuan. "'Jiu.erqi' zhizhi wudou cuoshi qianding yilai, Feng xian Liansi dazaqiang shao zhua jianlun" (Brief statement about the beating, smashing, looting, arson and kidnapping by Liansi since the signing of the "September 27" measures to curtail armed conflicts). January 1969.

Xuhai ban Feng xian paolian daibiao tuan. "Zhi Xuhai ban lingdao xiaozu he zhongyang ban de Mao Zedong sixiang xuexi ban zong bangongshi de xin" (Letter to the leading group of the Xuhai Study Class and the general office of the Center-sponsored Mao Zedong Thought study class). July 11, 1969.

Materials Issued by the Liansi Faction (in Chronological Order)

Feng xian zhengfa hongse geming zaofan zong silingbu. "Feng xian wenhua da geming yundong zhong juliu anjian cheng pibiao" (Application form for authorizing arrests made during Feng County's Cultural Revolution movement). February 12, 1967.

Feng xian zhengfa hongse geming zaofan zong silingbu. "Feng xian 'paoda silingbu lianhe zongbu' de qingkuang zonghe" (An overview of the situation regarding Feng County's "Bombard the Headquarters Allied General Headquarters"). March 18, 1967.

Feng xian wuchan jieji geming zaofan pai lianhe silingbu. "Guanyu xuanchuan, xuexi, zhixing zhongyang liuyue liuri 'tongling' de guanche yijian" (Opinion on carrying out the dissemination, study, and implementation of the Center's June 6 "orders"). June 10, 1967.

Hongxin zhanshi. "Jiu Shao Wen shi cuowu de—ping nonggan xiao lianhe zaofandui 'jiu Shao Wen jiu de hao'" (Grabbing Shao Wen is mistaken—an assessment of the agricultural cadre school allied rebel brigade's "The seizing of Shao Wen was done well"). June 17, 1967.

Paolian yibing. "Paolian de dafangxiang zaojiu cuo ding le" (Paolian's general orientation has long been mistaken). Handbill. June 20, 1967.

Feng xian wuchan jieji geming zaofan lianhe silingbu diaocha yanjiu zu. "Touji fenzi de dianfan, chumai linghun de zhuanjia—kan xianwei 'lianhe,' 'hongse' liang bingtuan gebie toutou angzang linghun" (Typical speculators and specialists in betrayal—see the filthy souls of the leaders of the "Lianhe" and "Red" Corps of the county committee). June 22, 1967.

Chouweihui yibing. "Wei ziji kelian de chouweihui er tanxi" (I heave a sigh for our pathetic preparatory committee). June 23, 1967.

Feng xian zhengfa hongse geming zaofan zong silingbu, "Yanzhong shengming" (Grave declaration). June 26, 1967.

Feng xian wuchan jieji geming zaofan pai lianhe silingbu, "Jiu '8·25' lianwei (paochou) qiangza Feng xian junguanhui yi shi zhengzhong shengming" (Solemn declaration concerning the Alliance Committee (Paolian preparatory) looting and smashing of the Feng County Military Control Committee on August 25). August 29, 1967.

Hanwei 178 hao tongling zhandoudui. "Paolian yi xiaocuo fachule wudou de dongyuan ling" (A handful of people in Paolian issue mobilization order for armed combat). June 27, 1967.

Feng xian wuchan jieji geming zaofan pai lianhe silingbu. "Xingfeng xueyu sa Feng nan" (Reign of terror in the south of Feng County). Jiu.yisan bao, February 20, 1968.

Shao Liyun. "Wode kongsu" (My accusation). Reprinted in Feng xian wuchan jieji geming zaofan pai lianhe silingbu, Jiu.yisan bao, February 20, 1968.

Xuhai ban Feng xian liansi daibiaotuan. "Wang Xiaoyu, Li Bude jiqi Xu Fang, Zheng Guoxin zai Xuhai diqu tuixing zichan jieji fandong luxian zhi yipai ya yi pai de zui'e" (The crimes of Wang Xiaoyu, and Li Bude along with Xu Fang and Zheng Guoxin in carrying out the bourgeois reactionary line of supporting one faction while suppressing another in the Xuhai region). August 6, 1968.

Yuan liansi zongbu. "Yuan liansi zongbu guanyu jige zhongda wenti de jiancha baogao" (Self-criticism of former Liansi headquarters regarding some major issues). May 20, 1970.

Documents Issued by Central Authorities (in Chronological Order)

Zhonggong zhongyang. "Zhonggong zhongyang guanyu wuchan jieji wenhua da geming yundong de jueding" (CCP Central Committee decision regarding the great proletarian Cultural Revolution movement). August 8, 1966. In Cultural Revolution Database.

Zhonggong zhongyang zhuanfa zhongyang junwei, zong zheng. "Guanyu jundui yuanxiao wuchan jieji wenhua da geming de jinji tongzhi" (Urgent notice on the great proletarian Cultural Revolution in military academies). October 5, 1966. In Cultural Revolution Database.

Zhonggong zhongyang. "Zhonggong zhongyang guanyu bude ba douzheng fengmang zhixiang jundui de tongzhi" (CCP Center's notice forbidding turning the spearhead of struggle toward the military). Zhongfa [67], no. 21, January 14, 1967. In Cultural Revolution Database.

"Zhou Enlai tongzhi daibiao Mao zhuxi, dang zhongyang, guowuyuan, zhongyang junwei, zhongyang wen'ge dui wuchan jieji geming zaofan pai da lianhe, da duoquan wenti zuo zhongyao zhishi" (Comrade Zhou Enlai relays important instructions to proletarian revolutionary rebels about the great alliance and great power seizure on behalf of Chairman Mao, the Party Center, the State Council, the Central Military Commission, and the Central Cultural Revolution Group). January 22, 1967.

Zhonggong zhongyang, guowuyuan, zhongyang junwei, zhongyang wen'ge xiaozu. "Guanyu renmin jiefangjun jianjue zhichi geming zuopai qunzhong de jueding" (Decision regarding the resolute support of the People's Liberation Army for the masses of the revolutionary left). Zhongfa [67], no. 27, January 23, 1967. In Cultural Revolution Database.

"Bixu zhengque duidai ganbu" (It is necessary to treat cadres correctly). Renmin ribao. February 23, 1967, p. 1.

Zhonggong zhongyang. "Zhonggong zhongyang zhuanfa zhongyang guanyu Anhui wenti de jueding ji fu jian" (CCP Central Committee transmits the Center's decision regarding the Anhui question and attachments). Zhongfa [67], no. 117, April 1, 1967. In Cultural Revolution Database.

Zhongyang junwei. "Zhongyang junwei shitiao mingling" (Ten orders of the Central Military Commission). April 6, 1967. In Cultural Revolution Database.

"Zhou Enlai Kang Sheng jiejian Shandong daibiao tuan Wang Xiaoyu Yang Dezhi deng ren de jianghua" (Zhou Enlai and Kang Sheng's speeches in a meeting with Wang Xiaoyu, Yang Dezhi, and other members of Shandong delegation). April 26, 1967. In Cultural Revolution Database.

"Zhonggong zhongyang, guowuyuan, zhongyang junwei, zhongyang wen'ge xiaozu, tongling" (Notice of the CCP Central Committee, State Council, Central Military Commission, and Central Cultural Revolution Group). Zhongfa [67], no. 178, June 6, 1967. In Cultural Revolution Database.

"Zhonggong zhongyang guanyu jinzhi tiaodong nongmin jincheng wudou de tongzhi" (Central Committee notice regarding the prohibition of the incitement of farmers to enter the cities for armed combat). Zhongfa [67], no. 218, July 13, 1967. In Cultural Revolution Database.

"Zhonggong zhongyang, guowuyuan, zhongyang junwei, zhongyang wen'ge xiaozu guanyu buzhun qiangduo renmin jiefangjun wuqi, zhuangbei he gezhong junyong wuzi de mingling" (Orders of the CCP Central Committee, State Council, Central Military Commission, and the Central Cultural Revolution Group forbidding the seizure of weapons, materials, and other military supplies from the People's Liberation Army). Zhongfa [67], no. 288, September 5, 1967. In Cultural Revolution Database.

"Zhou zongli zai jiejian Xuzhou diqu tielu, meikuang xitong, Xuzhou shi liangpai geming qunzhong zuzhi fuzeren he jundui lingdao tongzhi shi de zhongyao zhishi" (Premier Zhou Enlai's important instructions in meetings with leaders of revolutionary mass organizations from the Xuzhou Prefecture railway and coal systems and Xuzhou City, and leading comrades in the military). December 30, 1968. In Cultural Revolution Database.

"Zhongyang shouzhang jiejian Mao Zedong sixiang xuexi ban Xuhai ban de jianghua" (Talks by central leaders when meeting with the Xuhai group in the Mao Zedong Thought study class). May 26, 1969. In Cultural Revolution Database.

Zhonggong zhongyang. "Zhongguo gongchandang zhongyang weiyuanhui bugao" (Proclamation of the Central Committee of the Chinese Communist Party). Zhongfa [69], no. 41, July 23, 1969. In Cultural Revolution Database.

"Zhonggong zhongyang dui chengli Jiangsu sheng Lianyungang shi geming weiyuanhui de pishi" (The CCP Central Committee's response to establishment of Lianyungang Municipal Revolutionary Committee). Zhongfa [69], no. 64, September 25, 1969.

"Zhongyang shouzhang dui gesheng Mao Zedong sixiang xuexiban chengyuan de jianghua" (Speeches by central leaders to the members of the various provincial Mao Zedong Thought study classes). October 17, 1969. In Cultural Revolution Database.

Zhonggong zhongyang. "Guanyu daji fangeming pohuai huodong de zhishi" (Instructions regarding striking against counterrevolutionary sabotage activities). Zhongfa [70], no. 3, January 31, 1970. In Cultural Revolution Database.

Zhonggong zhongyang. "Guanyu fandui tanwu, touji daoba de zhishi" (Instructions regarding opposing corruption and speculation). Zhongfa [70], no. 5, February 5, 1970. In Cultural Revolution Database.

Zhonggong zhongyang. "Guanyu fandui puzhang langfei de tongzhi" (Notice regarding extravagance and waste). Zhongfa [70], no. 6, February 5, 1970. In Cultural Revolution Database.

Wu De. "Wu De guanyu qingcha 'wu.yiliu' de jianghua" (Wu De's speech on the "May 16" investigations). December 20, 1971. In Cultural Revolution Database.

Ji Dengkui. "Ji Dengkui zai guowuyuan huibao ganbu huiyi shi de jianghua jingshen" (The essence of Ji Dengkui's speech at the cadre reporting meeting of the State Council). March 31, 1972. In Cultural Revolution Database.

Wu De. "Wu De guanyu qingcha 'wu.yiliu' de jianghua" (Wu De's Speech about the "May 16" investigations). April 1972. In Cultural Revolution Database.

Zhonggong zhongyang. "Zhonggong zhongyang, zhongyang junwei guanyu zhengxun dui sanzhi liangjun wenti de yijian tongzhi" (Notice of the CCP Central Committee and Central Military Commission on questions about the three supports and two militaries). Zhongfa [72], no. 32, August 21, 1972. In Cultural Revolution Database.

Zhonggong zhongyang. "Guanyu zai pi Lin pi Kong yundong zhong jige wenti de dafu" (Responses to certain questions that have arisen in the Criticize Lin Biao and Confucius Campaign). Zhongfa [74], no. 12, April 10, 1974. In Cultural Revolution Database.

Zhonggong zhongyang. "Guanyu jiaqiang tielu gongzuo de jueding" (Decision on strengthening railway work). Zhongfa [75], no. 9, March 5, 1975. In Cultural Revolution Database.

Zhonggong zhongyang. "Pizhuan 'Zhonggong Jiangsu shengwei guanyu Xuzhou diqu guanche zhixing zhongyang 9 hao wenjian de qingkuang xiang zhonggong zhongyang, guowuyuan de baogao'" (Relaying with instructions "Report to the Central Committee and State Council by the Jiangsu provincial party committee on the thorough implementation of central document no. 9 in Xuzhou Prefecture"). Zhongfa [75], no. 12, June 2, 1975. In Cultural Revolution Database.

Zhonggong zhongyang. "Guanyu nuli wancheng quannian gangtie shengchan jihua de pishi" (Instructions on striving to complete the annual production plan for iron and steel). Zhongfa [75], no. 13, June 4, 1975. In Cultural Revolution Database.

Zhonggong zhongyang. "Pizhuan Deng Xiaoping zai zhongyang junwei kuoda huiyi shang de jianghua" (Relaying Deng Xiaoping's speech at the enlarged Central Military Commission conference). July 15, 1975. In Cultural Revolution Database.

Zhonggong zhongyang. "Zhuanfa Zhejiang shengwei 'Guanyu zhengque chuli tuji fazhan de dangyuan he tiba de ganbu de qingshi baogao'" (Circulating Zhejiang provincial party committee's "On the correct handling of those who were rushed into party membership and promoted as cadres"). Zhongfa [75], no. 16, July 17, 1975. In Cultural Revolution Database.

Zhonggong zhongyang. "Zhuanfa guowuyuan 'Guanyu jinnian shangban nian gongye shengchan qingkuang de baogao'" (Relaying the State Council's "Report on the production situation during the first half of this year"). Zhongfa [75], no. 17, July 17, 1975. In Cultural Revolution Database.

"Zhonggong zhongyang tongzhi" (Notice issued by the CCP Central Committee). October 7, 1976.

Zhonggong zhongyang. "Guanyu Hua Guofeng tongzhi ren Zhongguo gongchandang zhongyang weiyuanhui zhuxi, Zhongguo gongchandang zhongyang junshi weiyuanhui zhuxi de jueyi" (On the decision to appoint Comrade Hua Guofeng to the posts of chairman of the CCP Central Committee and the Central Military Commission). Zhongfa [76], no. 15, October 7, 1976. In Cultural Revolution Database.

"Zhongyang zhengzhiju tongzhi jiejian Peng Chong, Xu Jiatun tongzhi shi de tanhua jilu" (Minutes of the talks between Politburo comrades and comrades Peng Chong and Xu Jiatun). October 7, 1976.

"Zhonggong zhengzhiju lingdao tongzhi shiyue qiri wan zhi bari lingchen zai si shengshi san junqu fuze tongzhi huishang de jianghua (genju jilu zhengli)" (Speeches by leading comrades of the Politburo at a meeting with responsible comrades from four provinces and cities and three military regions on the evening of October 7 and early morning hours of October 8 [compiled from minutes]). October 7–8, 1976.

Zhonggong zhongyang. "Guanyu jianguo yilai dang de ruogan lishi wenti de jueyi" (Resolution on certain problems of party history since the founding of the nation). June 27, 1981. In Cultural Revolution Database.

Zhonggong zhongyang. "Guanyu qingli lingdao banzi zhong 'sanzhong ren' wenti de tongzhi" (Notice on the problem of cleansing the 'Three Types' from leading groups). Zhongfa [82], no. 55, December 30, 1982. In Cultural Revolution Database.

Zhongyang zhengdang gongzuo zhidao weiyuanhui bangongshi. "Guanyu zuohao qingli 'sanzhong ren' diaocha heshi gongzuo jige wenti de tongzhi" (Notice on several problems in verifying the investigation work of "Three Types"). April 26, 1984. In Cultural Revolution Database.

Zhonggong zhongyang. "Guanyu qingli 'sanzhong ren' ruogan wenti de buchong tongzhi" (Supplementary notice on various problems in the investigation of "Three Types"). Zhongfa [84], no. 17, July 31, 1984. In Cultural Revolution Database.

Documents Issued by Regional and Local Authorities
(in Chronological Order)

Zhonggong Feng xian weiyuanhui. "Zhonggong Feng xian weiyuanhui pizhuan xianwei zuzhibu guanyu jiaqiang dang de jianshe wenti de sange baogao" (Feng County party committee transmits organization department's three reports on strengthening party building). May 13, 1966.

Zhonggong Feng xian xianwei xuanchuan bu. "Guanyu kaizhan wenhua da geming xuexi de tongzhi" (Notice on unfolding the study of the Cultural Revolution). May 25, 1966.

Zhonggong Feng xian weiyuanhui. "Guanyu chengli xianwei wuchan jieji wenhua da geming lingdao xiaozu de tongzhi" (Notice on the establishment of county party committee leading small group for the great proletarian Cultural Revolution). July 20, 1966.

Zhonggong Feng xian weiyuanhui. "Guanyu shuqi xunlian chuzhong, nongzhong jiaozhiyuan de tongzhi" (Notice on summer training sessions for junior middle school and agricultural middle school teachers and staff). July 22, 1966.

Zhonggong Feng xian weiyuanhui. "Pingfan tongzhi" (Rehabilitation notice). January 25, 1967.

Zhonggong Feng xian weiyuanhui. "Guanyu pingfan wenti de jinji tongzhi" (Urgent directive on the question of rehabilitation). January 30, 1967.

Feng xian gongan ju. "Feng xian gongan ju gonggao" (Public notice of the Feng County public security bureau). February 20, 1967.

Feng xian geming zaofan pai linshi jiandu shengchan weiyuanhui, Feng xian renmin weiyuanhui. "Guanyu fenpei huafei de tongzhi" (Notice on the distribution of chemical fertilizer). February 23, 1967.

Feng xian geming zaofanpai linshi jiandu shengchan weiyuanhui, Feng xian renmin weiyuan hui. "Guanyu renzhen zuohao shanyu yumiao yongmei gongying gongzuo de tongzhi" (Notice on carrying out well the distribution of coal for the raising of sweet potato seedlings). February 28, 1967.

Zhongguo renmin jiefangjun Jiangsu sheng Feng xian renmin wuzhuangbu shengchan bangong-shi. "Guanyu chengli xian shengchan bangongshi bing qiyong yinzhang de tongzhi" (Notice regarding the establishment of the county production office and its use of official seals of government). March 8, 1967.

Zhongguo renmin jiefangjun Jiangsu sheng Feng xian junshi guanzhi weiyuanhui. "Guanyu jianli zhua geming cu shengchan di yi xian zhihuibu de tongzhi" (Notice on the establishment of the frontline command post for grasping revolution and promoting production). April 8, 1967.

Jiangsu sheng Feng xian junguanhui zhua geming cu shengchan di yi xian zhihui bu. "Guanyu zhaokai zhengzhi gongzuo huiyi de tongzhi" (Notice on the convening of the political work conference), April 21, 1967.

Zhongguo renmin jiefangjun ji zi 283 budui gongzuozu ji 6174 budui zhu Feng xian sanzhi liangjun budui. "Guanyu 'paolian' wenti de diaocha baogao" (Investigation report on the "Paolian" question). July 6, 1967.

Zhongguo renmin jiefangjun Jiangsu sheng Feng xian renmin wuzhuangbu dangwei. "Gei Feng xian renmin de yi feng gongkai xin" (An open letter to the people of Feng County). August 20, 1967.

Zhongguo renmin jiefangjun Jiangsu sheng Feng xian junshi guanzhi weiyuanhui, Jiangsu sheng Feng xian renmin wuzhuangbu. "Lianhe shengming" (Joint declaration). August 25, 1967.

Jiangsu sheng Feng xian renmin wuzhuangbu. "Zhongguo renmin jiefangjun Jiangsu sheng Feng xian junshi guanzhi weiyuanhui yanzheng shengming" (Solemn declaration of the People's Liberation Army Military Control Committee of Feng County, Jiangsu Province). August 28, 1967.

Feng xian shengchan bangongshi. "Guanyu qiyong gongzhang de tongzhi" (Notice regarding the use of official seals of government). November 3, 1967.

Feng xian Paolian he Feng xian Liansi daibiao. "Feng xian liang pai guanyu liji zhizhi wudou de shitiao xieyi" (Feng County's two factions on the ten-point agreement to immediately end armed combat). March 5, 1968.

Zhang Zhixiu. "Zai Feng xian liangpai zhizhi wudou xieyi qianzi yishi shang de jianghua" (Speech at the signing ceremony by two Feng County factions of the agreement to end armed combat). March 5, 1968.

Xuhai ban Feng xian daibiao tuan. "Guanyu luoshi 'qisan,' 'qiersi' bugao, liji tingzhi wudou, shoujiao wuqi de xieyi" (Agreement on implementing the "July 3" and "July 24" orders to immediately halt armed battles and surrender weapons). September 27, 1968.

Xuhai ban Feng xian daibiao tuan. "Guanyu choujian Feng xian geming weiyuanhui de shishi fang'an" (On preparations for the establishment of the Feng County Revolutionary Committee), June 10, 1969.

Liushiba jun dangweihui. "Liushiba jun dangweihui guanyu guanche luoshi 'jiuda' jingshen de jige wenti de baogao" (Report of the 68th Army party committee on some questions regarding the thorough implementation of the spirit of the Ninth Party Congress). July 27, 1969.

Zhongguo renmin jiefang jun liushiba jun. "Gei Feng xian, Pei xian guangda geming qunzhong de yi feng xin" (Letter to the broad revolutionary masses of Feng and Pei Counties). August 19, 1969.

Zhonggong liushiba jun weiyuanhui. "Guanyu chengli Jiangsu sheng Lianyungang shi geming weiyuanhui de qingshi baogao" (Report on the request for instructions regarding the establishment of the Lianyungang City revolutionary committee). September 12, 1969.

Zhonggong liushiba jun gongqu weiyuanhui. "Guanyu chengli Jiangsu sheng Feng xian geming weiyuanhui de qingshi baogao" (Report on the request for instructions on establishing a revolutionary committee in Feng County, Jiangsu). September 16, 1969.

Zhonggong liushiba jun weiyuanhui. "Dui liushiba jun gongqu dangwei 'guanyu chengli Jiangsu sheng Feng xian geming weiyuanhui de qingshi baogao' de pishi" (Comments on the report from the party committee of engineering unit of the 68th Army on establishing a revolutionary committee in Feng County, Jiangsu). September 17, 1969.

Liulingliusan budui zhu Feng junxuandui linshi dangwei, Feng xian geming weiyuan hui. "Guanyu guanche zhixing Xuzhou zhuanqu geming weiyuanhui 'Yingjie weida lingxiu Mao zhuxi "qi.erjiu" guanghui pishi yizhou nian tongzhi' de baogao" (Report on thoroughly carrying out the Xuzhou Prefecture revolutionary committee's "Notice on welcoming the first anniversary of the great leader Chairman Mao's Glorious 'July 29' Comment"). May 14, 1970.

Feng xian geming weiyuanhui qingdui bangongshi. "Guanyu dangqian qingdui gongzuo de jidian yijian" (Opinions on current class-cleansing works). June 25, 1970.

Feng xian geming weiyuanhui. "Guanyu wuchan jieji wenhua da geming zhong liang, qian, wu qingli de yijian (huiyi taolun gao)" (Suggestions regarding the problem of grain, funds, and supplies during the great proletarian Cultural Revolution [meeting discussion draft]), July 21, 1970.

Feng xian geming weiyuanhui. Jian bao 13, August 16, 1970.

Feng xian jiguan ganbu Mao Zedong sixiang xuexi ban. "Zhang Liansheng tongzhi daibiao yuan Paolian zongbu xiang quan xian renmin zuo guanyu wuchan jieji wenhua da geming zhong jingyan jiaoxun zongjie huibao" (Comrade Zhang Liansheng's summary report to all the people of the county, representing the former Paolian headquarters, regarding the lessons learned during the great proletarian Cultural Revolution). August 27, 1970.

Feng xian jiguan ganbu Mao Zedong sixiang xuexi ban. "Li Zongzhou tongzhi daibiao yuan Liansi zongbu xiang quan xian renmin zuo guanyu wuchan jieji wenhua da geming zhong jingyan jiaoxun zongjie huibao" (Comrade Li Zongzhou's summary report to all the people of the county, representing the former Liansi headquarters, regarding the lessons learned during the great proletarian Cultural Revolution). August 27, 1970.

"Fennu jiefa Yang Zhengxiang fandui Mao zhuxi, duikang dang zhongyang de taotian zuixing" (Angrily expose Yang Zhengxiang's monstrous crimes of opposing Chairman Mao and resisting the Party Center). In *Xuzhou shi tielu fenju junguanhui, geweihui Mao Zedong sixiang xuexi ban jiefa cailiao zhuanji (shisan)*, October 14, 1970.

Feng xian daji daohui men linshi bangongshi. *Qingkuang jianbao*, no. 4, January 7, 1971.

Jiangsu sheng Feng xian geming weiyuanhui zhenggong zu. "Guanyu zhaokai Zhongguo gongchandang Feng xian di liuci dahui de xuanchuan tigang" (Propaganda outline regarding the opening of the Sixth Feng County Communist Party Congress). April 20, 1971.

Zhonggong Xuzhou diwei. "Xuzhou diwei dianhua huiyi jilu" (Minutes of the telephone conference of the Xuzhou Prefecture party committee). September 7, 1971.

Zhonggong Feng xian xianwei. "Guanyu yijiuqiyi nian geming, shengchan de jiben qingkuang he jindong mingchun gongzuo anpai yijian" (Regarding the basic situation in revolution and production in 1971, and suggestions about arranging work this winter and next spring). January 3, 1972.

Feng xian gongan jiguan junguanhui. "Qingkuang jianbao, disanqi, sanyue fen di, she qingkuang" (Situation report, no. 3, Enemy's activities and social situation in March). March 28, 1972.

Feng xian gongan jiguan junguanhui. "Dangqian gongzuo de jidian yijian" (Several suggestions regarding current work). July 7, 1972.

Feng xian gongan jiguan junguanhui. "Qingkuang jianbao, dijiuqi, jiuyue fen di, she qingkuang" (Situation report, no. 9, Enemy's activities and social situation in September). September 28, 1972.

Feng xian geming weiyuanhui. "Feng xian 'siwu,' 'wuwu' jingji fazhan guihua (cao'an)" (Feng County's economic development plan for the fourth and fifth five-year plans). March 1973.

Feng xian gongan jiguan junguanhui, Feng xian geweihui zhengfa zu. "Guanyu Sunlou gongshe fanxinzhan douzheng shidian gongzuo de zongjie baogao" (Summary report on the provisional methods practiced in Sunlou Commune to fight against enemy's psychological warfare). April 10, 1973.

Feng xian gongan jiguan junguanhui. "Qingkuang jianbao, disiqi, siyue fen di, she qingkuang" (Situation report, no. 4, Enemy's activities and social situation in April). April 28, 1973.

Zhonggong Feng xian weiyuanhui. "Guanyu chengguan zhen deng ershiyi ge jiceng dangwei gaixuan de pifu" (Reply regarding the revised selection of members of the party committees of the county seat and 20 other basic-level committees). May 25, 1973.

Zhonggong Feng xian weiyuanhui. "Guanyu Ji Xingchang, Chao Daiqin deng liu tongzhi renzhi de tongzhi" (Notice regarding the appointment of Ji Xingchang, Chao Daiqin, and four other comrades). October 6, 1973.

Feng xian gongan jiguan junguanhui. "Qingkuang jianbao, dishiliuqi, shiyue fen di, she qing-kuang" (Situation report, no. 16, Enemy's activities and social situation in October). October 30, 1973.

Feng xian gongan jiguan junguanhui. "Qingkuang jianbao, dishiqiqi, shiyiyue fen di, she qing-kuang" (Situation report, no. 17, Enemy's activities and social situation in November). November 28, 1973.

Feng xian geweihui zhengfazu. "Guanyu dui shehui da qingcha de qingkuang baogao" (Report on the status of the social cleansing investigations). January 17, 1974.

Zhonggong Fengxian weiyuanhui. "Guanyu Song Chuanhe deng tongzhi zhiwu renmian wenti de tongzhi" (Notice on the appointment and removal of Song Chuanhe and other comrades). February 15, 1974.

Zhonggong Feng xian weiyuanhui. "Shao Wen tongzhi zai xian nongcun sanji ganbu huiyi shang de jianghua, jianjue guanche luoshi zhongyang 21 hao wenjian, duoqu pi Lin pi Kong he quan nian nongye shengchan xin shengli" (Comrade Shao Wen's speech at the county's three-level rural cadre conference, resolutely carry out central document no. 21, strive for new victories in the Criticize Lin Biao and Confucius Campaign and annual agricultural production). July 29, 1974.

Zhonggong Jiangsu sheng weiyuanhui. "Zhonggong Jiangsu shengwei dianhua zhishi" (Telephone instructions from Jiangsu provincial party committee). August 14, 1974.

Zhonggong Feng xian weiyuanhui. "Guanyu He Quanfu deng shiba wei tongzhi zhiwu renmian tongzhi" (Notice on the appointment and removal of He Quanfu and 17 other comrades). October 3, 1974.

Zhonggong Feng xian weiyuanhui. "Diwei fuze tongzhi zai Zhonggong Feng xian xianwei changwei huiyi shang de zhishi" (The prefecture leaders' directives at the county party standing committee meeting). September 4, 1975.

Feng xian renmin fayuan. "Jiangsu sheng Xuzhou diqu zhongji renmin fayuan xingshi panjue shu" (Criminal judgment passed by the People's Court of Xuzhou Prefecture, Jiangsu Province). September 24, 1975.

Zhonggong Feng xian weiyuanhui. "Guanyu jiejue qingcha yundong zhong liangshi gongying wenti de tongzhi" (Notice on how to resolve the problems regarding victims' grain rations during the investigation campaign). October 15, 1975.

Zhonggong Feng xian weiyuanhui. "Guanyu Qin Yuxuan deng san tongzhi zhiwu renmian de tongzhi" (Notice on the appointment and removal of Qin Yuxuan and two other comrades). November 27, 1975.

Zhonggong Feng xian weiyuanhui. "Guanyu gongshe wuzhuangbu ganbu renzhi wenti de tong-zhi" (Notice regarding the question of offices held by commune People's Armed Department cadres). December 18, 1975.

Zhonggong Feng xian weiyuanhui. "Tongzhi" (Notice [on the Tiananmen incident]). April 7, 1976.

Zhonggong Feng xian weiyuanhui. "Zai shengwei zhaokai dianhua huiyi shang Peng Chong tongzhi de jianghua" (Comrade Peng Chong's speech on provincial telephone conference [on Hua Guofeng's appointment and Deng Xiaoping's purge]). April 8, 1976.

Zhonggong Feng xian weiyuanhui. "Tongzhi" (Notice [on commune PAD cadres' position and public administration]). April 8, 1976.

Zhonggong Jiangsu shengwei. "Xu Jiatun tongzhi zai di shi xianwei shuji huiyi jieshu shi de jianghua" (Comrade Xu Jiatun's speech at the conclusion of the conference of prefecture, city, and county party secretaries). December 9, 1976.

Zhonggong Feng xian weiyuanhui. "Yin Shibin tongzhi zai ge gongshe dangwei fuze ren huiyi jieshu shi guanyu chuanda guanche zhongyang gongzuo huiyi jingshen de jianghua" (Comrade Yin Shibin's speech at the conclusion of the conference of party leaders of various communes regarding the spread and implementation of the spirit of the central work conference). April 29, 1977.

Zhonggong Feng xian weiyuanhui. "Jianjue luoshi Hua zhuxi zhuagang zhiguo de zhanlüe juece, cong daluan zouxiang dazhi" (Resolutely implement Chairman Hua's strategic decision to grasp key issues regarding state administration and move from chaos to order). May 12, 1977.

Zhonggong Feng xian weiyuanhui. "Zai Hua zhuxi zhuagang zhiguo zhanlüe juece zhiyinxia liji xingdong qilai jianjue dahao sixia zhe yi zhang—Yin Shibin tongzhi zai quan xian guangbo dahui shang de jianghua" (Take actions instantly under the direction of Chairman Hua's strategic decision to grasp key issues regarding state administration, resolutely win the battle of agricultural production in summer season—Comrade Yin Shibin's speech at the all-county broadcast meeting). May 22, 1977.

Feng xian zong gonghui. "Guanyu zhengjian jiceng gonghui zuzhi de baogao" (Report on the adjustment of basic-level labor union organizations). June 22, 1977.

Feng xian niukui zengying bangongshi. "Guanyu niukui zengying gongzuo de baogao" (Report regarding the work of reversing deficits and increasing surpluses). November 3, 1977.

Zhonggong Feng xian weiyuanhui. "Gaoju Mao Zhuxi de weida qizhi, yanzhe dang de shiyi da luxian, wei gao sudu fazhan wo xian gongye er fendou—Zhang Benshu tongzhi zai Feng xian gongye xue Daqing xianjin daibiao huiyi shang de jianghua" (Raise high the great banner of Chairman Mao's Thought, follow the line of the 11th Party Congress, strive to rapidly develop our county's industry—Comrade Zhang Benshu's speech at the Feng County conference of learning from Daqing in industry advanced representatives). March 17, 1978.

Zhonggong Feng xian weiyuanhui. "Lu Shaoshi tongzhi zai xianwei sanji ganbu huiyi shang de jianghua" (Comrade Lu Shaoshi's speech at the three-level cadre conference of the county party committee). December 1, 1978.

Zhonggong Feng xian weiyuanhui, Xuzhou diwei gongzuo zu. "Guanyu Feng xian yanzhong weifan caijing jilü wenti de diaocha baogao" (Investigation report on the problem of serious violations of financial discipline in Feng County). December 12, 1978.

Zhonggong Feng xian weiyuanhui. "Guanyu chexiao wenhua da geming chuqi dui yibufen tongzhi chezhi baguan, kaichu dangji deng chuli jueding" (Decision on reversing the Cultural Revolution decisions to fire and remove from office and expel from the party certain comrades). February 15, 1979.

Zhonggong Xuzhou diwei. "Guanyu Feng xian yanzhong weifan caijing jilü wenti de tongbao" (Circular on the problem of serious violations of financial discipline in Feng County). March 20, 1979.

Feng xian hecha bangongshi. "Guanyu 'Shahe fangong tuan' jia'an de diaocha ziliao" (Investigation materials on the false case of the "Shahe Anti-Communist Group"). January 1, 1987.

Zhonggong Xuzhou diwei. "Guanyu dui Hou Li dingxing he chuli yijian de pifu" (Response on the opinion regarding the verdict and sentencing of Hou Li). January 17, 1987.

Zhonggong Xuzhou diwei. "Guanyu dui Zhang Guichun dingxing chuli yijian de pifu" (Response on the opinion regarding the verdict and sentencing of Zhang Guichun). February 25, 1987.

Zhonggong Feng xian weiyuanhui. "Zhonggong Feng xian weiyuanhui hecha 'sanzhong ren' gongzuo zongjie" (Feng County party committee summary of work in verifying the investigations of "Three Types of People"). June 18, 1987.

INDEX

Page numbers in *italics* refer to illustrations.

A NOTE ON THE TYPE

This book has been composed in Arno, an Old-style serif typeface in the
classic Venetian tradition, designed by Robert Slimbach at Adobe.

Printed in the USA
CPSIA information can be obtained
at www.ICGtesting.com
JSHW080922300923
49421JS00004B/213